Hopkins
Re-Constructed

Hopkins Re-Constructed

LIFE, POETRY, AND THE TRADITION

JUSTUS GEORGE LAWLER

CONTINUUM • NEW YORK

1998

The Continuum Publishing Company
370 Lexington Avenue, New York, NY 10017

Printed in the United States of America

Library of Congress Cataloging-in-Publication Data

Lawler, Justus George.
    Hopkins re-constructed : life, poetry, and the tradition / Justus
George Lawler.
       p.   cm.
    Includes bibliographical references and index.
    ISBN 0-8264-1058-8
    1. Hopkins, Gerard Manley, 1844–1889. 2. Christian poetry,
English – Catholic authors – History and criticism. 3. Poets,
English – 19th century – Biography. 4. Influence (Literary, artistic,
etc.) 5. Jesuits – England – Biography. I. Title.
PR4803.H44Z7113   1998
821'.8 – dc21   97–20641
                                                      CIP

To T. Josephine Lawler, O.P.
a sister and a Sister

Contents

Preface

Few readers would answer in the affirmative to the Browning-esque query, "Did you once see Hopkins plain?" Rather the response is likely to be, even a century after his death, "How strange he seems." This is a book that seeks to see Hopkins plain, to see him as Hopkins himself would have wanted to be seen by his imagined contemporary readers. Such readers would have shared his liking for Milton (over Dante), for Marvell, Herbert, Vaughan (largely on religious grounds), for Dryden, Pope, and ("crazy") Blake, as well as much of Keats and Tennyson (the latter originally on esthetic grounds). These imagined readers would also have appreciated, if not embraced as their personal ideals, both the native "Saxon" strain in language and the native "Catholic" strain in religion.

It is in the light of this poetic, this linguistic, and this religious tradition that I shall consider some of Hopkins's most celebrated poems. That they are so celebrated and that they are among the most widely read of Victorian poetry indicates that "this tradition" is not so alien or incomprehensible or obscure — all adjectives applied to the poet and his work — as the received critical opinion suggests. But because it is the religious tradition which will probably be less familiar to the typical reader — even of a book about a religious poet — I will try to limit discussion of theological, ecclesiastical, and devotional matters to what most deeply affected Hopkins personally and in relation to his poems.

Some technical issues must be considered, but the treatment will be as brief as necessary and as accessible as I can make it; moreover, since these are recurring matters throughout the book, they and what they imply will gradually become more and more familiar to the reader. But they, too, will not be as recondite or esoteric as conventional interpreters have asserted; even theology can be made relatively "plain." Also, concerning this religious tradition, I will be attending closely to biblical and liturgical influences, to feasts, ceremonies, and prayers, since these were the daily fare on which Hopkins's spiritual life and concomitantly his poetry were nourished. All of these factors (and a few malefactors, that is, perpetrators of the fiction of Hopkins's density and obscurity) will be examined in the first three chapters.

Some additional prefatory comments are called for. First, I have randomly used inclusive language throughout, except when referring to Hopkins's own chosen terms. For example, the phrase, "Men go by me," could not be subject to gender parity without distorting the meaning of the poem. We have to do in this study with the play of language, with uniquely conceived and uniquely constructed esthetic objects, with works of *wonder* and *pleasure,* not of social or political reform. And here I introduce the kind of traditional touchstone that shall be invoked throughout this book: *omnia admirabilia sunt delectabilia.* This is merely to labor what should be obvious: that is, these are poems of pleasure not of propaganda. And it is ingredient in my "methodology" that these touchstones — what used to be called *sententiae* — still speak cogently to latent memories and longings in the reader.

The focus, I repeat, is on the play of language, and on our leisured playing on that instrument, Hopkins's own poetic language. We are out of the domain of language as utilitarian vehicle, as instrument of ideological persuasion, whether of Faustian straining and striving, of Kantian "Herculean labor," of Arnoldian "high seriousness," or even of Hopkins's Catholic proselytism.

Second, I have inserted only a very few, but important, footnotes — even to the point of possibly excessive parentheses in the body of the book — so that as little as possible distracts from the poems and their commentaries. Third, for each poem treated in detail, I have supplied the complete text — however frequently interrupted by gloss or explication — to spare the reader having to collate the discussion herein with the poems in another anthology, collection, or edition.

*A*cknowledgments

First, I must express indebtedness to the administration of St. Xavier University. Never have administrative officials from the highest to the lowest echelons been so dedicated to the status and activity of an individual faculty member: from my Weekend College accommodations, to my decennial sabbatical, to my teaching, indeed from top to bottom, their attention to educational and personal detail has been conspicuous; and to say that this has set the tone of the institution from janitors to executives would be to labor the obvious.

I must also express similar sentiments to the Chair of the English Department, Professor Judith Hiltner, for her innumerable memoranda, her personal concern for my academic future, her heartfelt admonitions concerning pedagogy, her adjustments to my schedule, her openness on all sides of controversial issues, as well as her exemplary scholarship on Philip Freneau, which has provided me with a model I trust I can emulate. Lastly, there is Thomas Deegan, Director of Graduate English, who counseled so many of his charges into my courses, whose uncountable contributions to scholarly publishing have been truly inspirational, and finally, whose laborious ponderings over the weightiest administrative matters bespeak the gravity he so laboriously manifests.

•

Paulo maiora canamus. Having repaid in kind the syndics and peers of this institution, I turn now to my colleagues and coworkers, however less titularly grand than those I celebrate above. My greatest debt is to Ursula Zyzik, a Jagiellonian-trained philologist, a true lover of literature, and a determined researcher who traced down obscure sources and provided materials without which neither this nor its predecessor volume, *Celestial Pantomime,* could have been completed. To Heidi Epstein, a musician and feminist theologian, I owe innumerable moments of wisdom and of wit. Christopher Kaufmann has proved to be over the years an invaluable guide in matters both practical and speculative, as well as an inspiring model of diligence. To Werner Mark Linz and the Continuum team I am grateful for loyalty, patience, support, and solidarity; to James Finn Cotter and Joseph J. Feeney, S.J., for their gracious encouragement of earlier drafts; and finally to "those lovely lads" Tom, George, and Rich.

Introduction

"So Be Beginning"

My original subtitle, *Poetic Normality in Relation to Literary and Religious Tradition,* was intended to evoke the first major study of the poet, W. H. Gardner's two volumes subtitled: *A Study of Poetic Idiosyncrasy in Relation to Poetic Tradition.* A less allusive title might have been worded along the lines of Albert Guérard on Hopkins's close friend and editor, *Robert Bridges: A Study of Traditionalism in Poetry.* This would have been less cumbersome, but "traditionalism" is now a word that has negative overtones — hence the present subtitle: *Life, Poetry, and the Tradition.* Guérard, like Bridges and the first generation of Hopkins critics and commentators (e.g., Herbert Read, E. E. Phare, C. Day Lewis), writing after the second edition of the poems had appeared, viewed Hopkins as either outside the tradition or a "rebel" against it.

This is not to suggest I am engaged in a tardy debate with Gardner and his contemporaries — much less an attempt at refutation — nor any kind of rival effort in terms of subjects and scope. As to Gardner, his work was and is massive, and for its time, exhaustive in its coverage. My original subtitle was merely intended to suggest a corrective effort that would seek to read some central poems in the light of a historical and structuralist understanding of the poetic tradition, and of a broadly defined "Catholic" understanding of the Western Christian theological and philosophical tradition.

Concerning the "structuralist" component, I am using the word as defined in an earlier work: *Celestial Pantomime: Poetic Structures of Transcendence* (second edition, 1994). As to

"Western Christian," the terms are self-defining, and anyone familiar with Hopkins studies will know that there are scores of titles of books and essays on Hopkins emphasizing almost every conceivable aspect of these religious themes. My disenchantment with such studies will be detailed in the second chapter, and occasionally spelled out in the body of the book.

The underlying thesis is that Hopkins's "idiosyncrasy" has been so emphasized and even exaggerated that several unfortunate consequences have resulted. (The word "idiosyncratic" has itself been misinterpreted as it evolved to a pejorative from Socrates, through Francis the *idiota* of Assisi, through Dante who followed "his own course," to Prince Myshkin whose life, in its standardized translation, is called *The Idiot*.) First, the uninitiated reader either simply refuses to seriously consider the poems at all, or confronts them with critical defenses bristling with doubt, fear, or animus. Such a reader cannot hear the poet speak in his own voice, and so feels confirmed in her antagonist mood. Second, the preoccupation with idiosyncrasy encourages academicians to ferret out the most arcane and exotic readings of the poetry, on the specious grounds that if the text is acknowledgedly awry, critical interpretations are licensed to be askew.

This is to embrace with a vengeance the principle of *lectio difficilior,* which in its original sense had less to do with interpretation than with editing — as when the great Dantist, Scartazzini, affirmed that of several variants the most complex should be adopted because scribes and redactors are *simplificateurs*. But the textual problems in Hopkins are negligible compared with those in classics of an earlier era, and Norman MacKenzie, premier editor and commentator on Hopkins, has probably resolved (short of new discoveries) most of what is open to resolution. Third, the emphasis on idiosyncrasy inhibits the open-minded novice reader from drawing on his own intellectual and imaginative resources — on his own preunderstanding, if you will — when considering the poems.

Of these three consequences, the presumably authoritative voice of the members of the iatrogenic school of critics, seeking out abstruse and obscure readings, has probably been most damaging because it perpetuates the very problem it should solve: clarification of the text in its original setting and in the context of contemporary understanding. But such interpretations, as we shall see in the next chapter, are not merely bewildering and confusing; they are often just capricious speculations. And this, also, raises obvious deterrents to the common reader's access to the poetry.

Nor in this process of occlusion and deformation is Hopkins himself entirely guiltless. What the present writer regards as his most winning trait, a kind of childlike candor, has not served him well. Thus in a letter to Robert Bridges (April 27, 1881) he observed: "Alas, I have heard so much about and suffered so much for and in fact been so completely ruined for life by my alleged singularities that they are a sore subject." Nor did Bridges, loyal friend though he was, minimize these "alleged singularities" in the introductory comments to his first edition of the poems: "Mannerism, Oddity, Obscurity" was his indictment. And Hopkins seems to some twentieth-century readers indeed quite odd; but much of that oddness comes precisely from the poems being so related to the richest traditional formulas — linguistic, religious, philosophical — which have gradually become empty slogans, so that the poems also suffer from the perception of being something akin to archeological remnants. I am not talking here about Hopkins's adoption of a seemingly antiquated diction; that is an entirely different issue which I will address in the context of specific poems. Though, for now, it might be beneficial to recall his comment to Coventry Patmore (August 16, 1883): "I look on archaism as a blight." Therefore, another goal of this undertaking is to reinvigorate these basic traditional principles, now become obsolescent, but still evocative or virtually self-evident for most readers.

Escape/Inscape

For example, when teaching the poems, I have found it distracting if not utterly otiose to devote energy to making sensible interpretive applications out of such Hopkinsian coinages or usages as "counterpoint" or "logaoedic" rhythm, "outrides," "hangers," "*cywydd*," "*cynghanedd*," and others to be mentioned shortly. (Though I will pay homage to this last term from Welsh prosody — which means literally, "symphony," usually in the form of a combination of alliteration and homophones, and which Hopkins called "chiming" — in my choice of chapter titles and subtitles.)

On the other hand, the axiom, maxim, catchphrase, or *locus communis* from the philosophical, religious, and Jesuit tradition which undergird Hopkins's mature poems, and which collectively are as it were etched in the memory of so many of his readers — these shorthand formulas supply invaluable interpretive clues. I proffer from the Jesuit lexicon, *Age quod agis,* loosely, "whatever you do, do well"; *Contemplativus in actione,* loosely, "blend the active and contemplative life"; *Agere contra,* loosely, "go against the grain." And there are among others from the philosophical/religious lexicon, *Agere sequitur esse,* loosely, "what one does flows from what one is"; *Intellectus* vis-à-vis *ratio,* loosely, "immediate intuition as opposed to analytic, discursive, syllogistic reasoning"; *Gratia presupponit naturam,* loosely, "the supernatural is not in conflict with the natural, but the former builds upon the latter"; *Nullam obicem ponere,* loosely, "sanctification comes provided one is open to it and raises no obstacles"; *Admirabile commercium* (from the Christmas liturgy), loosely, "the interchange between the heavenly and the earthly."

Though initially these various *sententiae* may sound to the contemporary reader alien or incomprehensible, nevertheless by the very frequency of their use as well as their manifest centrality to Hopkins's vision, they will become as familiar as would in other settings such phrases as *lex non scripta, in medias res, ius inter gentes, persona non grata,* and so on; in sum, by mere contextualized repetition their significance will become virtually self-revelatory as they themselves will become recognized as second nature to Hopkins, implicit in his daily life, and explicit in his poetry.

It may seem to many readers highly unlikely that these theological and philosophical apothegms are going to be immediately and precisely understood in this present secularized era. To that

I can only say such an unlikelihood must be tested in the actual reading of the poetry in their light. But I can offer an example of the persuasiveness of such *topoi* among twentieth-century readers who are not only thoroughly secularized, but also culturally outside the Western philosophical and theological world centered on the Mediterranean Basin.

Anyone who has read William Empson's *Milton's God* (1961) recognizes the personal obscurantism behind his biased "demythologizing" for Asian students of the retributively vengeful deity he claimed to have discovered in *Paradise Lost* and to be so shocking to his auditors. On the other hand, several years later (1975), D. J. Enright, explaining to these same non-Western students what might be called the Judeo-Christian vision, remarked *In a Choice of Milton's Verse* that "the Christian myth in some of its elements exerts a greater persisting influence on — or is more actively central to — not only our ethics (increasingly international) but also the darker places of the human psyche than is often supposed, even (or especially) by its conscious adherents." *That* is the myth that is embodied in the above themes and *topoi*, and these are the "maxims" or *sententiae* which, though superficially obscure, animate each poem of Hopkins, and elicit an almost instinctively sympathetic response within the typical educated reader. In fact, Enright describes himself as unexpectedly moved when teaching in the Far East the poems of Hopkins to his "young though ageless Catholics." "Catholic" is here used ironically since he describes his students as being "not Christian either by conviction or, laxly, by environment." If young people in Asia can be affected by Hopkins's themes and images, how much more should readers nurtured in the Western tradition itself? Of course, these Latin tags and encapsulated truisms are ancient, and like so much of the past subject to entropy and obsolescence, but when read in conjunction with the poems, they repristinate and regenerate.

Thus I have found this attrition by time and desuetude to be a minor factor in the alleged popular consensus that the poems are obscure and "difficult." As I have noted, any moderately literate reader finds herself responding to these themes from the tradition, almost intuitively comprehending them, because whether couched in traditional formulas or in the language of today, they do awaken foundational and therefore deeply affecting configurations of the universal human psyche: themes such as openness to being, seasonal change, cloud symbolism, convergence of horizons, starry patterns, unity in variety, and so on. Hence I would reemphasize it is not the obscurities of the religious or cultural tradition, but the clutter of decades of fatuous glosses and the sheer repetition of stereotyped misjudgments that have frightened off our once-idealized common reader, and that have contributed to the received wisdom that Hopkins's poetry is exotic, arcane, odd.

But it must be admitted that here, again, Hopkins is his own greatest obfuscator. Consider his directives to Bridges for so transparent a sonnet as "Hurrahing in Harvest": " . . . (sprung and outriding rhythm.) Take notice that the outriding feet are not to be confused with dactyls or paeons, though sometimes the line might be scanned either way. The strong syllable in an outriding foot has always a great stress and after the outrider follows a short pause. The paeon is easier and more flowing." A daunting instruction, but totally irrelevant to appreciating the poem. And one can only imagine the reaction of the first readers of his "Author's Preface on Rhythm," where he admonishes: "Remark also that it is natural in Sprung Rhythm for the lines to be *rove over*, that is for the scanning of each line immediately to take up that of the one before, so that if the first has one or more syllables at its end the other must have so many the less at its beginning; and in fact the scanning runs on without break from the beginning, say, of a stanza to the end and all the stanza is one long strain, though written in lines asunder." "One long strain," without question — but embodied in a prescription Hopkins himself violated, as A. E. Housman noted after receiving a copy of the first edition from Bridges. "He [Hopkins] does not make it [sprung rhythm] audible; he puts light syllables in the stress and heavy syllables in the slack, and has to be helped out with typographical signs explaining that things are to be understood as being what in fact they are not."

Among such signs are the quasi-musical markings in which Hopkins placed great store as interpretive keys: brackets, eliders, ictuses, arses, ligatures, slurs, twirls, and a battery of diacritical notations. Their significance to the esthetic impact of the poems can be deduced from the fact that they are never totally and exactly reproduced except in virtually inaccessible photocopy. And this is true even of Norman MacKenzie's almost flawless "variorum" of 1990. Nor was there any widespread objection to the omission of Hopkins's typographical signs in the established and esteemed "Oxford Authors Series," under the title *Gerard Manley Hopkins* (1986), with the subhead, "A Critical Edition of the Major Works" — nor, I say, was there widespread objection when the editor of this volume, Catherine Phillips, observed casually but honestly: "Cost and editorial opinion at Oxford University Press have restricted metrical marks in the text to simple stresses." So much for the hermeneutical symbols Hopkins thought essential to the reading of his poems.

Moreover, Hopkins's knowledge of music and musical notation remained equally quirky and amateurish. It was as unimportant in his own time as it is a century later. When he had submitted his views and a sample of his composition to the musicologist Sir Robert Stewart, he was whimsically derided — and this, in 1886, three years before his death. Stewart wrote: "Indeed my dear Padre I *cannot* follow you through your maze of words in your letter of last week. I saw, ere we had conversed ten minutes on our first meeting that you are one of those special pleaders who never believe yourself wrong in any respect.... Nearly everything in your music was wrong.... What does it matter? It will be all the same 100 years hence." And it is.

Scop's Scope

Other than an awareness of the utter singularity and uniqueness Hopkins attached to each individual creature (an awareness which one can get from attending to the poetry itself), not much more is needed for an appreciation of alleged obscurities in the major poems than a general understanding of traditional philosophy and theology, and of the continuum of British poetry — certainly much less than is needed for an appreciation of John Donne or George Herbert. Even the Scotism, which Hopkins imagined underlay this sense of individuality, is in his writings philosophically vague, however on occasion theologically ingenious and precise — but still largely irrelevant, except symbolically, to the poetry as such.

Moreover, the language he himself put into currency to express his sense of the "uniqueness" of all created beings, though novel and fresh, is consistently inconsistent. Ponderous pages have been devoted to sorting out, systematizing, and debating such marvellously creative coinage as: inscape, instress, pitch, sake, splay, neap, cleaves of burl, an install, and so on. For those concerned with biography or linguistic creativity or intellectual history, all of these neologisms singly or together may be of interest and importance, and some will indeed recur in my second biographical chapter. But for the poems, such language is of little utility to the careful reader who, if she can grasp without extensive paraphrase Browning and Rossetti or Stevens and Crane, will have no great difficulty with Hopkins.

After this brief introduction, chapter 1 will be a severely negative criticism of some of the more extreme and eccentric interpretations of Hopkins's work, and chapter 2, an equally negative criticism of interpretations of Hopkins's life, with particular emphasis on Robert Bernard Martin's homoerotic "reading."

Those who are more interested in the poetry than in its curious critical reception, or more interested in the poetry than in allegations about its author's private life, may want to omit or postpone chapters 1 and 2, and move immediately into the substantive and positive contributions of the last five chapters. Those two earlier chapters constitute an important clearing of the ground, but they may be of more interest to the specialized student than to the general reader. In any case, after the present introduction, the bulk of the book, the five last chapters, will focus on representative poems — among Hopkins's most popular — which will be read in light of their place in the British literary tradition both in terms of themes and in terms of structural patterns. The themes, I have noted, are generally conventional — natural beauty, seasonal change, the human plight, and so on — though here treated by a passionate believer and knowledgeable student of the theological and devotional heritage of Catholicism, albeit with a Jesuit accent.

Hopkins was emphatic on the importance to poetry of what he called "pattern," and what I will be treating under the broad heading "structures," particularly those I analyze in *Celestial Pantomime*: circularity, parenthesis, enjambement, coda, prepositionalizing, refrain, and most importantly, complementarity — as this latter term had been used in quantum physics, and has since been adopted by sociologists, theologians, mathematicians, behavioral scientists, and of course literary critics. Because each of these structural patterns will be clarified in the context of the poetry, I am merely enumerating them now, though the reader may find it helpful to consider them in the fuller sweep of the earlier book, a book that John Hollander generously described as "an ultimate act of comprehending Hopkins, and of going beyond the limitations of his theories of meter and music" — and, finally, a book that led to this present effort to redeem Hopkins from the arch-especial specialists and to place him in the more accessible sequence of British poetry and Western religion. It is my hope the book will prove to be a work of *nova et vetera,* a work that presents new readings in the light of my original subtitle: Normality in Relation to Literary and Religious Tradition.

I: _S_choliasts and _S_ciolists

"At a Third Remove"

Those who grew up during the period that was called _le renouveau Catholique_ may remember that some of its most noteworthy figures were translated by one Gerard Hopkins: though I have not the least idea whether the latter translated such justly celebrated authors as Charles Péguy, Paul Claudel, Georges Bernanos, Gabriel Marcel, Henri Bremond, Jacques Maritain, et al. But during the period after World War I, Gerard Hopkins was one of the major translators of serious European literature, including several novels by Mauriac. There was in the United States a more or less parallel movement commemorated in a book by a Jesuit, Calvert Alexander, called _The Catholic Literary Revival._ Unfortunately, like Charles Homer Haskins's _Renaissance of the Twelfth Century,_ or J. J. Walsh's _The Thirteenth, the Greatest of Centuries,_ the contents did not quite live up to the title — a phenomenon that engendered among some American Catholic intellectuals the ironic _mot:_ "Yes, we have no Bernanos." But it was to the then (1918) unknown name of the future translator, Gerard Hopkins, that we owe the now very well known name of his uncle, Gerard Manley Hopkins.

Robert Bridges, fearing confusion as to the authorship of a collection of poems he was editing by a virtually unknown Victorian Jesuit, later decided to insert the now famous middle name, Manley — which the poet had almost never used during his lifetime — to avoid any such possible confusion. This well-intentioned gesture subsequently gave rise to several invidious equivocations relating to what Yvor Winters was the first to call G. M. Hopkins's "effeminacy" (1949), and to what a recent biographer of the poet, Robert Bernard Martin (1991), would emphasize at the very beginning of his book as "The Importance of Being Manley" — canards we shall examine later.

My intention in these first and second chapters is neither to trace the history of Hopkins's critical reception nor to examine in detail his biographies. As to the latter, in chapter 2, I will examine cursorily the earlier biographical treatments while concentrating on the two most recent and most nearly definitive lives of Hopkins. Concerning critical reception, here in this first chapter — and in the rest of this book — it will be made abundantly clear where I stand regarding the mass of interpretations, glosses, paraphrases, commentaries, even parodies that has grown up around so small a body of poems. For now, I will emphasize that my purpose is not to engage in the kind of comparative evaluation to which the poems were subjected during the first period of their acceptance into the canon of "minor" works, roughly from 1930 (the second edition) to Geoffrey Hartman's *The Unmediated Vision* (1954) and J. Hillis Miller's *The Disappearance of God* (1963). (A survey of the criticism during that period was made by W. H. Gardner [1949], by Todd Bender [1966], and by G. Roberts [1987].) Miller had some signal peers writing illuminating essays or entire books — Robert Boyle, Geoffrey Hartman, F. R. Leavis, Paul Mariani, James Finn Cotter, and William Noon — but for the most part, the criticism was carping, defensive, and subjective, particularly among the presumed creators of that loose congeries of like and unlike spirits known as the "New Critics." Though the major figures, Blackmur, Daiches, Donald Davie, Eliot, Empson, Richards, even Winters, all praised Hopkins as an innovator, the praise was often niggardly by reason of its immediately subsequent focus on a multitude of picayune flaws or alleged verbal oddities in scores of poems, with the consequence that, until Hillis Miller, Geoffrey Hartman, and Paul Mariani, along with a small group of Jesuits and ex-Jesuits, there was no sustained effort to get into the esthetic foundations of Hopkins's theopoetics.

Rather, the alleged foundations rested — roughly from the

1930s to the 1950s — on such stereotyped notions as: creation-mirrors-creator, poet-as-prophet, Jesuit-as-preacher, Catholicism-as-salvation, or on the alleged conflict between these various attributions. Such truisms and polarizations were pretty much standard fare for structuring the poems among the first two generations of critics, while the entire undertaking was bolstered by unabashedly exploiting the *OED* for every Hopkinsian linguistic obscurity, archaism, neologism, or putative solecism.

The New Critics rarely considered the basis of Hopkins's diction and rhetoric, of his effort to compress all words into the one Logos (Hartman, Miller), or of his effort to see in rhyming contrarieties a greater and greater purchase on the harmonics of the unity-in-Trinity theme known technically as "perichoresis" (and closely examined by James Finn Cotter). Instead most New Critics, fascinated by the pedagogical utility — often dependent on sloganeering about "irony" and "paradox" — of a basically ahistoric method were caught up in acrimonious and ultimately fruitless debates over such matters as, for example, the meaning in "The Windhover" of ambiguities relating to "dauphin," to "my heart in hiding," to "my chevalier," and finally to that gnawed and clawed polysemous crux, "buckle." When all these "issues" remained controverted and unresolved — as if irresolution were not the very definition of a classic — the burden of flawed art was often laid upon the extravagances of the poet, not upon the opacities of the critics.

Among this varied group, including Blackmur, Daiches, Donald Davie, Eliot, Empson, Richards, Winters, and assorted epigonal hangers-on: among this heterogeneous but relatively unified phalanx the animus was often so blatant it seemed understandable only in terms of extraneous, nonpoetic factors. There was little openness to Hopkins on his own terms, and the judgments were either globally subjective opinings usually on moral or religious matters, or cavils over verbal trickery, linguistic self-indulgence, lack of unity, untraditional poetic practice, and so on. The following is a representative sample: "coarse and clumsy assonance" (Middleton Murry);

"girlish tenderness masked by ruggedness" (Edward Sapir); "intellectually stiff" (Richards); "decadent" (Davie); "uncontrolled rhythm...unchecked emotionalism" (E. E. Phare); "miscellaneous images," "self-righteous," "stereotyped assertions...empty epithets" (Winters). And so on and on — all in marked opposition to Hopkins's dictum: "The most inveterate fault of critics is the tendency to cramp and hedge in by rules the free movements of genius."

But as I have noted, I am not writing a history of Hopkins criticism. In fact, I intend to do the opposite in this first chapter. I intend to sketch the eccentricity, the aberrancy, indeed the absurdity of so much of what has been written on his poems, and I attempt this with a view, first, to clarifying how it is that poems which are so widely known — however slim the total corpus may be — can be so outrageously misread; and, second, to justifying my own circumvention of much of what has passed during the last couple of decades among the successors to the original New Critics for serious analysis and interpretation.

As to the first issue, I will proffer enough examples to validate my assertion, and will tentatively suggest a reason for so blatantly egregious a *practice* (and it is with "practical criticism" that we have to do). As to the second issue, though I believe I have examined, over the past thirty-five years of annually lecturing on some aspect of Hopkins, virtually everything of real or presumed significance, my own readings have been based on criteria not usually recognized among those we might think of as Hopkinsinians *de métier.*

Thus, I am writing as a nonguildy party, that is, as a reader who believes that on controverted or seemingly obscure issues, the bias should favor not the analyst but the author. Lest this appear arbitrary, I hope I can bring forth enough examples of the primacy of the latter that the reader can make her own determination as to whether my option is justifiable. Equally, with my second hermeneutical principle (and also another of those *sententiae* I introduced above): *per simile simile percipiens.* This is merely to say, as I did less aphoristically in the introductory comments on tradition, that one poem is the best interpreter of another poem. A consensus of critical views must of course be taken into account. But with a poet such as Hopkins where the most contradictory and antagonist opinions on every conceivable *and* inconceivable interpretive crux have been brought forth — indeed, have been flaunted, almost it seems, precisely because of their aleatory, stochastic nature — unanimity prevails only with regard to the most truistic banalities, and one is compelled (or I at least feel compelled) to rely on a principle of exegesis from Hopkins's own religious heritage: Interpretation Is *in* the Tradition. That is, the text must be read in the light, first, of the poet's total *oeuvre*, and, second, of the historically cumulative factors — poetic, theological, social, personal, and so on — that influenced that work.

From the perspective of knowing the "poet's total *oeuvre*" nothing seems more arbitrary and unhelpful than the implications of T. S. Eliot's query (1933): "Who now, for the pleasure of it, reads Wordsworth, Shelley and Keats even, certainly Browning and Swinburne and most of the French poets of the century — entire?" (Who, indeed? And could one ever imagine a James Huneker or a Howard Taubman, for all their time-proven misjudgments, raising such a question of, say, Mozart, Brahms, and Berlioz, *even*?) Hopkins himself in a letter to Patmore commented on precisely this issue of "totality": "Are Virgil's Georgics and Bucolics read more or less for his having written the Aeneid? Much more. So of Shakspere's and Dante's sonnets. It was by providence designed for the education of the human race that great artists should leave works not only of great excellence but also in very considerable bulk."

Of course, as so often with Eliot, this canny simulator of modernist conservatism, he was protecting his flanks against anticipated assaults upon his own sparse and meager verse productivity — for which the "poetic dramas" would later allegedly compensate. But the response to *his* question could only be three other questions — though less Olympianly couched: what has happened to C. S. Peirce's "The sense of a symbol is in its translation into another symbol," or to Gaston Bachelard's "L'image ne peut être étudiée que par l'image," or to that axiom cited above, "Interpretation is in the tradition"? However idiosyncratic Hopkins's language and theories of versification may appear, his themes and images, as previously noted, are a summation of what is richest in the English poetic tradition and in the Western religious tradition.

As to my first clearing of the ground, the citation of the strange vagaries of much published Hopkins criticism in the last couple of decades, I shall be as brief as possible but as detailed as necessary. Moreover, to avoid needless polemic embarrassment, I shall provide only the year of publication and the source, rarely the titles or authors. (The former should be sufficient for anyone wanting to track down the latter.)

And, in the overall, I intend to avoid discussion of religious jargon or symbols that, unless precisely defined and precisely applied, can be invested with such universal significance as to be meaningless. Thus I shall not consider such omnibus *topoi* as, for example, the "sacramental," "incarnational," "evangelical," "Eucharistic," "Trinitarian," "Christic," "Ignatian," and so forth ...in Hopkins — adjectives followed by whatever obliquely relevant substantives one can pluck from any thesaurus of collective abstractions: for example, "influence," "vision," "perspective," "dimension" — again, and so forth.

Whims/Whams

Hopkins, I repeat, wrote out of a lengthy tradition remarkably rich in poetic and religious language and imagery (and in his case, singularly rich in arcana and esoterica), but to invoke any or all such *tradita* as blanket principles of interpretation or *en bloc* solutions to hermeneutic *cruces* is to smother his quite micrometric preciseness of figures, tropes, and verbal schemes in vapid esthetic or pietistic jargon. Thus I shall, as noted above, for the most part bypass works with such titles as *The Trinitarian Perspective in*...or, *The Patristic Theme in*....

I begin with an example of exactly this kind of omnibus jargon. In *The Hopkins Quarterly* (1985 — *HQ* in the future) the functionless noun is "perichoresis"; meaning, as noted above in its serious usage by Cotter, the circumincession of persons in the Trinity. But in the article I refer to we read *in re* "God's Grandeur" that, "The movement of the poem is from Father through Son to Spirit": no matter that in orthodoxy — and Hopkins was, if anything, orthodox — the Spirit proceeds from Father *and* Son (*filioque*); no matter that the presence of the Son in the poem is merely asserted not evinced; no matter that perichoresis is here defined as the three persons "dancing together" (a pretty translation but inaccurate and here much overworked as explanatory device); no matter that "reck his rod" is viewed as cryptogram for "wreck his rood," and that "oil *crushed*" refers to crucifixion — though the gospel of John is explicit about Jesus not being "crushed" in any fashion: "they did not break his legs." As for the highfalutin "perichoresis," it illuminates nothing in the poem and is merely employed as a kind of talismanic invocation.

In *HQ* (1974), under the heading "Romantic Structure and Theme in 'The Windhover,'" the three key words are so vague one could have titled the piece "Victorian Pattern and Content...." Similarly, a 1972 book, *Gerard Manley Hopkins and the Victorian Temper* (much indebted to a superior work, *The Poet as Victorian*), could as readily have passed muster under the heading *Romantic Temper*, so amorphous are the presumably distinguishing traits. In *HQ* again (1985), on "Hopkins and Vaughan," after proffering several cross-allusions which are either religious commonplaces or highly dubious links, the one direct bond, Romans 8, explicitly mentioned by both poets, is never adduced.

In *HQ* (1990), *bizarrerie* is canonized in a treatment of Hopkins and "Troubadour Poets," where his *pudeur* "helps to explain why there are only nuns, little girls, female martyrs, and the Blessed Virgin representing women in his poetry. They are the furniture of his Neo-Platonism, to be more specific, of the distancing mechanism of his 'Catholic' version of *amour courtois.*" (This clearly defies analysis: laminated are women/ Neo-Platonism/Catholic/*amour courtois.*) But, of these "represen- tations of women," common sense would suggest that they are merely the furniture of priestly celibacy, and have nothing to do with Provence, *Stilnovisti,* or Ficino.

Subsequently, of Hopkins and troubadours we are informed by this same author that: "[I]n 'It gathers to a greatness, like the ooze of oil / Crushed,' Hopkins may have been treating the *Catholic* Logos as the female consort, or emanation of the dis- tinctively male 'God' of the Hebrews" (emphasis added). Thus we are to embrace the notion that the God of the Hebrews is now the source of Plotinian emanationism. But regardless of this *non sequitur,* the female "consort" has always been identified not with Logos but with Sophia, that lovely figure hovering at the side of the Creator in Michelangelo's Sistine Chapel depiction.

New wonders are heaped upon new wonders — and of course always with an air of breathless discovery, and in the language and imagery of the most recondite scholarship: "Resorting to all but private code language [which code this author has 'cracked'], Hopkins writes 'ooze' when he really means to signify that *ou- sia* . . . is-es [*sic*], that is, acts as the Is of cosmic energy. If this is true, then 'ooze' should be recognized as a portmanteau word consisting of *'ous' and 'is.'* " (This reads like a *sic* joke, but this is the exact wording of the quotation.) Now, James Finn Cotter (whom I have cited twice on perichoresis) has written a brilliant "gnosticizing" study on Hopkins's christology (1972), so I am not here objecting to any glyphic arcana — or even Raymond Lul- lian or Reuchlinian "Catholic" kabbala — but only to the sheer arbitrariness of tying poor Gerard Hopkins to everything from Plotinus to Courtly Love.

A final dismal *exemplum:* though in fact the troubadours wrote in *langue d'oc,* we are solemnly told by our cryptanalyst that "Hopkins is using Troubadourian strategies" in "oil / Crushed" by linguistic allusion "to *langue d'oil*" (I am not fabricating this!) — all quite obvious to the "peer reviewers" of the *HQ* who have readily submitted to the *exousia* of this hierophantic author. I assume, given our resuscitated medieval trope, there were "twelve peers" voyeuristically engaged in assaying Hopkinsian *pudeur* and *amour*. ("Out of the tomb, we bring Badroulbadour" [Stevens].)

The Explicator (1963) first identified the fall, gall, gash of "The Windhover" with Christ's crucifixion, an identification repeated as established fact by virtually every professional Hopkins student since. Omitted are the gospel data that traditionally Jesus falls *three times;* and that "gall" in the poem cannot be a noun relating to Matthew's description of Jesus' being given "gall to drink" ("*gall themselves*"). The "gash" is, more or less acceptably, the piercing of his side — though how the blood and water that flowed from that wound correlate with "gold vermilion" is never explained. In *HQ* (1983) and in several other places in the commentaries, this eisigesis is embraced to enforce the notion that the entire poem is cruciaxional — now with the added notes that the bird in flight looks briefly "like a crucifix," and that "the kestrel's vertical ascent intersects the line of dawn, thus forming a cross" (*QED*).

This "ascent" is worried to excess in a 1989 book, *The Contemplative Poetry of Gerard Manley Hopkins,* where the adjective not only is omnipresent and presumably probative, but also is related to a previous work, *"Mined with a Motion"* (1984), the latter proffering a detailed and highly conventional reading of Newman's *Grammar of Assent* — soberly related to "ascent," as that of the "kestrel" (this latter an "in" term betokening professional status) in the "formation of a cross," as above.

And this in turn — such is the lend-lease nature of these exchanges — allows for some more up-to-date religious theorizing in that same 1989 work on "contemplation": "Gerald May, a modern interpreter of contemplative psychology [a discipline undefined], tells us that contemplation involves both an *open awareness* and a focused, sharpened *attention*." But this fairly obvious generalization leads to some curious gender stereotyping that most contemporary women would regard as little short of appalling (the author *is* a woman and this *is* 1989). The author assists the reader in understanding Gerald May's gnome by adding: "In contemplation, a *feminine, open awareness* combines with *masculine attention*" (emphasis added). And without a break, that sentence is followed immediately by the even more quaintly dualistic polarization of heart and mind: "This line [of May] also plays with the traditional [and gender-stereotyped] definition of prayer as a 'lifting up of the heart and mind to God.' " I have emphasized the date of publication because even the most militant "politically incorrect" writers approaching the last decade of this century would hardly dream of equating "feminine" with "heart," and "masculine" with "mind." Are we returning to Gilligan's Island, involved in a different vice, or merely witnessing another postmodern *paglia al vento?*

Perhaps the ultimate triumph of the therapeutic in Hopkins studies is *Send My Roots Rain* (1981), devoted to what the author first calls the ENG hypothesis, which is subsequently elevated into the ENG "principle" (no typo for ONG, no shorthand for Hopkins's penchant for old *Eng*lish, nor even an acronym for "Electronic News Gathering"), but a "developmental," or maybe "object-relations" notion used, the author says, like ESP — though with no connection, it is affirmed, to the latter. Having long ago vowed with Auden never to "commit a social science," I assumed ENG was some kind of approved acronym from the vast symbolic armamentarium at the disposal of exercitants of the discipline called "archetypalism" — a field that began to flourish contemporaneously with Hopkins criticism, and with much the same impercipient speculation, mummery, and hokum.

One can imagine the startlement that ensued on discovering what these upper cases (no higher court of appeal here) stood for: E = Encagement, related to "The Caged Skylark"; N = Naturation, related rather "woodenly" (cf. "Binsey Poplars") to appreciation of nature; G = Grace, related to the theological concept of divine assistance. Through this ENG grid, which also blurs the natural and the supernatural — or mixes *Apfeln und Engeln* — are sieved the equivalents of what ordinary folk call depression, acceptance, and religion: with half the book applying each trait to the poems,

half to the poet — fearful symmetry indeed. After this engrossing
if not engulfing notion has been engraved on the memory (if not
engaged by the intellect) one can only be grateful at the absence
of *branché* engenderment talk — though possibly not, because the
author does refer to what I take to be some kind of androgynous
deity: "a *Deus Abscondita.*" In any event, the final pronounce-
ment from our indeterminable analyst is (fittingly polysyllabic):
Hopkins "articulates a phenomenology of the ENG experience."

Now, I am here concentrating on explications which, although
no literate reader could embrace them, at least have the small
merit of some linkage with the text. I have not discussed the
penchant for the superiorly postured critic to indulge in totally deracinated asseveration with no discernible basis in a given poem,
save the critic's own subjective opinion or strabismic perception.
When, for example, I read Walter Ong's article "Bird, Horse, and
Chevalier" in 'The Windhover'" (*HQ*, 1974), I cannot embrace
his conclusions — as I shall attempt to show — but I can see how
he arrived at them, how they relate to Hopkins's text, and how
he correlates the context of the poem with an allegedly similar
Shakespearean context.

Nevertheless, I do find disingenuous the treatment as commonplace of a technical term previously archaic, and now utilized as
universally accepted within the guild. Thus Ong, again regarding
"The Windhover": "It has long been well known [but only since a
professional Hopkinsian discovered it in the *OED*] that the 'rung'
is a term from the manège referring to a horse circling or 'ringing'
around his trainer." But, of course, it hasn't been well known at
all, and since Ong's essay is titled "Bird, Horse, and Chevalier,"
presumably the echoes of "ménage à trois" are sufficient to lend
credence to a highly dubious assumption. "Manège" is simply a
translation of "handle," as in *manus*. But this is a minor matter,
illustrative of the coercive power of derivative received wisdom in
the guild.

More disturbing in Ong, though as I say, not without textual
foundation, is the heavy reliance on "psychological" categories of
what might broadly be termed a "Jungian," "mythic," "Gestalt"

nature, so that every specific image of Hopkins melds into every other (as with many of Joseph Campbell's reconstructions), and thus bird, horse, and man are all separately or collectively at one point or another in the poem identified with Christ. This is justified because presumably myths are relatively fluid narratives of general applicability, that is, are "agglomerative," to use another blanketing *Schlagwort*. Thus, the "fire that breaks" applies, the reader is told, to "the bird-steed *or* the bird-rider-steed" (as though it mattered little). And since we have the bird's flight related to a "rein," the fire can also relate to a horse: "even 'the skate's heel' carries a strong suggestion of a horse's hoof"! And so cumulatively dependent on one another are these critics that a decade and a half after Ong's conflation, Robert Bernard Martin's biography (which I take up in detail in the next chapter) can insouciantly affirm of the last line of "Felix Randal" that "part of the splendour...is achieved by the invocation of the drayhorse-Pegasus-chevalier-Christ association *that had run through so much of his* [Hopkins's] *poetry*" (emphasis added). Where we had bird, horse, and man amalgamated in Ong, we now have a draught horse identified with chivalry, with Pegasus, and finally with Christ.

Thus from a bird's flight related to a "rein," we derive a horse; from a horse, then a centaur; from a centaur, then a *flying* horse; from a flying horse, then a Pegasus — with all the mythic machinery of the tradition attached to each successive transmogrification; and so on, until every image is assimilated to every other image "in all its pointedness and in all its *vagaries*" (Ong's observation, my emphasis). Four years after Ong's ingenious agglomeration, another critic (*In Extremity*, 1978) would read the *entire* sestet of "Hurrahing in Harvest," with its reference to "a stallion stalwart," in the light of the Pegasus myth. This is Parmenides's "everything is everything" with a vengeance.

But since Ong was not only a critic writing then from the Center for Advanced Study in the Behavioral Sciences, but also a trained theologian, there is another ubiquitous principle at play which I mention only because it has also become a favorite tactic of archetypal and analytical critics — but here with a specifically religious twist. Since Christ is the "exemplary cause" of creation, since Christ is, as it were, creation's blueprint, everything reflects that one divine Idea, that divine Logos. All of this is theologically quite orthodox, but with fuzzy interpretive implications, as sketched by Ong: "Yet in his action, too, Christ gathers to himself the other images in the poem. The bird-horse-man theme effectively implements this gathering, for it provides the psyche with a long-standing and rich symbol of exuberant energy in which seemingly diverse elements are buckled into an exceedingly active and even incipiently other-worldly whole." But under the rubric "psyche, symbol, Christ-gathering, etc." almost anything can be justified, and in less sophisticated critics than Ong this, as we have seen, is precisely what does happen. Parenthetically I emphasize that this is early Ong, and not the Ong who brought his subsequent learning and insights to bear on, among other projects, the best biographical study of the poet's interior spiritual development, *Hopkins, the Self, and God* (1986). But it is in the name of "myth" and "Logos" that our previously cited and "cruciform"-obsessed critic (*HQ*, 1983) actually refers to the "flight plan" of the windhover. So, fasten your seat belts, raise your tray tables, and delve into encyclopedic ornithological lore as it relates to "a skate's heel," or to "the art of *patinage*" (*sic*) (but blessedly, no horses and thus no Pegasus here):

> Actually, two images are possible in this context [via a lot of ex-cruciating sudoriferous engagement with the *OED*]. If Hopkins is referring to the "running" or "fen" style of skating, the "skate's heel" itself might visually suggest a cross — "The heel is at right angles to the surface of the ice." A "bow-bend" in this style of skating could be only a simple parabolic curve — visually analogous to the path of the windhover's flight, or the line of dawn itself.... If, however, Hopkins' simile refers to the more modern style of "figure skating," the perpendicularity [*sic*] of the heel is no longer an operative image since the blades of such skates were curved

(*bowed?*) both heel and toe. The "bow-bend" in this style of skating has been taken to suggest a "figure-eight" — itself a criss*crossing* [*sic*] as well as a symbol of infinity on its side, though not precisely analogous to the windhover's flight. Furthermore, I think that the "fen style" of skating offers a more precise gloss of the simile since Hopkins probably knew that such figures were cut on the edges, not on the heels of ice-skates. Either image may be taken to suggest an unstated analogy with the cross. A less probable interpretation of the simile glosses "skate" as a member of the genus *Rajidae* [one R. W. Ayers first identified "skate" with the fish of the same name], in which case the preposition *on* requires that "bow" denote the *bow of a ship*. Such a "skate" is itself cruciform, or "winged" like the falcon....

And on and on into the intensest inane, even though Wordsworth had said it all: "... spinning still / The rapid line of motion, then at once / Have I, reclining back upon my heels, / Stopped short; yet still the solitary cliffs / Wheeled by me..." (*The Prelude,* I, 455 ff.).

In *Gerard Manley Hopkins and the Language of Mystery* (1991), the author, generally sensible though long-winded, goes on for five pages about the banal play on "up" and "down" in "The Starlight Night," ignoring not only Hopkins's own, "I lift *up* heart, eyes, *down*" (in "Hurrahing in Harvest"), but the widespread recurrence of the topos — for example, a couple of non-Jesuit jesters: Crispin conceived "his voyage to be / An *up* and *down*." Thomas Nashe's clown sings: "Trip and go, heave and ho' / Up and down, to and fro"; Stevens's fishes go "in many directions / Up and down"; the "Virgilian Cadences" of "Notes toward a Supreme Fiction" are, "up down, / Up down"; Crispin, again, goes "up and down between two elements"; Browning's "Lippo" (40), his "Andrea" (189), and his poet in "How It Strikes..." (4) all execute these same cadences. And our ultimate voyager was "taught by the heavenly Muse to venture *down* / The dark descent, and *up* to reascend": a trajectory reversed in the grand and touching proem to book VII (12–16). Again, it is axiomatic — poetry is its own best interpreter: *per simile simile percipiens*.

Then we have concepts treated like amulets (no Shakespearean allusion), as when the mere presence of parallel structures is taken as a critical virtue (and with thanks to but no creative use of James Kugel on Psalmodic patterns). Thus our student of "contemplative psychology" rather self-gratulatingly announces: "I read 'Pied Beauty' as one large antithetical parallelism." Or again: "The relation between the parallel clauses of 'The Windhover's' first tercet is duplicated by that between the parallel clauses of the final tercet.... Thus, the two tercets are parallel to one another." (We just said *that,* but in any case, so...?) Of the "sillion" and the "gash gold": "Both these images have antithetical structures." Indeed, but what is the point of treating antithesis as though it were some kind of mantra? Exposition and exhortation are not explication. *So,* where is the seal-that-*so* feature?

But enough of jargon and *opus-operatum* reification. I will close with a little unvarnished subjective opinionizing: *Meinung* as in *Mein.* In the aptly titled *In Extremity,* it is decreed of "The Bugler's First Communion" that "the boy's father is described with unwitting grotesqueness as 'an English sire.' It is regrettable that such a grossness should result from Hopkins attempt to avoid monotonously obvious patterns." It is also regrettable that this author did not "avoid monotonously obvious patterns" like "grotesqueness" / "grossness." This kind of finicky edict attaches to one of Hopkins's most characteristically brilliant lines (original author's italicized stutters): "Or *t*o-fro *t*ender *t*rambeams *t*ruckle a*t* the eye." (This is also a line that Charles Williams, editor of the second edition of the *Poems,* found "funny" — much to the vindicating delight of Leavis.) The *In Extremity* gloss: "The trinket effect of all those dentals is at odds with the trundling bulk of 'tram' and of 'beam' which, anxious though one may be [why?] to make it refer to a ray of light, *suffers in association*" (my emphasis to stress the lameness of this "curtal" proof). Nor do I know what could be "trinketing" about consonants neon-lit by repeated italics. In fact, what we have here are what the Scholastic philosophers called transcendentals: tram = trans; beam = be-am.

Even more significant in the light of my generalized focus on structures, and more particularly on the pattern of complementarity of wave and particle in Hopkins, is the fact that this allegedly "trinketing" line perfectly embodies what is now being called the "wavicle" hypothesis: the dentals *do* break up the line into particles or quanta, and we are in one sense talking about *rays*, that is, about energy which is wavelike or cymatic. In short, this embodiment of being "at odds" and "suffering in association" with its context is an excellent illustration of one of the theses on structural patterns, particularly that of complementarity, central to this discussion. All this cumulative detail is admittedly tiresome, but one final "cinematic" wrap (mainly because it brings us back to Stevens). Our trinketeer notes: "Hopkins failed lamentably on one or two occasions to make himself understood, and those occasions do not become less lamentable when his letters provide the necessary gloss." But as Holly Stevens brings out repeatedly, the problem is with the blinkered paraliterate, not with the glossy letters. With Hopkins, as with Stevens, one is always amazed at how the most seemingly obscure texts become epiphanic through their authors' plain-spoken *éclaircissement*.

"Time is our tedious song should here have ending," so what follows will be brief and litanic, though, I trust, serviceable. We have the esteemed student of Victoriana who repeatedly refers to Chartreuse Cathedral (having forgotten her ecclesiastical history and her Stendhal); and who also, nearer to home, repeatedly refers to Felix Randa*ll*; and who titles an essay, after a perfectly sensible hint from Hillis Miller, "The Windhover as Symbol of 'Diabolic Gravity.'" (The windhover as "levity's rainbow" would be more appropriate.) We also have the author of the definitive biography (1992) referring to a Dominican "monk."

We repeatedly (three times over a decade in *HQ*, and most recently in *G. M. H. and the Language of Mystery*) have the received tradition launched by Gardner that "The Starlight Night" has as guiding image an auction! See (or rather, hear) for oneself: Look, Look: buy then, bid then; all is a purchase, all is a prize. How could the nonventure capitalist have missed this? Though there is the problem that people bid, and *then* buy; and having made the purchase cannot win the prize. (Oh, unhappy, unhappy lottery.) The same poem, for unexplained reasons, is also discussed in *HQ* (1980) under the rubric, "The Game-Motif in Gerard Manley Hopkins's Sonnets." We have had the ENG "principle," earlier; maybe now we have the "Jeopardy" hypothesis.

I think I can cap, clear, and clinch all this by my penultimate example; that of a critic who had called Bridges a "rat" and who, when denounced in print for using "bar-room" talk, replied as follows: "I am Boston Brahmin born and bred, Pilgrim-fathered and DAR-mothered, a Wellesley-Cape Cod independent, none of which ever took me near a barroom. My deliberate selection of one three-letter word ('rat') was amply supported with several indisputable facts. What I do not understand is why critics choose not to admit that those facts exist" (*HQ*, 1983). What *I* do not understand is whatever happened to plain old-fashioned *odium theologicum*.

Finally, among the components of this chronicle of follies, I have saved the most deracinated, outlandish, and groundless as coda to this chapter. In a Foucauldian, Lacanian, and pseudo-Bloomian exegesis, *Hopkins against History* (1995) proposes (and this is the foundational thesis of the entire book) that in "The Windhover," the much-controverted "Buckle" is a direct reference to the historian Henry Thomas Buckle. Now, I have always been sympathetic to Benjamin's notion of poetry as entailing a kind of "magic," but it would take blind faith in wizardry to find in Hopkins's "Buckle" even the faintest allusion to a contemporary historian — unless, of course, in that same line one found in the word "act" a reference to another historian (and a Catholic one, at that), Acton: the poem *was* dedicated belatedly to "Lord." I have just described this exegesis as deracinated, outlandish, and *groundless*. In those terms, as conjoined with this exegete's abuse of poetic "magic," it seems therapeutic to suggest he is in need of more chthonic and less djinn. *Genug.* Until I take up "The Windhover" in my sixth chapter, the Buckle stops here.

Class and Cause

Many of these citations are clearly not merely unconventional or eccentric, but dotty and crankish. Yet how can this be? These are academicians, professors of literature and religion, publishing in learned journals or in books from university presses. Does this not indict whole fields and whole groups of scholars? The answer is, of course, it does, and it should. The specific explanation relating to Hopkins studies has already been adumbrated. So seemingly slight a body of work tempts slight attention to the poems themselves. The original creative studies I referred to earlier have depleted the field: contamination by the examples above might tempt one to say, the ooze of oil field. So what is now left are geological improvisations equivalent to the desperate construction of offshore rigs ("ramps against the shore"); or the academic counterpart of drillings through slag and shale, and in the end coming up with little that is energizing — but with much that does pollute the intellectual environment.

The more generalized explanation is the universally recognized collapse of academic standards, and the fragmentation of scholarly disciplines. That is a reality few will deny, though the macabre may welcome it as an expression of a post-posthumous *Tendenz*. But collapse and fragmentation are consequences not causes of senescence. In the humanities, the very allusion above to *textus receptus* suggests an opposite but equally oppressive drift which canonizes repetitive sterility. The pressure to publish brings about an implosion of the trite *and* the revolutionary (compare the perennial cold-nuclear-fusion claims) that generates the chaos to which all the above citations attest. These are problems for the academy in general, and in any case are not my business here (as they are — and well-solved — for Terry Eagleton in *The Illusions of Postmodernism*). But if we have established Societies for the Analysis of Social Anomie, institutionalized Structures for

Deconstructionism, surely we can survive Centers for the Study of De-centering.

However, even entirely apart from this universal intellectual entropy, there remains a seemingly insoluble problem in the humanities as such where the methods and perspectives of the physical sciences now predominate. The assumption is not only that the goal is a novel, revolutionary, and definitive discovery, implicitly motivated by the vulgar competitiveness enshrined in Kendrew and Watson on the double helix (whose intellectual infirmity only Irwin Chargaff had the courage to attack); but that such a discovery can only result from the compilation of every strand of minutial research, the accumulation of which inevitably, it is presumed, leads to new knowledge. (Here the *monitum* is: "Give 'em enough rope.")

But it is Charles Taylor who has most emphatically pointed out that, as opposed to the physical sciences, there are very few foundational "data" in the humanities, little cumulative "knowledge," only more and more insights deriving rather from scholarly intuition than from assembly-line remodeling and redesigning of prior "research." After twenty-five years, Mariani's, Hartman's, Miller's, and Cotter's commentaries on Hopkins's poetic achievement, far from being obsolete, remain, along with Gardner and with a few other works from the postwar period, more useful and more enriching than virtually anything from the last couple of decades — again exception being made for Ong on Hopkins and the self, and for the textual discoveries of MacKenzie. So the spiral descends from the academy in general, and then to the humanities in particular.

But again, why the concentration on Hopkins? Why do so many explicators sound like parodies from that early Hopkins admirer, Louis MacNeice: "Some on commission, some for the love of learning, / Some because they have nothing better to do / Or because they hope these walls of books will deaden / The drumming of the demon in their ears. / Cranks, hacks, poverty-stricken scholars, / In pince-nez, period hats or romantic beards / And cherishing their hobby or their doom" ("The British Museum

Reading Room")? I have already adumbrated an answer to this question, so this is by way of summation.

There is, first of all, the fact that Hopkins's is so slim a body of work that it tempts the facile (or the rushed dissertation writer) to imagine it is therefore easily comprehensible. There is, second, the fact that Hopkins's work has been subject of study for roughly a mere half-century, and, as with most untested hypotheses, "anything goes." Moreover, the intrinsic ambiguity of Hopkins's texts, the singularity of his language, which Bridges unwittingly overemphasized, and his quirky, but oh so winsome, personality — all allow free play to the most unwarranted, most uncontrolled assumptions: again, as exemplified in the citations above, and in the sheer volume of vacuous critical studies. (If the flood of books and monographs on Hopkins continues unabated, his profile will be second only to that of Dante as universally recognizable even among non–poetry lovers.) Third, there is the fact, unique in literary studies of a major/minor figure, that virtually every substantive idea in Hopkins, every proper noun, whether thing, place, or person, is indexed in the four volumes of letters, private spiritual writings, devotions, and sermons. This explains why in almost every book on Hopkins, the identical quotations appear and reappear, incessantly — so that, to take a curious example, if a given author wants to describe Hopkins's penchant for punning, there will be a list of such puns in the index, all lying at hand for exploitation.

Repetition is only one side of the problem. The other is that a moderately perceptive student, recognizing this stenobathic phenomenon (unfortunately the *mot juste)*, will then seek radically different, and *épatant,* applications and explications in order to break out of this prefabricated narrow mold of Hopkinsian themes and lore: with the result that in the pursuit of the new broad vista, the most absurd and utterly unutterable proposals will be calmly and soberly envisaged as serious and profound discoveries by those travailing in these realms of dross.

There is, finally, the more delicate matter of all of such factors converging on Hopkins's Catholicism. Notwithstanding all commendable ecumenical talk and deeds, English-language Catholicism is still freighted with nineteenth-century bogies and clichés, with the baggage of a parvenu lower-class culture, and in North America, with that of an immigrant, largely Irish, religious style. As a result much Catholicism and probably almost all "Jesuitry" are still viewed even by enlightened academicians as a kind of hybrid reduction of something foreign, mysterious, even sinister — as though the Jesuits were heirs of the Knights Templars. Witness in Hopkins studies the self-consciously well-intentioned, and thus labored, clarifications of religious feasts and practices (e.g., the Sacred Heart, mental prayer, the Ignatian *Exercises*); of theological and philosophical concepts (e.g., the Real Presence — usually gotten wrong — infallibility, hypostatic union, free will, *media scientia*, angelology); of institutions (e.g., monastic life, Oratorians, tertianship).

More particularly in the United States, the situation is not improved by the fact that until recently there has been very little difference among the "public" socioreligious values described by Roman Catholic writers from James T. Farrell, through J. F. Powers and Flannery O'Connor, to Mary Gordon. The themes and images of the last are in continuity with those of the first — all, broadly speaking, being reactions to WASP stereotypes from the turn of the century.

Eithne Wilkins in *The Rose-Garden Game* (1969), a sophisticated socioanthropological study of the symbolism of beads in Eastern and Western religious traditions, describes present-day attitudes to one Catholic devotion: "But there is a vague, dim opposition and prejudice against the rosary, a passive and latent resistance rather than a conscious dislike. A Protestant, if roused to comment, will use some such phrase as 'mumbling of beads.'" Elsewhere, she notes of this particular devotional practice: it "suggested the Middle Ages, an Edwardian novel I had never read, and some old crone with a black shawl over her head, toothlessly mumbling Hail Mary, at her cottage door in Ireland or Italy."

Not only devotional practices but theological concepts and religious "lifestyles" are all reified as exotic or alien: as topics to be sociologically analyzed from a distance, never to be entered into as the living entelechy of an evolving society. Hence all those negligible essays, to which I referred above, on Hopkins's contemplative, sacramental, incarnational, mariological, etc., vision, perspective, dimension, again, etc. As late as 1986, Catherine Phillips, daughter of Norman MacKenzie, could affirm that "Hopkins's 'oddity and obscurity' still cause sufficient difficulty to suggest that Bridge's [1918] criticisms have some validity."

The sincere, thorough, dedicated, non-Catholic scholarly representative of the regnant culture comes to this mysterious religious poetry as would an American New Age anthropologist (if such exist) to the study of Cuban Santería or Brazilian Pentecostalism. As Karen Brown's work has shown, it takes years, even decades, to understand these "alien societies" from the inside. This is why the best work on Hopkins has been done not necessarily by Catholics, but certainly by Jesuits who have lived in and from this tradition. They have put the lie to the old confabulations and brought closure to the old dreary issues: Was he being used by the Society, abused by the Society, frustrated by the Society? These are generally pointless questions conceivable only by outsiders for whom the "Society" itself is viewed as sinister, anachronistic, and incomprehensible.

I would even venture to suggest that only someone who had spent several years in a Catholic religious community, preferably one like the Jesuits, could answer such questions with the requisite empathy. Maybe "in partial fulfillment of the requirements" for a dissertation on Hopkins, students should spend a year in a Jesuit novitiate, this last an institution non-Catholics invariably get confused with its denizens, called "novices" — witness Stevens in "The Idea of a Colony": "Shrewd novitiates / Should be the clerks of our experience." What then of that chronicle of follies sketched above concerning the poet, his works, and his days? What opinions, judgments, interpretations, and so on, can be tolerated? Again, that is beyond the scope of this book, but in brief one may suggest that in a post–post-period, when it is solemnly affirmed that the old "narratives" have lost much of their cogency, perhaps the old practical *sententiae* may still supply guidelines: *securus iudicat orbis terrarum; consensus fidelium* — to invoke a couple that still are useful; or closer to home, Madisonian federalism; or even, "the authority of interpretive communities." Neither of these latter is epistemologically well-grounded, but they may be pragmatically useful for arriving at moderately credible collective standards.

II: *The Biographical Perverse*

"Lies My Life"

What I want to do in this chapter is briefly survey Hopkins's biographies, and after that examine in detail the two most recent lives which may be said to bring all previous scholarship up to the 1990s. Since one of these lives has proved highly controversial in its treatment of Hopkins's undergraduate years, this examination will also allow me to discuss the early poems that will enter the body of this book only briefly and fragmentarily.

In the three decades after the appearance of the second edition of the poems, virtually every book, essay, or even brief allusion relating to Hopkins's adult life centered, as noted earlier, on one and/or another of the following conflicts: Anglican/Roman, ascetic/esthetic (Newmanite/Paterian), priest/ poet, communal Jesuit/isolated maverick, Thomist/"Scotist," high aspiration/low attainment, moral scrupulosity/sensual ardor — in short, as a fellow Jesuit and Hopkins's first memorialist remarked: "Never was a squarer man in a rounder hole." Some of these conflicts were simply resolved by negating one horn of the dilemma, for example, "Anglican"; most others were never resolved, but the tension was sublated, as the poet was put at the service of the priest; the high aspiration subordinated to the demands of the clerical life; the "Scotism" internalized in theological speculation and occasionally in some of the poems. (I have been signaling the "Scotism," because I am not sure it is really at play in most of the poems — but of this, more in the following discussion.)

One alleged conflict, curiously preoccupying agnostics like I. A. Richards and Yvor Winters, that between Hopkins's Catholicism and skepticism, was never resolved because there is no evidence it ever existed outside of those critics' imaginations. There was physical and mental depression; there was disappointment at his priestly mission; there was distress at the condition of the Irish church; there was temptation to despair, and briefly to suicide in the face of the fruitlessness of his intellectual and poetic efforts; but there was nowhere any sense of loss of faith. In fact, the same passages attesting to the strength of his religious convictions are so endlessly repeated in every commentary that they are now trotted out verbatim in virtually every book on the poet.

The tension of priest, Jesuit, and "Scotist" — with perhaps too much stress on the latter — had been fully and satisfactorily explored by the indefatigable Gardner, subsequently by John Pick, and by several other critics, including Christopher Devlin, W. A. M. Peters, J.-G. Ritz, William T. Noon, Robert Boyle, Thomas Alford, James Finn Cotter, and most recently and originally, Walter J. Ong. Even though many of these are Jesuits, for reasons I have set forth in the preceding chapter, in no case does one get the impression of anything other than experienced insight into aspects of Hopkins's life and spirituality; never does the interpretation of Hopkins's trials and tensions take the form of "protecting" a co-religionist or confrere. Complete lives, written as it were from the "outside," have been less successful. There is a fictionalized and moderately tendentious early biography (1947) by Eleanor Ruggles, and four more recent, derivative, but brief introductions to the man and the poet by Bernard Bergonzi (1977), Paddy Kitchen (1978), Graham Storey (1981), and Gerald Roberts (1994). All in all, for a poet of the recognized influence of Hopkins, it is a rather skimpy list, with only in 1995 a sketch in the *Dictionary of National Biography*.

The absence of serious biographies is not from want of materials since almost all of what appears to be the extant and relevant prose documentation is now readily accessible. Hopkins even had close relatives who survived him up to the period of World War II and who have been a fruitful source, however random, of information. Norman MacKenzie in 1989 published an excellent facsimile edition of the early poems and notebooks with truly exemplary textual reconstructions and a cogent introduction, though perhaps marred by "psychoanalytic" interpretations. The sermons and devotional writings have long been available, and there have been four, successively expanded and annotated, editions of the poetry — with a fifth (definitive and exhaustive) by MacKenzie published in 1990. There are two periodical publications devoted to Hopkins; and bibliographical entries relating to the poet now approach the astonishing figure of three thousand.

Norman White in 1988 (*HQ*) suggested that the main "blockage" responsible for the paucity of serious biographies lay in the "difficulty of being adequate to both...the poetry and the Jesuitry" — thus perpetuating the same conflict that one thought had been definitively laid to rest two decades before, and also ignoring what I have already described as the most original study of the character of Hopkins the man, Walter Ong's *Hopkins, the Self, and God*. It is possible that White was merely building up a sense of anticipation for his own biography, long gestating and finally appearing in 1992. But regardless of publishing strategies, his was a book worth waiting for: extensively researched and relatively unbiased. Of course, it has its flaws, to which I shall return after considering in detail White's only competitor, a somewhat smaller but at least in this decade a much more consequential and modish (i.e., "politically correct") biography, Robert Bernard Martin's *Gerard Manley Hopkins: A Very Private Life* (1991).

Still, even an extended notion of "privacy" is incapable, in light of the mass of material indicated above, of explaining at this late date the fact that we have only two substantial critical biographies. Studies of the poetry abound, even to excess. But this is probably due to the fact, noted in the previous chapter, that so small a body of work tempts authors to assume it means easy comprehension. So we have full-length books focused on the ordering of the *six* "terrible sonnets'" for example, *"Inspirations Unbidden"* (1981), occasionally insightful but containing more than a tolerable share of deconstructionist jargon, and displaying an ignorance of Catholicity which, I have also noted earlier, is more or less endemic in Hopkins studies — beware of authors like

Harris, who refers to *St.* Thomas à Kempis, or like Overholser (1991), who has Hopkins "brought into the church by Dr. Henry Newman," or, finally that vexing Victorianist, also cited earlier, who repeatedly asserts that Arnold visited "Chartreuse Cathedral," and who should do penance with a novena to St. Bruno or by memorizing Blake in "An Island in the Moon," on Thomas Sutton, "for he did build a house / For aged men & youth..." — the "house" being the Charterhouse. And that Carthusian illustration reminds one that we also have voluminous and otiose studies by the same author devoted to Hopkins the Victorian, although that theme had been ingeniously and sympathetically analyzed by W. S. Johnson four years earlier (1968). So the question remains, Why so few broad-gauge and scholarly lives?

Newman

The answer is, alas, that Hopkins is the clerical and academic embodiment of quiet desperation. His adult life sifts out into a tiny plateau of quotidian banalities; there are not even any cliffs of fall until the very last years. One could say much the same of Newman during his Catholic period, forty-five years, approximately that of the whole of Hopkins's life. But what makes Newman enduringly appealing is that after his conversion he delighted in, indeed gloried in, focusing the most subtle and supple intelligence of the age on some of its most crucial philosophical, historical, and theological issues. Therein resides the continuous allure of the man. The poetry and the theological writings of his Anglican period — excepting only *The Arians* and the *Justification* essay (*Development* is a Catholic work) — are never read except by romantic reactionaries or apologetical burrowers; though in the actual events of Newman's Tractarian career there is always the somewhat perverse fascination of encountering an authentically devout religious fanatic of the sort that would cross the street to avoid greeting a friend who was deviating toward monothelytism, or some other heterodoxic horror. This contradiction between the Anglican Newman and the Catholic was summarized by Hopkins in 1864: "I assure you Dr. Newman, the extremest of the extreme, so extreme that he *went* beyond the extremes of that standard and took a large faction of his side with him, *is* a MODERATE MAN" (*sic*). That this moderate man had to defend himself against trying to revive the Inquisition, and was thought of by Dr. Arnold as a "thug" (in the subcontinent sense), might also explain Hopkins's fascination with a real inquisitor, the Savonarola of George Eliot's encyclopedic enumeration, *Romola*.

But with Newman, as a Roman Catholic publicly pledged to the defense of a system that was grinding him up, as the most famous convert to an institution that feared him and treated him like a mere schoolmaster (as for much of his life in Birmingham he indeed was), there came into full linguistic tension a rhetoric of unparalleled mysticism, of noetic sensibility, and of moral and psychological acuity. (Abbé Bremond's "mystère" should be translated "paradox.") Even more, there came into play a mastery of classical polemic styles (Hopkins was wrong that Newman's prose was merely Oxford high-table talk writ large), and an almost infinite capacity for philosophical and theological accommodation, qualification, adjustment, refinement — all usually culminating in a logical stranglehold on his opponent. One is reminded of the true-blue zealot in "Hudibras" (Newman *had* evangelical roots): "A rope of sand he could twist / As tough as any Sorbonist." As for his relations with Rome, one may compare the virulent but conventional and conservative attack by the Anglican Newman on de Lamennais with the sympathetically insightful Catholic appreciation of the latter, even when denounced by Rome as an apostate and heretic. The reason, of course, is that Newman was being subjected to attacks similar to those launched against de Lamennais.*

One might compare, as well, that detailed catalogue of churchy politicking in the *Apologia* (certainly the most boring autobio-

---

*Compare Newman's bitter Anglican essay, "The Fall of de Lamennais," in *Essays Critical and Historical*, vol. 1 (1872), with his comment to Matthew Arnold, "Perhaps La Mennais will be a true prophet after all" (*Unpublished Letters of Matthew Arnold* [1923], 60; cf. also *Lord Beaconsfield's Correspondence with His Sister* [1886], 208).

graphical classic of the modern era) with the sinuously wrought argumentative tissue of *The Present Position* or of *Anglican Difficulties* — all culminating in the intertwined strands woven so cleverly together in the unseverable cable of "The Letter to the Duke of Norfolk," composed in defense of a papal teaching on infallibility to which Newman was fundamentally unsympathetic; and the marvel is that the letter is done with no hypocrisy, no dissimulation, no verbal subterfuge, no resort to scholastic legerdemain about "thesis"/"hypothesis," "inopportunism," and so on.

As one antagonistic critic said (with unwitting wisdom) of that most densely textured and most insidiously persuasive work of British religious philosophy, *A Grammar of Assent,* the argument entails linguistic and verbal mechanisms as subtle, varied, elusive, *and* as overwhelmingly effective as the spritely "aerial kind" in the "Rape of the Lock." But in *A Grammar* we have dianoetic sylphs, psychological fays, phronetic genii. It is little wonder that Hopkins offered to edit the work for a broader audience.

And now heirs of this Newmanian legacy have thirty volumes of correspondence as engaging as that of Keats, and as cutting and witty as that of Byron. With Newman, *the writings are the events,* and hence his *and* their endless appeal. Ironically, the "great event" of Newman's Catholic years, the tardy red hat, came not as homage to his intellectual sovereignty or as exoneration of his Catholicity, but merely as satisfaction of a condescending whim of that same Duke of Norfolk to whom the infallibility essay was addressed. (No end of Howards here.)

Tennyson

To invoke a Tennysonian family pun: from Te Deum to tedium — from Newman to Hopkins. With the latter, the prose writings are thin, with little social, political, or theological significance; they are occasionally witty, occasionally whimsical, occasionally perceptive, especially when discussing his own poems, but usually humdrum. As to the correspondence, it is all with poets no one other than doctoral students reads today. Bridges's *Testament* remains a very pretty piece of Platonism, where Hopkins as Jesuit is briefly introduced. But Bridges's poem remains what Hopkins himself called "munch."

Hopkins's early journals are embarrassingly mawkish and understandably narcissistic, save when relieved by compulsively fascinating oddities, while his Balliol essays are pretentious and ambiguous. Hopkins is an author who did nothing of any public note, though as observed he wanted to capitalize on Newman's *Grammar* — only to be chillily dismissed by the great man. What *can* a biographer say about a bright star (not of Balliol) so unsteadfast? about a figure who after his undergraduate years becomes more and more a caricature of the British eccentric, and a stereotype of the Victorian amateur ceaselessly dabbling in matters beyond his competence? and about one who finally becomes physically and spiritually straitened, delivering oddly boggled sermons, ministering to parishioners with whom he had little in common, and ultimately facing death at the prospect of correcting reams of student papers? Who would have thought the heart source of fiery animation could be snuffed out by an examination? — a Byronic allusion to Keats played on by Hopkins's earliest cartoon and recorded pun, when faced with, not correcting but passing, what he called at age fourteen, "examination/exanimation."

And Hopkins himself realized this failure of expectations, from the frustration expressed in his undergraduate, "The Alchemist in the City," to one of his last Irish poems, "The shepherd's brow...." On the one hand, Hopkins must have recognized himself as almost the literal contradiction of all those ill-fated young Jesuits — Kostka, Berchmans, Gonzaga — whose Collects would affirm that, "in a short span fulfilled a long life"; while, on the other hand, he is almost the avatar of St. Alphonsus Rodriguez whom, in an ad hoc but revelatory sonnet, he described as living "those years and years... of world without event." What is there to say about this Hopkinsian sequence of "nullity and dullity" (Keats), except that from such nonevents emerged the most

original lyrics in English during the hundred years from early
Tennyson to early Auden? And *that* — as would opine catholic
Stevens, who remained ambiguous about Hopkins — is a verita-
ble "lalapalooza" of poetic achievement: a noun from the 1920s
now curiously invoked only by rock musicians exercising their
own brand of sprung rhythm.

But alas, again, all of *that* relates to the extraordinary poetry, not to the quotidian history. Faced with a *life* that would
bore to the core anyone except other Catholic converts or poetic devotés, what could a modern biographer do except galvanize
such inanation by whatever means might shock the contemporary
consciousness (or unconsciousness)? With Hopkins those means
are limited, if not nonexistent. What could redeem so publicly
vacuous a narrative, a story where the visible plot of the main
character is so blanketed in *Alltäglichkeit?* What indeed, except
to discover or to fabricate a secret, hitherto undisclosed "private"
life — as in the subtitle of Martin's biography? And what would
be more private than the sexual life of an ascetic, celibate, Jesuit
priest?

Unlike Hopkins's earlier, and quiescently frustrated, biogra-
phers (Paddy Kitchen excepted), this is the tack Martin takes as he
turns the other chic and introduces among his *dramatis personae*
the very most private of parts. Moreover, one had feared worse to
come, as suggested by the only other major biography then loom-
ing (leering?) on the horizon, that projected by Norman White,
whose meticulously diligent researches over the years in *HQ* never
compensated for lickerish judgments: for example, the decrial of
admirers of Hopkins for expecting "his life to provide uplift, biography as a brassiere"(1988) — maybe a typo for brasserie. In
any case heady brewage here. Happily, White later took a higher
road, and nothing like this appears in his 1992 biography.

Readers of Martin's *Tennyson: The Unquiet Heart* (1981)
never felt he was forcing a thesis, certainly not one related primarily to sexuality. The reason has certainly to be that with Tennyson
there *is* enough excitement, enough achievement, enough close
relationship with the major figures of the day (Gladstone, Fitz-

Gerald, Maurice, the Rossettis, the Carlyles, the Brownings, Emerson, Margaret Fuller, Froude, Manning, Wilfrid Ward, not to speak of Soapy Sam and the Widow of Windsor); with Tennyson there is enough lunacy, quinsy, angina, addiction, sexual pathology, melancholia, neurasthenia, hypochondria (almost all the ailments from book XI of *Paradise Lost*); with Tennyson there is enough public controversy ("Christopher North," Bulwer-Lytton), enough public honors (laureateship, lordship, and finally Abbey enshrinement); with Tennyson there is enough of everything that attracts the generality of readers and that obviates the need for any extraneous enticements. *All, unfortunately, unlike Hopkins.*

I am not saying that Martin deliberately and pervasively distorts Hopkins. Martin was, at least initially, both too serious and too conscientious a scholar for that kind of exaggeration — though he seems excessively dependent for factual and organizational data on Bernard Bergonzi's 1977 study. But I think Martin is driven out of sheer desperation (at least in the beginning of the book, and probably in the beginning of his writing of it) to sensationalize certain alleged character traits of Hopkins and certain events alleged to have occurred in his life: self-centeredness, delicacy, solitariness; susceptibility to female and maternal influence with a corresponding antagonism to the male and the paternal; late-developing prurience; effeminacy, autoeroticism, and narcissism. Once Martin has set this course he becomes more and more obsessed by such real or imagined traits that by the central chapters of the book he has locked himself into an interpretation which leads to a *provably* warped view of Hopkins.

I shall take up shortly the methods and techniques which result in this mutilated portrait. But first it must be said that I have no "political" interest in this or that reading of Hopkins's sexual inclinations as teenager, undergraduate, or priest. Religious history, and none more emphatically than that of nineteenth-century England, testifies that one cannot confine gaiety all to the laity. I am concerned only with the implications of the dumbfounding absence of evidence for Martin's overarching thesis, indeed the axis of the entire work: that is, *one* allegedly sexually charged meeting with *one* presumably congenial aspiring young convert, Digby Mackworth Dolben, was "the most momentous emotional event of Hopkins's undergraduate years, probably *of his entire life*" (emphasis added).

However, I want to return to the Tennyson of Martin's earlier biography, the Tennyson called by his critics a "eunuch" (strangely unmentioned by Martin, who elaborates fancifully on Hopkins's use of the word), and hypothesize for Tennyson a life as bland and vacuous as that of Hopkins. Through what lens would Martin then have examined that life?

Incipit In Memoriam. Arthur Hallam not only would be center stage, but would be omnipresent in every act, whether documentable or not, even unto the final scene where as old men Gladstone and Tennyson were still arguing over to whom Hallam had been more devoted. Instead, gliding by *In Memoriam* — pious homage to the Corydon *topos* from Virgil to Gide — and scores of other explicit, nonconjectural, public witnessings, Martin concludes (because he has to get on to other more interesting Tennysonian *gestes*): "The bluff openness [of a comment by Tennyson] is surely evidence of his lack of self-consciousness about the matter [seemingly erotic language], which would not have been true had he been aware of having sexual feelings for Hallam." "Bluff" is a minor hermeneutical key. How can a practitioner of that most virile of English traits, bluffness, have homosexual longings?

I have already noted that Martin's first chapter on Hopkins is tendentiously titled, "The Importance of Being Manley," as though the attainment of "manliness" were a burden for Hopkins — this, notwithstanding his detailed and lengthy defense of Keats's "distinctively masculine powers," "manly virtues," and so on, his repeated commendation of Bridges's poetry for its "manliness," and his condemnation of Bernardino Luini's "exquisite grace refined almost into effeminacy." Part of the problem concerning "manliness" is that the word is used in its Romantic, even Byronic, sense, whereas Hopkins used it in its "deep-structural" poetic sense, derived, according to Donald Davie, in a critique (1961) of Walter Scott, from Pater. And if one finds the introduction of Pater here ironic, it is merely further evidence of how tainted one may be by the superficial and attenuated Romantic notion of masculinity. For Pater masculinity certainly did not entail anything like bluff, male assertiveness. Rather it was the esthetic "full consciousness of what one does, of art itself in the work of art, tenacity of intuition and of consequent purpose." Says Davie persuasively, "It is this, an energy of apprehension which, so far from running wild, seeks out of itself the structures to control it, which makes a piece of writing masculine or manly, as Pater and Hopkins understood those terms." Lastly, and often overlooked by commentators like Martin, is that what bothered Hopkins was never his middle name, virtually unused by him, but what he thought of as his "unpoetic" surname.

But Martin accepts none of this exoneration, and goes on to treat as authoritative the most oft-cited study of Victorian religiosity and homosexuality, David Hilliard's "Unenglish and Unmanly" (1982). Regrettably, for Martin's purposes the essay is self-defeating since, while purporting to be "liberal" and "modern," it not infrequently reinforces Hemingwayesque, limp-wristed, campy-pop platitudes. (Another *monitum:* beware of authors, like Hilliard, who believe Newman had a "religious brotherhood" *at Littlemore*).

Moreover, the Puseyites and Anglo-Catholics Hilliard focuses on were all obsessed with liturgical peripherals: colorful processions, pseudo-Gothic vestments, Gregorian incantings, dramatic thurifications, and so on, all matters of *utter* indifference to Hopkins, whose sister Milicent he described as "given to Puseyism..., mummery nunnery. Consequently she will be directed by some Ritualist which are the worst hands she could fall into: these men are imperious, uncommissioned, without common sense, and without knowledge of moral theology." (Hilliard stresses this nexus of unmanliness and ritual as seen by four-square Church-of-England types, though he ignores the fact that this nexus is not necessarily historically bound, as evident by the as-yet unstudied history not only of nineteenth-century Anglo-Catholic ritualists but of their twentieth-century counterparts.)

But back to Martin's non-"parallel lives" of Tennyson and Hopkins. Martin, after his "bluff" clincher, and to get the whole matter of Tennyson's possible homoeroticism out of the way and to proceed to the *real* Tennyson, his works, ailments, achievements, et al., continues thus: "But, some critics would say, wanting to have it both ways [*sic?*], his [Tennyson's] lack of awareness is the final proof of how deeply sexual his feelings were, since he had to deny them to himself. Possibly, but there can be no discussion in the face of such a claim." Unfortunately, there is a great deal of discussion, in fact total dependence, by Martin on precisely such a claim regarding Hopkins: that is, since we can't validate textually the "secrets" of Hopkins's "private life," that very fact indicates how deeply interiorized and how skillfully disguised such secrets were.

Martin continues the Tennysonian exonerative process by noting that the "pairing of friends such as Hallam and Tennyson was both common in the [Cambridge] Apostles and perfectly open," and presumably therefore of only incidental biographical significance. It was left to Geoffrey Faber on those other *[Oxford] Apostles* (brackets supplied) to make such friendships central to the narrative, however furtive and tainted they were assumed to be. But not so with Martin on Hallam, Tennyson, and their circle. "Such deep but *frank* [another exculpating term like "bluff"] feelings were by no means confined to the [Cambridge] Apostles." Then Edward FitzGerald and John Allen are introduced by Martin: the former "described his college friendships as more like loves, and Thackeray remembered Cambridge with a sigh: 'What *passions* [original italics] our friendships were.'" So much for Tennyson. But there is no reprieve for the-soon-to-be-converted and ultimately ordained Hopkins, who had met the alleged object of *his* "passions" no more than once for a few hours in a single day out of the whole of his life.

But we do have a small problem, overlooked by Hilliard, concerning literary and epistolary conventions. The language of

FitzGerald and Thackeray, which would not have shocked their contemporaries, and which would not shock — to take an example out of the air — the members of Robert Bly's New Masculinity movement (or so I assume), might very well disturb the frail ego of the present post–feminist-terrorized male generation. I thus proffer a hypothetical situation: let us suppose we did not know the lengthy and detailed Hopkins-Bridges correspondence (two-volumes plus), and someone with Martin's ferreting inclinations were to discover letters *from the 1880s* in which Hopkins addressed Bridges (as indeed he did), as "dear Heart," how might this be exploited by neurotic, threatened emulators of machismo some sixty years later? Would, then, not a seamless tapestry of homoeroticism have been woven?

Philters

Now everyone knows that all exclusively male — or female, for that matter — societies are going to generate erotically explosive emotions to a greater or lesser degree depending on a wide spectrum of circumstances. Prisoners, prep-schoolers, soldiers, and seminarians will be particularly susceptible to what have variously been related to "piffles," *le vice anglais,* "crushes," and so on. (There was even some years ago a sociological treatise on the homosexual bond among pirates that was reviewed under the title "The Jolly Rogers"; and everyone remembers Whistler's gibe that a projected drama by Wilde should be called *The Bugger's Opera.*) Much of this represents a way of demeaning what is alien, as with accusations of "temple prostitutes" by the Hebrews, or as with British and Italian references to syphilis as "the French disease." But much of this also represents rudimentary physiological and psychological data — with, *contra* Martin, certainly no more relevance to Hopkins than to Tennyson: in fact, much less to Hopkins, or certainly much less that is documentable and nonconjectural.

There are scores of vigorously heterosexual poetic fragments by Hopkins (and one major poem) before he became immersed in the hot-house atmosphere of Oxford; and there are no poems from his Jesuit years that strike me as particularly homoerotic — and that emphatically includes "To What Serves Mortal Beauty," which is simply Hopkins's *ars poetica* on the power of *intellectus* versus *ratio*, of insight vs. analysis: "Where a *glance* master more may than *gaze*." I have already suggested the likely reason why *le vice anglais* is so central to Martin's *Hopkins*: it provides a unifying theme, and it titivates an otherwise uneventful narrative. No one doubts the intensity of Hopkins's undergraduate relationships — nor his life-long, and hardly abnormal, fascination with the beauty of the body. Though it should be noted that in the notebooks there are no sketches of males except one cartoon of himself, and at least four drawings of young women — of which Martin, along with all other commentators, makes no mention. Nor does he mention, save dismissively, Hopkins's first major poetic undertaking: "A Vision of the Mermaids" — a poem Hopkins also illustrated, like the drawings of young women in the early notebooks.

Martin here endorses the critical cliché (derived from Bridges, and our first instance of his noble-spirited but disastrous poisoning of the critical wells) that this important early poem is "unfortunately" Keatsian, whereas it owes more to the Tennyson of "The Lotus Eaters," just as Hopkins's even earlier "Escorial" is totally indebted to Tennyson's "Palace of Art." Martin further criticizes "A Vision of the Mermaids": "One has the feeling that here he is writing dutifully." But all the evidence indicates that this was a topic of his own choice. It was not a Highgate School prize poem, and had Hopkins been of a different bent he could just as well have written in emulation of Arnold's "The Forsaken Merman." Again Martin: "[I]t takes a moment to realize that it [the poem] is drenched in sensuous images without ever suggesting the sexuality [*meaning*, "homosexuality"] that lies behind almost all of his mature poetry." Apart from the difficulty many of us have, even after lecturing on Hopkins for decades, in recognizing this omni-latent sexuality, this proves to be pure *ipse dixit*.

"A Vision" *is* a mature poem evocative of the precocity of the young Milton or of that exhibited in "Endymion." Moreover, the images of "A Vision" are intensely "heterosexual," and are renewed twenty-four years later in Hopkins's enthusiastic description of a mermaid by Edward Burne-Jones: "a stroke of truly artistic genius." Whatever covert sexual strain there may be in the later Jesuit poems, when it exists at all, is almost invariably related to the allegorical mysticism derived from traditional readings of the Song of Songs.* In "A Vision" we have exuberant (literally) descriptions of the female body; we have a scene of ravishment by "Summer" as a "glorious wanton" (parallel to the beginning of Milton's "Death of a Fair Infant," written when he was the same age as Hopkins); we have a richly erotic passage (42–51) even to a *congressus* of red and blue parallel to Browning's in "Popularity" (41–55), a poem of homage by Browning (homosexual? *c'est à rire*) to Keats published seven years before Hopkins wrote "A Vision." And we have much more. (Boyle, *Metaphor in Hopkins* [1961], even finds in "A Vision" echoes of the metrics of *Paradise Lost*.)

The ineluctable, and for me distressing, conclusion is that Martin cannot see the heterosexual beam (to-fro tender trambeams) for the homosexual biographical mote in his own eye. Thus there is no mention in Martin of Hopkins's obvious infatuation with his two cousins (whom he met while still "homosexually" obsessed): "what charming country cousins I had"; the one had "beautiful eyes, a bright complexion, black hair tied with blue bands, and a pretty figure all in muslin"; the other was described, most curiously, as "more of the Charles II beauty in character [Nell Gwyn, Catherine Peg?] with cherry lips." Nor does Martin mention a friend's recently acquired wife whom Hopkins "found danger-

---

*The spiritual tradition known as *Brautmystik* has been criticized by contemporary feminists for the cultural misogyny that gave birth to the tradition whether in Jewish or Christian commentaries on the Song of Songs. The criticism is unquestionably well founded, but the fact remains that as a historical phenomenon the "relationship" of God to world or of Christ to soul did give priority to the masculine. For further detail see the footnote on p. 72.

ously attractive," nor another friend's wife with whom Hopkins committed "spiritual adultery."

But that few of Martin's omissions or his slanted eisegesis illuminate either Hopkins or the poems themselves (not even the one poem that is central to his thesis of an omnipresent and life-long homoerotic preoccupation) raises the question of why one would bother to discuss at length Martin's textually unverifiable allegations. The question is more acute since the putatively crucial poem alluded to above has been utterly evacuated of any possible sexual significance by several studies that I will cite shortly and that are overwhelmingly persuasive, except for readers with either a private agenda, certainly like Auden and possibly like F. O. Matthiessen, or a desperate need to say something provocative, like Martin.

Nevertheless, I must confess, Martin is not a Geoffrey Faber — whose blunderbuss tractate Hilliard describes as a "classic" — whom Martin characterizes as "the authority on the personal life of the earlier members of the Oxford Movement"; much less is he a Michael Lynch, who writes, in of all places an academic vehicle (*HQ*, 1979), about the need to "recover" for contemporary gays Hopkins's homosexuality and "pedophilia." *N.B.*: it is the judgmental accuracy *not* the "recovering" that is at issue. (It is synchronicity — or absurdity — with a vengeance for a partisan of Lynch to invoke probatively the "gaygear" of "The Leaden Echo...," since the word happens to describe "girlgrace"!) Nor, finally, is Martin a Michael Dacey, whose title speaks for itself: *Gerard Manley Hopkins Meets Walt Whitman in Heaven* (1982) — where Lytton Strachey also enters.

Parenthetically I would note that as with the classic instance of Dostoevsky's Alyosha, it is not unusual for candor, openness, and mystical porosity to attract, like negative polarizations, a sort of gross devotion posturing as personal kinship; this, even to the point where Hopkins's delicacy and sensitivity are read as warrants for, of all things, the "dehumanizing of females" (Lynch). But it is hardly dehumanization Hopkins exercises in Dublin when describing to Bridges, "Ladies, girl graduates [who] look nice in gowns"; or when he observes to Patmore, with a whimsical comment on his own sisters, "that nothing in good women is more beautiful than just the absence of vanity"; or when he is extensively cited in the texts marshaled in the introduction to MacKenzie's edition of *Early Poetic Manuscripts and Notebooks* (1989). We see more of this "negative polarization" in Dacey, who versifies like a caricature of the typical MFA in "Creative Writing": for example, we get this brand of wit in a presumably self-exonerating and self-consciously heterosexual poem — "Glory be to God for dappled things, like hips / The white grip of elastic still marks, a mons / Fur rides electrically, and, look, see, there, ah, / The achieve of, the mastery of, a mouth...."

Martin for all his uncreative misprisions is never as squalid as that, so the question remains: Why would one devote as much space to his work as I am here doing? The first answer is that, perhaps merely by default, Martin's book has received a great deal of attention — for example, *The New Yorker* no less (October 6, 1991). Martin's was by far the most thorough life we had until the appearance of Norman White's *A Literary Biography*. And by the mere fact of priority, Martin has been invested with considerable credibility. Both answers would justify attention to his book — but not in these introductory chapters.

Here, my interest in Martin's undertaking is purely hermeneutical. The book is a masterpiece of highly nuanced tendentiousness which makes — to take an example out of the Bloomsbury air — *Eminent Victorians* look like a pedestrian exercise in socialist realism. I have suggested above Martin's motivation, probably unwitting in the beginning but subsequently intentional as he gets trapped by his own strategies. Nevertheless it is the strategies engendered by that motivation that are important because they have already had an influence on a drastically revisionary reading of Hopkins's life. Martin is also worthy of detailed study because he transcends the self-serving, clumsy reductionism of Lynch, Dacey, et al., and *seems* driven by the textual evidence itself.

Because of space limitations, I will focus initially on only two cumulative themes of Martin which allegedly support his larger thesis of "homoeroticism" — recognizing the anachronism of the term. First, Hopkins's relation to his father; and, second, Hopkins's (presumably Whitmanesque) preoccupation with male "bathing" — never "swimming." Other motifs could have been chosen, but I am illustrating hermeneutical drifts, not supplying exhaustive critiques; so two will do. Lastly, I shall take up in more detail the crucial poem (in Hilliard, transmogrified into *"a series of sonnets"*) which is presumed to validate the existence of that "most momentous emotional event of Hopkins's undergraduate years, probably of his entire life."

Fathers

Adducing antagonism on the part of Hopkins toward his father is a desiderandum because in popular psychology, and in unreconstructed Freudianism, such antagonism is a precondition of homosexuality. (Presumably one should set aside self-evident experience of scores of homosexuals everyone knows whose affection for their fathers is manifest, sincere, and public — there are even organizations proclaiming such filial and paternal love.) But we have to do here with conventional wisdoms and The Big Theory of homosexuality, even though Freud on Hopkins is about as useful as Joyce Kilmer, who at least *did* read the poetry and wrote about it.

The insinuation comes early in the context of a critical review by Hopkins's father (in *The Times*, no less, and obviously no duffer he) of *In Memoriam* condemning Tennyson's "enormous exaggeration of grief" (precisely the opposite of Verlaine's judgment on *In Memoriam*), and his expressions of "amatory tenderness" regarding Hallam. Martin glosses: "Since both aspects of Tennyson on which he [Hopkins's father] lands with such heavy irony were characteristic of his son and *at least implied* [emphasis added] in his poetry, we could hardly expect great sympathy between Hopkins father and son, and indeed they probably felt little." The supposititious "implied" and "probably" will later become "explicit" and "certainly." A sinister *non sequitur* is Martin's arbitrary observation that the young Hopkins climbed trees as a boy, thus "preserving the distance between himself and his family that was always so important to him."

The first mention of Newman is "of the man who was to become his model, even his religious father." (We are spared here Lynch's "gayfatherly relation" of Newman to Hopkins, though I am a bit surprised we don't have Pater *pater*.) Later we are told by Martin that "Newman had a particular significance for him [Hopkins] as a priest for whom the formal address of 'Father' had a good bit more meaning than mere conventional usage." Never mind that Newman discouraged use of the title "Father," except among his fellow Oratarians at Edgbaston, and disliked it on more personal grounds as smacking of Irish/Italian Catholicism. During his first year at Oxford, Hopkins "often seems to be stroking his parents' apprehension, as if there were a slightly nervous truce *beneath* [emphasis added, meaning "secret"] the affectionate surface." But this is the kind of truce every undergraduate arranges as he experiences his first heady liberation from old ties — indeed, this *is* the very recipe for "undergraduateness," and one which every sensible parent takes with a heavy dose of irony.

Martin's insinuation becomes dissimulation anent some experimental jocose verses by Hopkins about a domineering husband and father titled, "By Mrs. Hopley." Of this we are told, "It is ... impossible to miss the hostility to his father latent" in the poem, with Hopkins "scarcely bothering to conceal the combination of Manley and Hopkins in the name." All very cogent save for the fact that in the standard commentary on the poems, on which Martin relies extensively and which he cites in his bibliography (MacKenzie, *A Reader's Guide*, 1981), MacKenzie *corrects* that earlier reading (*The Poems*, 1967) conflating Hopkins/Manley into the portmanteau "Hopley," which Martin without any justification tendentiously elects to follow. In any case, in this standard 1981 commentary, Mrs. Hopley is identified as the wife of a schoolmaster imprisoned "for causing the death of a pupil through severe discipline" and to whom the wife wrote affectionate letters. Hopkins's poem, then, would be a not atypical undergraduate's attempt at mocking his own remembrances of the arbitrary punishments imposed on him by a tyrannic headmaster (all very documentable), in this case, J. B. Dyne at Highgate School.

The only verifiable evidence of serious friction between father and son came, as one would expect, at the latter's announcement to his family of his conversion. His letter to his parents evinces what Cardinal Manning in a different context called "the ruthless talk of undergraduates." The letter *was* ruthless, and was described by his father as showing "inexcusable selfwill and obstinacy" — a relatively mild reaction considering the arrogance of the announcement. With some condescension Martin notes: "It would be hard to disagree with Mr. Hopkins, who called the long document a 'hard & cold' letter, but a sympathetic reading of it makes it clear that Gerard felt he was all but fighting for his life." Possibly Hopkins *did* feel this, but the interpretation makes one wonder about how deeply academicians can get immersed in documents expressive of the ethos of an earlier age, and about how forgetful they may become in the process of such immersion about their *own* relations with their *own* children. A twentieth-century father, even a twentieth-century father who is also a scholar like Martin, would probably end up saying something to the effect of: "You've got a family that loves you tremendously; lighten up." Again, anachronistic, of course, but the young Hopkins, all of whose letters showed an irrepressible delight in whimsy, slang, bad puns, and so on, just might have come to his senses. *Autre temps... Trop de zèle,* are the chapter headings here.

What wouldn't have brought Hopkins to his senses would be solemn and "sympathetic" asseverations made in the hindsight of twentieth-century scholarship on the most important "conversion" since Newman's — to wit, such epic dronings as: "The worst was over and Hopkins had reached his goal. He had become a Roman Catholic, he had asserted his independence, and in the complicated structure of his familial allegiances [a

complication to be memorized, not investigated], he had substi-
tuted Newman for the father figures of Liddon, Pusey, perhaps
Jowett..., and Mr. Hopkins himself." But, in historic fact not
in Freudian conjecture, this single and singular breach over the
conversion was soon healed.

All subsequent letters of Hopkins, particularly in the volumes
centered on Bridges and Dixon, are replete with affectionate references to his father, companionable sarcasm about the latter's
poetic and etymological explorations, about his hobbies and his
habits. In short, letters from a mature and gentle man to a loving
and loved father; a father, finally, with whom Hopkins enjoyed
collaborating on a technical book published two years before his
death, *The Cardinal Numbers.* No Newman here; merely a mis-
cellany in which both father and son indulged their idiosyncratic
penchant for numerology, symbolism, astral/spectral theory, and
other scientific and cryptoscientific arcana. (All soberly treated in
Thomas Zaniello's *Hopkins in the Age of Darwin,* 1988.) Of all
of that, nothing in Martin.

And though Martin discusses one of the last sonnets, "To
seem the stranger...," he sees in it no corrective of alleged paternal alienation, notwithstanding the explicitness of: "To seem
the stranger lies my lot, my life / Among strangers. Father and
mother dear, / Brothers and sisters are in Christ not near." Nor,
to put an end to this discussion, did I note cited here one of the
most moving letters from Hopkins's father at the time of his son's
conversion, when both were taking too seriously his son's veiled
and thoughtless threats of permanent alienation. Manley Hopkins
wrote: "I shall not touch on this morning's letter — further than
to say that the manner in which you seem to repel & throw us
[father and mother] off cuts us to the heart. All we ask of you is
for your own sake to take so momentous a step with caution &
hesitation; have we not a right to do this? Might not our love &
sorrow entitle us to ask it? & you answer by saying that as we
might be Romanists if we pleased the estrangement is not of your
doing. O Gerard my darling boy are you indeed gone from me?"

But there was no way he could ever be gone from his father,

for Hopkins owed to him not just life and love, but the source of his most deeply rooted themes and images. Manley Hopkins was a shipping insurance actuary (who hoped his son would join him in the firm) and thus professionally occupied with seamanship, with marine hazards, and of course with the kinds of shipwrecks that inspired Hopkins's two most sustained poetic efforts. From his boyhood abstinence from liquids for three weeks because this was emulative of "seamen's sufferings" to reading in the last year of his life Richard Henry Dana's *Two Years before the Mast,* Hopkins showed himself a true son of his father.

Bathers

"Water socialism" was a goal of scores of major midcentury political reformers. George Godwin was typical in his optimism about public bathing, and he affirmed, "The cost of cleanliness can now no longer be pleaded as an excuse for dirt." This, in 1854 in sooty London where the fastidious Gerard Hopkins was growing up, albeit exurbanly. It is not difficult even today to understand why bathing was then a passion and a necessity. Yet Martin's treatment of the phenomenon borders on the apocalyptic. There are in his book sixteen pages of illustrations, all save the final one clearly relevant to Hopkins's life. This last, truly climactic, half-tone is a reproduction of Frederick Walker's painting titled simply *Bathers.* Beneath it in Martin's sequence of illustrations is an enlargement of the middle section of the painting (occupying three-fourths of the page) with frolicking nude youths, genitalia and all, clearly portrayed.

The function of the reproduction, initiates will immediately realize, is to make the connection with Thomas Eakins's depiction of a similar scene, invariably (almost compulsively) reproduced in every book on Whitman. The relation of Hopkins to Whitman has been exhaustively and inconclusively analyzed, and all the relevant texts are presented by Humphrey House and Graham Storey in the journals, by Claude Colleer Abbott in the three volumes of letters, and in the last couple of decades by innumerable articles. Implicitly the relation is either erotic (two homosexuals), esthetic (two prosodic innovators), or political. Whitman was revered in England almost exclusively as the poet of "democracy," while Hopkins had semiseriously referred to himself as "in a manner a Communist," and was much absorbed by conditions among the working class, about which he wrote one of his most affecting poems.

The "relation" is encumbered by some readings of "the beast from the West" in "Andromeda" as representing Whitmania, though no one so far as I know has bolstered the identification with Swinburne's "To Walt Whitman in America," written eight years before "Andromeda": "A blast of the breath of the West," with its detailed catalogue of free-thinking modernist "vices." This at least is geographically accurate, unlike other candidates, for example, Newman's "Liberalism." (Though a case can be made for Adrienne Munich's identification with emerging American suffragism in *Andromeda's Chains* [1989]).

The Whitman issue is presumably open, with Yvor Winters, a foaming phobic, initiating the attack on one side of the divide, with Auden and Matthiessen, initiating the defense on the other. But not much of this is relevant to my present hermeneutic concerns. What is relevant is that there is no evidence Hopkins knew Walker's *Bathers,* whereas there is some evidence (first mustered by Paul Mariani) that another Walker painting (*not* reproduced here), *The Plough,* described by Hopkins as "a divine work," may have inspired "Harry Ploughman," a poem whose metrical freedom worried Hopkins that it might appear Whitmanesque. Whence then the two reproductions of *Bathers* among the relatively few illustrations in Martin's book?

Martin lays his first mine in a footnote on p. 4, where Walker is described as "the man who was to become his [Hopkins's] favorite Victorian painter," but a favoritism based largely on Walker's premature "Keatsian" death. In fact, Hopkins's pictorial enthusiasms are full of contradictions. Thus he wrote of John Millais (whom he subsequently would criticize): "I see that he is the greatest English painter, one of the greatest of the world." Martin then leaps from p. 4 with its first mention of Walker to pp. 390ff., so that the book is bracketed by discussion of this particular painter. Unfortunately Martin's discussion is (intentionally?) duplicitous.

The context of that discussion is Hopkins's fragment "Epithalamion," written for his brother's wedding; the poem opens with a description of swimming, which for Martin immediately elides into Walker's *Bathers.* A close analysis reveals tortuous prose, and lengthy and (perhaps intentionally) distracting irrelevancies — which I italicize: *"The use of such a word as 'Fairyland,' describing the bathing place, may connect the poem specifically with Stonyhurst and the Hodder* (see p. 200 for his letter about the pool there)." But "the pool" where the narrator (not necessarily the poet) swims is *not* that where the Walkerian youths are gamboling. Martin continues immediately: "What seems more significant [Than what? 'Fairyland'?] is that the scene he [Hopkins] describes is very like that in Frederick Walker's painting 'Bathers,' *which the artist considered one of his most important works, and on which he had worked intermittently almost until his death in 1875."* This garblement (Walker worked on works) and this irrelevant detail may be mere pedantry, but I strongly suspect it is intended to divert the reader from the speculative *non sequiturs* which follow.

Martin continues (and here I again italicize the supposititious assumptions): "Hopkins *had probably seen* the painting exhibited in 1868, although he does not mention it specifically in his discussions of Walker's works." But if the work had filled him with such enthusiasm it is more than curious that Hopkins doesn't mention it. "Almost twenty years later he was still writing enthusiastically, *almost obsessively,* about his [Walker's] paintings and about the etchings of them made by R. W. Macbeth, whose studio he [Hopkins] visited with his brother Arthur where *it seems probable* he saw at least a reproduction of 'The [*sic*] Bathers.' " (The clumsy syntax and erroneous title are revelatory hermeneutical keys.) But it (the subtending argument) does not only not "seem probable," it *is impossible* by Hopkins's own words. Hopkins refers to several Walker pieces by name (*not* including *Bathers*), criticizes one of them, mentions that "the news of his [Walker's] death gave me a shock," and then observes of the reproductions that "most of them [were] new to me."

But if Hopkins had "probably" seen *Bathers* in 1868 it could hardly be new to him "twenty years later." The fact is there is no evidence of Hopkins's ever seeing the painting, and *a fortiori* no evidence of his enthusiasm for it, and finally, no evidence that the painting is related to "Epithalamion." For all these reasons, this painting by Walker is not included among the many Walker reproductions in the definitive study of Hopkins's pictorial interests (*All My Eyes See: The Visual World of Gerard Manley Hopkins* [1975]). Whence therefore in Martin's selection of illustrations, the reproduction of this particular painting, along with an enlargement — lest the viewer miss anything — of a section of it? The clue is immediately forthcoming, as Martin without interruption goes into a discussion of Walt Whitman, Thomas Eakins, and Philip Dacey's doggerel. (But of course no mention of, say, Stevens's "A Lot of People Bathing in a Stream": that would be too untendentious.)

It is not duplicity but ignorance which leads Martin to conclude of the "Epithalamion" fragment that "the energy of the poem has depended upon his celebration of the physical [code word for we know what], and with the weak attempt to wring allegory from what he has loved for itself [nude swimming], he leaves the poem unfinished." Of "wringing allegory" I shall write shortly. But a piece of physical evidence, which Martin knows since he reproduces it, is the autograph of the poem, which was undeniably written in class while Hopkins was proctoring student examinations, the burden of correcting which he lamented frequently during his Irish years as the cause of so many "unfinished" projects. There is also the tendency of Hopkins, as he said years before, to succumb to "spooniness" on the subject of marriage.

As to the alleged frustration consequent on trying to allegorize bathing and marriage, for Martin it might exist. But for Hopkins it simply didn't. The conjunction of the two subjects is a common-place of the tradition in which Hopkins had been reared from his days as a Jesuit novice to his Dublin period. I do not want to seem excessively recherché, but the fact is Martin (who refers to a "Father [sic] Pick") and most Protestant students of Victoriana, as noted earlier, are woefully ignorant of that particular tradition. Though it must be acknowledged that such ignorance does not afflict Wendell Stacy Johnson's quite sensible "Sexuality and Inscape" (*HQ*, 1976) — though he does find sexuality in Hopkins's reference in "Epithalamion" to the water as "flinty kindcold element." In fact, the less strained allusion is to the patristic term *"photismos"* for "baptism," where the complementarity is of water = cleansing, and flintspark = illumination. (It is worth noting that in the context of "complementarity," Einstein's term "photon" was extended to other forms of wave-particle energy.) As to bathing and marriage, the *locus classicus* is the Patristic summary in Odo Casel's "Baptism as Bridal Bath of the Church."* This study is a synopsis of what Hopkins would have known intimately from the Office for the Epiphany cycle, and from his familiarity with the tradition of "bridal mysticism," as exemplified in the life of St. Gertrude. (That tradition is central to understanding "The Wreck...," where Gertrude is invoked, and to understanding Hopkins's sense of "profanation" at Patmore's *Sponsa Dei*.) The cardinal liturgical texts are the antiphons from Vespers, so ancient and so immemorial that I cite them in full: "Three wonders have distinguished the holy day that we celebrate. Today, the star has led the magi to the crib; today, the water has been changed into wine at the wedding banquet; today, Christ has willed to be baptized by John in the Jordan...." The second is more pertinent: "Today, the Church is espoused to the heavenly bridegroom, for in the Jordan Christ *bathes* away her sins, the magi hasten with gifts to the royal wedding, and the guests are gladdened with water made wine." If this remains too recondite

---

*"Die Taufe als Brautbad der Kirche," *Jahrbuch für Liturgiewissenschaft* 5 (1925): 144ff. For a popular, and illustrated, treatment, see J. G. Lawler, "Epiphany, Feast of Light," *Jubilee* (January 1968).

for those outside the tradition, I proffer Wallace Stevens, intuitive discerner of foundational myths: "...one's Sunday *baths,* one's tootings at the *weddings* of the soul" ("The Sense of the Sleight-of-hand Man"). So much for Hopkins's "wringing allegory" out of bathing/marrying imagery.

Bothers

We come now to the Johannine Comma, the Donation of Constantine, the Ossian, the Thomas Rowley of Hopkins studies; in short to the biographical crux and the red herring — all relating to Martin's definition of "the most momentous emotional event" of Hopkins's life, when he met (for a few hours, if that) Digby Dolben.

How would a critical and putatively "standard" life of a poet proceed? Obviously there would be introductory genealogical material and descriptions of the poet's early years up to his first significant relationships and achievements. From then on — assuming this is not the *People Magazine* school of criticism — the poems would be both the point of departure and the thread linking all those other public and private events that would be filled out by correspondence, memoirs, contemporaneous references, and finally by the insights or distortions of subsequent research.

But it is the poems that are the bedrock on which the whole edifice stands. Apart from clinical or prurient interests, it is the poems alone that constitute the *raison d'être* of the biography. But though one must affirm that while they are substance and the rest are accidents, one must also affirm — in the name of the kind of "Catholic Aristotelianism" (*read:* Thomism) Hopkins studied as a Jesuit — that accidental change predisposes to substantial change. This is merely to say that notwithstanding the priority of the poetic text, that text must be reread in the context of various secondary materials as well as of each generation's understanding of what *is* both primary and secondary.

I thus begin at the beginning, that is, with the poems and fragments up to and including those allegedly relating to the "momentous" event which occurred in February 1865, and concluding with poems and fragments of 1866, the year of Hopkins's conversion. Concerning the "momentous" event, it is to be noted that for all its alleged centrality, we have neither week nor day nor hour, much less "moment." This conspectus will not be as lengthy and tedious an undertaking as at first glance it appears, since the period involved, except for some minor poems and fragments, is only about three years. I follow throughout the order and numbering in the fourth edition of the poems, and start with what are for the most part technical exercises by a very young man.

As one would expect many of them are derivative, imitative, experimental, not to say awkward and pretentious. Their intrinsic esthetic importance is usually slight, but they do provide a foretaste of future development, and may occasionally indicate genuine concerns of the author, concerns that go beyond mere matters of technique. I have already discussed the lovely "A Vision of the Mermaids," a conventional treatment in pentameter couplets (occasionally Hopkins appears to be counting out the syllables) and noteworthy also because it is the first *poetic* expression of the ubiquitous shipwreck motif: mermaids "ring the knells / Of seamen whelm'd in chasms of the mid-main, / *As poets sing.*" The last phrase reflects schoolboy Shakespearean pedantry as well as a self-consciousness about poetic craft that runs through almost all these early poems.

"Winter in the Gulf Stream" is a topical poem experimenting with terza rima. "Spring and Death," written in octosyllabic couplets, continues Hopkins's infatuation with seventeenth-century forms, in this case Milton's "Il Penseroso," first expressed in the lengthy fragment of the year before, "Il Mystico." (The seventeenth-century influence later comes to fruition in that Metaphysical marvel, "The Blessed Virgin Compared to the Air We Breathe.") Then follow several religious poems and fragments "of a very Catholic character," only two of which are of interest here because they are clearly imitative of that Browning whom Hopkins never ceased to excoriate: "A Soliloquy of One of the Spies Left in the Wilderness" and "Pilate" (no. 80). (One might suggest it is only very young poets who are afflicted by the Bloomian blight of anxiety over antecedents.) From this same period are several fragments, some with titles some without, but all having to do with seemingly impassioned, seemingly satiric relationships with women (nos. 79, 81 [175 lines], 82, 83 ["The Lover's Stars"], 87, 94 ["Miss Story's character! too much you ask"], 95, and 96 ["Seven Epigrams"]).

I cite only a few representative lines:

> Did Helen steal my love from me?
>   She never had the wit.
> Or was it Jane? She is too plain,
>   And could not compass it. (95)

> Miss M.'s a nightingale. 'Tis well
>   Your simile I keep.
> It is the way with Philomel
>   To sing while others sleep. ("On a Poetess")

> You ask why can't Clarissa hold her tongue.
> Because she fears her fingers will be stung. (96, iii)

Number 99 is a brilliantly wrought *ut pictura poesis* exercise on the transformation of Io (which predates by six months the "momentous" event of February 1865, but Martin spares us any aspersions about latent zoophilia: "like a brinded cow" — though on "horses" he is more incautious). There are lengthy fragments of a drama in blank verse ("Floris in Italy"); a pastoral romance in couplets ("Richard") thematically indebted to Wordsworth's "Michael," with a deft but self-conscious put-down of the master's prolix detail:

> ... The grass was red
> And long, the trees were colour'd, but the o'er head,
> Milky and dark, with an attuning stress
> Controll'd them to a grey-green temperateness,
> Making the shadow sweeter. A spiritual grace,
> *Which Wordsworth would have dwelt on* ... (iv)

Of all these, "Miss Story's character..." is most fascinating since we know its context from a letter of July 24, 1864, to Baillie — a letter preceded by another which is one of Hopkins's most quotably witty and proleptically Joycean. The earlier letter concludes: "Bay our negst beetigg be berry add birthful, but dow I have a cold. Your affegtiodate friedd, GERARD EB. HOBKIDS." *Satis.* Back to the Story story in the holiday-cum-exam-preparation letter of July 24 where Hopkins writes that he "has a hard time of it to resist contamination from the bawdy jokes and allusions of Bond and Hardy [fellow vacationers]. Hardy is always talking of debauching too, well-dressed girls but when he has introduced himself to them oh then he is very, very sick. [This last sentence was later obliterated.] We have four Miss Storys staying in the house, girls from Reading. This is a great advantage — but not to reading." The pun on Reading/reading indicates self-mocking infatuation; the resulting poem indicates *that,* along with a whimsically accepted rebuff.

The "Rape of the Lock" is not too far away:

> Miss Story's character! too much you ask,
> When 'tis the confidante that sets the task.
> How dare I paint Miss Story to Miss May?
> And what if she my confidence betray!
> What if my Subject, seeing this, resent
> What were worth nothing if all compliment!
> No: shewn to her it cannot but offend;
> But candour never hurt the dearest *friend.*
>
> Miss Story has a moderate power of will,
> But, having that, believes it greater still:
> And, hide it though she does, one may divine
> She inly nourishes a wish to shine;
> Is very capable of strong affection
> Tho' apt to throw it in a strange direction;
> Is fond of flattery, as any she,
> But has not learnt to take it gracefully;
> Things that she likes seems often to despise,

> And loves — a fatal fault — to patronize;
> Has wit enough, but less than female tact,
> Sees the right thing to do, and does not act....
> Married, will make a sweet and matchless wife,
> But single, lead a misdirected life.

Lastly, there is a ballad, "The Queen's Crowning," dated from December 1864, and beginning:

> They were wedded at midnight
>   By shine of candles three,
> And they were bedded till daylight
>   Before he went to sea.

...and so on, for thirty-eight "fits" that probably could have been extended more or less indefinitely.

What all do we have thus far, two months before the momentous event of February 1865? Certainly nothing that is particularly homoerotic — in fact, quite the opposite. We also do not have much that is autobiographically enlightening: Keats's "mused rhyme," Milton's "sights as youthfull Poets dream / On Summer eeves by haunted stream," a passage that also haunted Blake and Wordsworth — in fact, a text that haunts every young poet in the tradition. No one since E. M. W. Tillyard half a century ago read Milton's early Italian and Latin exercises in amorous verse as autobiographical; much less has anyone seriously (though some oddities do arise) suggested that Milton to Diodati, in a published exercise on a standard Renaissance theme, should be accused of the sexual obsessiveness now brought to bear on Hopkins and Dolben, and for which (unlike Milton to Diodati) there is no textual evidence whatever.

Why should twenty-year-old Hopkins be the exception among these other talented tyros, recognizably testing their skills in all the metrics and genres and through all the conventional *topoi*, particularly love poems and religious poems? Why should he alone be the subject of so contorted a reading? Apart from what

I have noted above — the appeal of scurrility and novelty —
I would also suggest the Anglo-Scotch Protestant suspicion of
and fascination with Catholicism in general, and "Jesuitry" and
celibacy in particular. Professor Martin declaims: "*Inevitably,* one
asks *today,* whether a commitment to celibacy is not a way
of *hiding from one's self or others* a psychological disinclina-
tion to marriage that stems from *instincts* having little to do
with religion" (emphasis added) — what a congeries: modernity,
deception, and mysterious instincts; all in the service of the homosexuality theme which follows illogically, but with Martin also
very inevitably. But I wouldn't *so* ask, having met as many non-
celibates with the same concealed disinclinations, and finding
them as normal as I do Martin; though I find the latter on celibacy
about as persuasive as Charles Kingsley in Hopkins's own time,
or Edward Said (1983) in ours. Said finds that Hopkins and his
like take refuge from the "failure of the capacity to produce or
generate children" in organizations "whose social existence was
not in fact guaranteed by biology." But this pretentious banality
is as true of the Palestine Liberation Organization as it is of the
Society of Jesus.

The historical reality is, again, that very little distinguishes
Hopkins from his celibate or noncelibate, married or unmarried,
homo- or heterosexual predecessors or contemporaries except
his lyric genius, and his all-redemptive slightly zany sense of
the comical and the whimsical. Both are what make him so
likable when compared with such strenuous, earnest, dedicated
(and often boring) spirits as young (miscible or immiscible) Tennyson, Arnold, Clough, Rossetti, Thomson, Swinburne, Lang,
Gladstone, Disraeli, or George Eliot.

But back to the wide prospect and (I suppose Martin would
suggest) the Asian fen of Hopkins's early development. From
January 1865 there is a fragment for another Wordsworthian narrative, "Stephen and Barberie" (though December is the month
suggested by MacKenzie). February (when the Dolben *rencontre*
occurred) or March sees the Blakean song of experience, "The
Summer Malison," which begins:

> Maidens shall weep at merry morn,
> And hedges break, and lose the kine,
> And field-flowers make the fields forlorn,
> And noonday have a shallow shine...

The anaphora, "and," continues clumsily for seven more lines. Hopkins also writes during that Lent and Eastertide several seasonal poems, as well as a number of poems celebrating the delights of Oxford.

These poems appear of a *slightly* more serious tenor and *probably* (the italics suggest *my* nuance and dubiety, because we still have to do with youthful poetic experiments) reflect the religious conflict between his love of Oxford, that home of lost causes, and his dying devotion to that ultimate lost cause, the Via Media of Anglicanism — a devotion buried in "The Alchemist in the City" (May 15) and resurrected seventeen years later in "The Leaden Echo...."

But there are also more manifestly conventional amatory verses similar to those of the previous year: for the first time, *à la* Milton, fragmented translations from Greek and Latin, for example, "Love me as I love thee. O double sweet!" (no. 161); "Why need the lovely roses of summer show their bloom? / That bloom is in the soft cheeks of a maiden"; and "I remember girl when your lot was a sad one" (no. 163). This theme is continued in some love poems of May and June, as is also the Oxonian theme during the same months.

In May there are three poems under the general title, "The Beginning of the End," that Bridges — ignorant of the *locus amoenus* theme as well as of most of the contemporaneous experimental poems and fragments (and publicly protective while privately critical of Hopkins's celibate vocation) — decades later misguidedly decreed should never be printed. Structured like conventional love poems ("My love is lessened and must soon be past"), they are *probably* poems of Hopkins's decision, made during this period, to end his relationship with the Anglican communion. (Again, I italicize the conjecture, since we still have to do

with juvenilia, however heartfelt.) The last poem in the sequence
employs the direct address (to Jesus?) so frequent in the later
explicitly religious poems; indeed, it reads like one of Herbert's
reprimands to his Lord:

> You see that I have come to passion's end;
> This means you need not fear the storms, the cries,
> That gave you vantage when you would despise:
> My bankrupt heart has no more tears to spend.

That Bridges totally misjudged the nature of the sequence is also
suggested by the even more exaggeratedly derivative and "book-
ish" character of these poems than is evident in any previous
ones. In the first poem of the sequence, after declaring, "My love
is less," the speaker affirms:

> That *less* is heavens higher even yet
> Than treble-fervent *more* of other men...

— echoing Browning's "Andrea" on those "who reach many a
time a heaven that's shut to me" (84) and "...so much less! /
Well, less is more" (77–78). The second sonnet, "I must feed
Fancy," echoes Browning's "My Star" and "The Statue and
the Bust" (especially 145–50) in the context of the astral lore
Hopkins later explored with his father. The third returns to
the dramatic codas of Herbert with a Keatsian comparison of
Hopkins's mood after the loss of *faith* in the church of his *youth:*

> The *sceptic* disappointment and the loss
> A *boy* feels when the poet he pores upon
> Grows less and less sweet to him, and knows no cause.

The Herbartian mode is even more intense, and more explicitly religious, in another "love" poem of a few months later
beginning:

> Love I was shewn upon the mountain-side
> And bid to catch Him ere the drop of day...

(Hopkins capitalizes the "H" in "Him"), again with a coda right
out of Herbert, in this case, "Redemption":

> You have your wish; enter these walls, one said:
> He is with you in the breaking of the bread.

Certainly in this last poem, and possibly in some of the others, what we have is that elision of eros and agape which is at the heart of the natural-supernaturalist vision, and which (I now make the transition to the Oxford eulogies) sees every lovely temporal *locus amoenus* as a foretaste of the blest kingdoms meek of joy and love ("Lycidas").

The companion-pieces celebrating Oxford, and written in a three-day period, are nos. 12 (i and ii) and 13. Again we hear the language of eros/agape, now with a Shakespearean accent:

> New-dated from the terms that reappear,
> More sweet-familiar grows my love to thee,
> And still thou bind'st me to fresh fealty
> With long-superfluous ties....

Then comes a description of Oxford's "charms" which

> ...may all be sought
> By other eyes, and other suitors move,
> And all like me may boast, impeached not,
> Their special-general title to thy love. (no. i)

"Long-superfluous" is intentionally ambiguous: (1) there is no need for traditional links, and (2) all links are about to be rendered superfluous in the light of the poet's Romeward journey.

These three poems are a tightly woven triad, with a clearly delineated evolution: in the first, *from the known and immediately present universal* experience of conventional Anglicanism ("all like me"); then in the second poem *to the known, the subsequent, and the singular* experience of conversion and the breaking of old bonds of friendship ("thus I come.... None besides me"); and finally *to the unknown and far future universal* experience of being fated to life among Catholics ("to many unknown men").

The latter phrase is the transition and preparation for the opening of the concluding (and "momentous") poem: "Where art thou

friend, whom I shall never see…?", with its echoes of Shakespeare's Sonnet 100, "Where art thou, muse…?" I here stress
the echoes (denominating the Shakespeare, *"S,"* and the Hopkins,
"H"):

> *S:* Muse, that thou forget'st so long / To speak of that
>   which gives thee all thy might
>
> *H:* friend whom I shall never see, / Conceiving whom I
>   must conceive amiss
>
> *S:* Spend'st thou thy fury on some worthless song
>
> *H:* Or sunder'd from my sight in the age that is
>
> *S:* straight redeem / In gentle numbers time so idly spent
>
> *H:* Or far-off promise of a time to be
>
> *S:* Sing to the ear that doth thy lays esteem / And gives
>   thy pen both skill and argument
>
> *H:* thou hadst borne proportion in my bliss. / That
>   likest in me either that or this
>
> *S:* make Time's spoils despised everywhere
>
> *H:* make all the virtues to abound

The echoes are muted with Hopkins soaring into the explicitly theological. But both Shakespeare and Hopkins are merely
writing in the traditional loss-and-gain mode (more explicit in
Newman's dismal conversion novel).

The evolution in all these Oxford exercises is also — again with
echoes of Herbert — allegorically rigged: *from the earthly profane*
("my pleasaunce"), *to the earthly sacred* ("this chapel side"), *to
the celestially sacred "altitudo"* ("God's dear pleadings").

Now, all of this seems to me the basic factual foundation
(youthful poet testing all the poetic waters while suffering one
major — in this case, religious — crisis) on which any biographer must build. It also seems to me to provide a coherent and
persuasive scheme of Hopkins's poetic development, a scheme

which sees him unidiosyncratically (the allusion is again to Gardner) integrated into the tradition; a scheme which doesn't scant his unique qualities; and, finally, a scheme which relies on verifiable data, not adventitious conjectures, far-fetched readings, or arbitrary and tendentious eisegesis.

Foisters

That Martin and the scholars on whom he depends would blur almost every salient feature of the above portrait is due to several factors. I have said enough about Martin's tactical choice of the scurrilous, and about his self-generated effort to enliven a seemingly uneventful narrative: to employ a Hopkins image, Martin has "the pearls without the string." But the fact is, there are only pearls; there is no golden thread of enticing events linking those luminously perfect poems. So it is of imaginary sexual threads that that string must be plaited. The result is a monochord endlessly, incessantly, dissonantly plucked by Martin with forced fingers harsh and lewd. Whence such obsessive harping?

Like all embarrassing questions, as Oscar Wilde insightfully told us, the answer is deceptively simple: it is that last infirmity of all researchers, the refusal to tend the homely slighted shepherd's trade, the need to make a discovery, to say something new, to be cited, quoted, memorialized. Alas, the hungry undergraduates and *PMLA* and *HQ* readers and writers look up and are not fed. *Ite domum impasti.*

What abets this whole process is something sanctified in the academy under such honorifics as "tradition," "received wisdom," "veterism," "dalliance with false surmise," and more recently "political correctness" — in short, at best inertia and at worst *corruptio optimi.*

The single source of all of Martin's outrageous interpretations is a simple and modest opinion which was tentatively proffered half a century ago during the infancy of Hopkins studies, which was subsequently embraced and elaborated by aimlessly questing

secondary researchers and which was, finally, through this same
gravitational drift reduced to the near-historical status embodied
in Martin's observation: "In recent years there has been a discernible movement among a few Hopkins scholars to minimize
the importance of his feelings for Dolben" allegedly expressed
in "Where art thou friend," analyzed above. That the "importance" remains unsubstantiated, that it is in fact mere guess, that
it rides roughshod over the poems, letters, memoirs, and so on,
indeed, over the whole of Hopkins's achievement — all this fades
in the climate of our hobby-horsical devotion to old authorities
(Coleridge).

That single source, the Itasca, which has since overflowed and
inundated the entire field, is a sentence by Humphrey House in
his preface to *The Note-books* (1937): "I think that the sonnet
'Where art thou friend, whom I shall never see,' though not entered in the book till April, is connected with Dolben; and that
is obscure because Dolben was closely bound up with the religious crisis." The "connection" is not even tenuous; it is nothing
more than that, on the manuscript page preceding the poem —
among a multitude of adnotations, most crossed out because they
list in the form of an examination of conscience various scru-
ples, personal foibles, vexations, and "temptations" — there is on
two lines out of a total of forty a forwarding address for Dolben.
Nothing more. But out of House's *creatio ex nihilo* has emerged
a world, a universe, a galaxy not of tentative speculation — but
of dogmatic asseveration. Moreover, if that poem on the page
following the preceding page crowded with crossed-out confessional foibles did indeed relate to some erotic connection with
Dolben (certainly a most confessable vice), the poem would also
have been crossed out as were several lines above and below it
(MacKenzie, *Early Poetic Manuscripts,...* plates 107, 159). Obviously it is not crossed out because the homoeroticism and the
"connection" itself are nonexistent.

Rudolf Bremer (*HQ*, 1980) skillfully traced the development
of this deformative process in "the academy of fine ideas," whose
members include Eleanor Ruggles, K. R. S. Iyengar, A. G. Sul-

loway, D. A. Downes, Bernard Bergonzi, and Paddy Kitchen. More cautiously, W. H. Gardner embraced the *possibility* of the relationship, as did tentatively Norman MacKenzie, only to discerningly reject it in a detailed analysis in his 1989 introduction to the notebooks, where he also provides the most thorough and balanced treatment thus far of Hopkins's alleged homoerotic tendencies. MacKenzie's is the indispensable study of the entire matter.

But what is astonishing about the evolution of the Hopkins-Dolben "Where art thou friend" nexus is that House offered no evidence whatever of Hopkins's "religious crisis" being "closely bound up" with Dolben and "Where art thou friend." What is even more astonishing is that none of House's emulative parrots proffer any additional "evidence" and merely repeat the same claim, almost invariably using House's words, occasionally with some irrelevant "creative" embroidery. I cite a typical comment from a book published after Bremer's study: "*Undoubtedly* linked with the crisis, in a *strong* if not clear way, was his meeting with the seventeen-year-old poet Digby Mackworth Dolben that February.... An obscure *but strongly felt* sonnet written in his diary in April, 'Where art thou friend, whom I shall never see,' was *almost certainly* addressed to Dolben" (Graham Storey, 1981). From Storey's embellishments italicized above it is not too far a leap to Martin's "most momentous emotional event."

Gardner (1949) detected the flaw in this argument regarding the April sonnet, since Hopkins had indeed "seen" Dolben two months before. Bremer and MacKenzie cite favorably W. Nowottny's attempt to resolve the issue by suggesting the influence of a poem by Friedrich Klopstock on Hopkins's sonnet — all pretty silly, and suggesting to me an emendation of Blake: "When Klopstock England defied / Uprose terrible Hopkins in his pride." Bremer's reading, though somewhat influenced by Nowottny, is elegantly simple: the poem has nothing to do with Dolben, and is a plea for sympathy from any future reader of Hopkins's own verse. Bremer's commonsensical interpretation is certainly not incompatible with the interpretation in my stereo-conspectus of all the poems of 1864–66 above, an interpretation totally at odds with that of Martin and all the domesticated House apes.

This chapter — like this book — is an exercise in a hermeneutic of suspicion. I have been engaged in a work of detection, detection of the ingenious strategies Martin employs to make plausible what remains an utterly dubious and tendentious thesis. Those strategies are threefold and at least as hoary as Quintilian. First, _circular argumentation_ (Martin is _princeps petitio principii_); second, _transformation of character_ (Hopkins is a sexual obsessive — and not merely as an undergraduate, which might at least be plausible); third, _repetitive reference_ (with Dolben invoked and evoked in contexts where he is the least likely referent). Antiquated rhetorical devices, to be sure, but here handled by a master.

As to the first, circular argumentation, Martin notes: "Not long after Dolben's departure [on _the_ day of _the_ momentous event] Hopkins made _one of his few cryptic_ references to him [Dolben] in his published diary. . . . _The laconic manner should not blind us to Hopkins's preoccupation._" (Unless otherwise noted all italics and bracketed materials are my additions.) According to Martin, it should not blind us because of what Humphrey House had arbitrarily conjectured. Further: "It _may seem_ . . . that Digby Dolben's name should occur oftener if he [Hopkins] were actually thinking of him _most of the time._ . . . Even in the original [of Hopkins's journals] the _comparative rarity_ of its appearance gives a _wholly false impression_ of its significance to Hopkins." In reality, of the hundreds of names, Dolben's appears only nine times, and four of these are in the context of Hopkins's "prideful" desire to be an instrument in Dolben's conversion to Catholicism. "Yet the thought of Dolben, interdicted as it was [by Hopkins's fear of spiritual pride], underlay _all of that sexually turbulent_ spring of 1865."

"_As one would expect of Hopkins_ [why?], only the _faintest air_ of hurt at Dolben's lack of response _was allowed to show in his diary and correspondence._" How do we know about this "faintest air" if Hopkins never "showed" it? "_A truer index_ of his *stifled feelings* is found in the series of poems he wrote after Dolben had first visited Oxford." But those poems are far more patient of the interpretation (youthful exercises, disenchantment with the *via media* of Anglicanism, etc.) I have sketched above, than of any reading that refers them to Dolben. Thus we have the obscure silence about Dolben in the prose writings explained away by the alleged clarity of the poetic writings — writings that in fact have no reference whatever to Dolben.

One may get an idea of how Martin determines the "truer index" of Hopkins's mind by Martin's reading of the second Oxford sonnet — referred to earlier — which is a simple description of one of the chapels as envisioned from the ground up. Martin notes: "Hopkins plays with the curious view of the world come from looking at things from an unexpected angle," which Martin defines as "topsy-turvy." He then adds that "unexpected angles" come from "the *unnerving new perspective on the world that love* [of Dolben] *brings*." Another of these circular *QEDs*: "Almost all the rest of the poetry Hopkins wrote in 1865 shows his coming to terms with what he realized was to be a solitary life. Probably *most lovers who feel rejected go through the same stage*." But what every reasonable critic without exception would say Hopkins was coming to terms with was family conflict, conversion, ordination, and celibacy — *not* sexual rejection by the momentarily visitated Dolben.

Lastly (though this list of tautologous arguments could be extended for pages), there is the matter of Dolben's demise. On returning from a holiday in France, Hopkins found a letter waiting for him telling him of Dolben's death. Martin cites accurately the Journal entry: "I found a letter from Coles, which had been waiting since the day I started for Paris, to tell me of Dolben's demise. See June 28." Nothing more. Martin glosses this utterly neutral entry (my emphasis, as always): "The last brief phrase is about as close as Hopkins came to indicating *overtly how deeply* Dolben's death had affected him, for it refers back to an entry in a previous volume of his journal, *now lost*, where he had *presumably entered* his own activities." The "depth" of Hopkins's "overt" feelings is based on a "presumable entry" in a journal which is "now lost." As to the depths of Hopkins's feelings in general, "these are to be *inferred* only by the turn of a phrase or occasionally *by a deliberate omission.*" But "inferences based on omissions" is the very definition of "question begging."

Martin continues: "There was, *of course,* a flurry of letters *back and forth* between [*sic*] Dolben's friends at his death." The unconscious deception on Martin's part probably explains the grammatical error. But in fact there was no flurry of anything. Martin omits the beginning of Hopkins's letter to Bridges since its tone undercuts everything Martin is trying to establish. The letter is casual throughout. The omitted beginning is: "Dear Bridges,— I heard of Dolben's death the day I returned fr. Paris by a letter fr. Coles wh. had been a week waiting for me. Edgell has since written me a few more particulars." Martin supplies the next few sentences accurately: "I have kept the beginning of a letter to you a long time by me but to no purpose so far as being more ready to write goes. There is very little I have to say. I looked forward to meeting Dolben and his being a Catholic more than to anything. *At the same time from never having met him but once I find it difficult to realise his death or feel as if it were anything to me.*" Martin, never one to relent, finds "shock and numbness" in these lines — but at least he does cite them, which is more than can be said of another Dolben-centered reading (R. V. Overholser, 1991) that omits this damning passage altogether.

However, any honest reader would be compelled either to take Hopkins's words at face value or to postulate that Bridges and Hopkins were conspiring in one of the great historical charades in nineteenth-century poetry. Dolben was Bridges's cousin; if some grand passion had existed Bridges would certainly have known of it, and it would at least have been implied in the correspondence. Instead Hopkins, after perfunctory inquiries about Dolben's death, continues with two paragraphs of Oxford gossip; and two months later in one paragraph out of a six paragraph letter tells Bridges: "It is quite true, as you say, that there was a great want of strength in Dolben — more of sense. Edgell told me he had some mortuary cards done and offered me one and till this minute I had never written for it." Martin omits the last sentence since, certainly, from his reading Hopkins would have papered the walls of his room with "mortuary cards." But Martin will not let dead Dolbens lie, so more guesswork is marshaled: "The letter that would *probably* tell us most *intimately* what Hopkins was feeling is his answer to Coles, who *had been privy to* both Hopkins's emotions and Dolben's. *But it has disappeared.*" The fact is we do *not* know it has disappeared; we do not even know whether it had *ever* existed, much less what it conceivably contained.

As to the second of Martin's strategies, obsessive sexuality, I have refuted it in the context of the poems, and I recommend MacKenzie's detailed confutation in his introduction to *The Early Poetic Manuscripts*. The sexuality in question is, of course, homosexuality. Early in the book, Martin tells us Hopkins "matured physically at a very late age. If we are to trust *their position in his notebooks as evidence of a firm date,* his notes on nocturnal emissions indicate that they did not occur regularly until he was well over nineteen years old." It is a basic hermeneutical principle that of all explanations the simplest and most comprehensive is to be favored: in this case, we have *no* significant detailed personal notes *of any kind whatsoever* until that "firm date." But Martin has a heavier agenda concerning this tardy maturation: "Since he achieved sexual maturity *so late* [now reified as undeniable *fact*], it is possible that as an undergraduate he was still passing through the phase of homosexuality that we are told [by whom?] is normal *in early puberty.*" Engaging the issue subsequently, Martin notes: "*Naturally enough* for a young Victorian, he thought of sins as largely sexual [but of the hundreds of confessional entries, missing evening prayers, killing an insect, distraction in chapel, uncharitable thoughts, etc., very few would be defined as "sins" even by a "young Victorian"], and the most recurrent *he recorded* were concerned with *masturbation.*" It matters little to Martin that the latter term is never used in the notebooks: "So painfully did it nag at his conscience that he used a repetitive abbreviation,

'O.H.' to indicate when he had fallen into *old* habits" — so we have an insoluble issue akin to Dr. Johnson's use of "M" in his diaries.

But is not *"old* habits" a curious term for one who, we were earlier told, "achieved sexual maturity *so late"* in his life? It also raises hilarious issues regarding the major poems, where every critic, except W. A. M. Peters (1948) and James Finn Cotter (1972), had thought Hopkins inconsistent in his use of the ex-clamations, "Oh," "O," and "Ah." What will the glossators do, for example, with the "O fair" and the "Let him *oh"* of "Henry Purcell" or the identical shift in "The Windhover"? Again, it would be the better part of simplicity and elegance to conclude, as does Felix Letemendia in his "Medico-Psychological Commen-tary," in MacKenzie's *Early Poetic Manuscripts:* "Because of the high degree of scrupulosity that Hopkins reveals in the Notes, it is impossible to know what significance can be attached to references to 'old habits,' and 'temptations' or 'impurities.' "

Let me terminate this noisome discussion with a twofold hope: first, that the use of particular-examen notes for the sacrament of penance will be as out-of-bounds to students of nineteenth-century figures as the use of psychiatric-session notes should be to students of twentieth-century figures; second, that we will not see the kind of *textus receptus* tradition launched by Humphrey House regarding Dolben duplicated regarding Hopkins's sexual-ity. Without a scintilla of proof, Martin continues: "One writer claims that Hopkins recorded 1564 sins in ten months, averaging five a day, and that 'Of these, 238 were sexual sins.' " The writer is Norman White, "Problems...," cited earlier, and the tradition is confirmed by Martin's concluding assertion, "This may well be true." Though one doesn't care for the calibration of such al-leged matters, it should be pointed out that "sexual sins" by this reckoning occurred twenty-four times per month. (Portnoy thou shouldst have lived in that hour.)

The third strategy, "Dolben Ubiquitous," is more easily coun-tered since his name is almost ceaselessly introduced at random and *à propos de rien,* apparently on the assumption that here familiarity will supersede critical contempt. Of "mortuary-cards" Edgell we are told: "There is little evidence that Hopkins thought well of him, but they were linked, *loosely but inescapably,* by their shared memories of Dolben" — this, nearly fifteen years after Dolben's death. Of the cry of the nun in "The Wreck...," we are told that her words "should have been evoked by the thought of Christ as lover is an idea that would have seemed familiar enough to generations of poets — and to Dolben in particular." Why to Dolben in particular? Nobody knows — except Martin. The jagged Edgell recurs as Hopkins spends "a fine August afternoon talking in Regent's Park, *presumably* about conversion and about Dolben...." During this same visit to London, Hopkins writes of another convert, "*they* call him F. Dominic," which Martin tells us "had obvious resonances for him [Hopkins] of Br Dominic, as Dolben had liked to be called." But it is the unknown "they," not Hopkins, who invoke the name Dominic. Of an early rebuff by another student *before entering Oxford,* Martin observes, "Gerard's disappointment was a rehearsal in small of his desolation three years later over Digby Dolben": disappointment and desolation that were experienced only in the imagination of Robert Bernard Martin, and, I here rest my case, that will inevitably be the lot of readers of *Gerard Manley Hopkins: A Very Private Life.*

Whiteners

I have cited Norman White several times in the above discussion, generally critical not of the accuracy of his research or judgments, but of his tone. However, Professor White appears to be a practitioner of a kind of *Formgeschichte;* or is what would be called in nonbiblical circles a "genre critic." Those citations were all from journal articles, where apparently more casual, even more colloquial language and imagery were viewed as acceptable. But in the finished book, *Hopkins: A Literary Biography,* a radically different mood prevails. Compared to Martin, White is more judicious, more restrained, and more scholarly and untendentious; as well as more thorough, particularly regarding what relates to Hopkins and to the larger social, intellectual, political, and ecclesiastical stage on which his life is played out.

There are, as I have already noted, flaws in the book, among which I would point, first, to the perpetuation, however modified, of the dichotomy between priestly and poetic vocation; second, without being as tendentious as Martin, White still gives too much credence to the myth of Dolben's importance; third, figures whose importance extends into the post-Victorian era are rarely identified. Thus Joseph Rickaby's role as an active social ethicist and in revitalizing Thomism is ignored; and Alban Goodier, later archbishop, is simply identified as a "boy with toothache" whom Hopkins encounters. More important, however, is White's succumbing to the same subjective fixations relating to the most trifling issues that — as I noted in the preceding chapter — have been the critical sociopathology of too many Hopkins studies.

I proffer only a few examples. Of "The Lantern out of Doors," we are told: "The poem's second voice, which speaks the intended clinching argument of Christ's interest, could be said also to lack a dramatic link with the first." But the obvious link is between "beam" = be-am, and "interest" = inter-esse. In "Spring," "the contrast [with the octave] of the sestet's interpretation is startling. . . . Tone, pace, and imagery have changed." But that is precisely what is meant by the "turn" in a sonnet. "Pied Beauty" advocates "a group of qualities . . . contrary to the orthodox." It is "an attack on the idea of God as the god of the conventional." But nothing could be more orthodox or conventional than the Scholastic aphorism, "Unity can only be imitated by multiplicity." "Ribblesdale" is denigrated as "a product of misanthropic broodiness, written in distinctive style, but without passion or urgency." How respond to this peremptory judgment? Of what seems to me Hopkins's most extraordinary Metaphysical poem — though he did not personally favor it — with conceits as brilliant as those of Donne and as extenuated as those of Crashaw, "The Blessed Virgin Compared to the Air We Breathe," White observes: "The metre . . . does not encourage originality, and the poem lacks power." Again, the second clause is plain *ipse dixit*, and the first is pure *non sequitur*: How could meters encourage "originality"?

In what I have called Hopkins's *l'art poétique*, "To What Serves Mortal Beauty?," White finds "deviousness," and continues with a virtual *catalogue raisonné* of gratuitous and piddling judgments — of the sort also detailed in the preceding chapter:

> Although the title of the poem refers to *meditation*, it [the title?] makes such a self-conscious attempt at archaic and poetic carved phrase [*sic*] that the *argument* is stanched before it can flow. It does not progress until after the caesural pause in line 3; there has to be a catching-up phrase, "See: it does this," to restart the progress of the meditation.... There is a clash between the question, which requires a *reasoned and syntactically framed* answer, and a group of direct responses of a quite different, *anti-rational,* unframed and disconnected kind..., without a *mediating* framework of *argument.* [emphasis added]

Is this an analysis of Hopkins's poem or of Friedrich Vischer's *Wissenschaft des Schönen?*

I will conclude this itemization of minor *and* mincing issues with White's comments on "Epithalamion": there is of course the now-conventional reference to Whitman, the ignorance of *Brautmystik,* which I discussed above, and then — what otherwise one would think a parody of the quirkiness of much Hopkins criticism — an "account of the undressing," which is "sadly comic..., because the boots come off after the trousers." Poor Hopkins, whose vow of chastity prevented him from sporting with Amaryllis, would have wondered: What boots it with uncessant care to write a marital hymn for a brother that could be subjected to this kind of attack?

Fortunately, for the most part such petty judgments are kept brief. Thus we have, blessedly, only a page and a half devoted to "The Windhover," and only a few lines to the ubiquitously polysemous "buckle." For a book subtitled *A Literary Biography* and of over five hundred densely packed pages, such "critical" parsimoniousness can only be applauded.

After these rather lengthy introductory and explanatory observations, I turn now to some of the major poems with a view to validating my original "claim" of Hopkins: poetic normality in relation to literary and religious tradition.

Primordial Complementarity

"Deep Down Things"

GOD'S GRANDEUR

The world is charged with the grandeur of God.
  It will flame out, like shining from shook foil;
  It gathers to a greatness, like the ooze of oil
Crushed. Why do men then now not reck his rod?
Generations have trod, have trod, have trod;
  And all is seared with trade; bleared, smeared with
      toil;
  And wears man's smudge and shares man's smell: the
      soil
Is bare now, nor can foot feel, being shod.

And for all this, nature is never spent;
  There lives the dearest freshness deep down things;
And though the last lights off the black West went
  Oh, morning, at the brown brink eastwards,
          springs —
Because the Holy Ghost over the bent
  World broods with warm breast and with ah! bright
      wings.

We begin with an utterance that has a flat, factual certitude about it: "The world is charged with the grandeur of God." There is nothing about this statement that would among Christians elicit debate, confutation, or challenge. It is not a remembrance or a hope. It is straightforwardly declarative; simple indicative, and neither subjunctive nor optative. There is nothing particularly metaphoric or "poetic" — though "charged" might be so read —

save to the degree all speech is metaphorically grounded. Indeed, if one were to consider this sentence abstracted from context, that is, abstracted from any kind of specialized prior knowledge, and treat the word "God" as merely a pointer or tag entailing no faith statement whatsoever, the observation is as coldly phenomenological as the equally flat-out factuality of something like, "Earth has not anything to show more fair..." than this city. Thus, it is not a "performative" or a self-implicating observation, one that demands further clarification from the speaker or fuller expectation in the listener; though obviously any word, phrase, judgment, contains implications that can be unraveled more or less indefinitely.

For Hopkins that the world is so constituted is merely a self-evident, self-validating, experiential response to reality as he conceived it in the light of his faith. So, from his perspective, this is a statement not of moral conviction but of *physical* certitude; and the latter is — for him in this instance anyway — more "solid" and factual than if he were engaging in Scholastic metaphysics (which, in theory as a Christian thinker, ought to be for him more cogent). But the plainness of tone indicates that here we are in the hard, commonsensical world of British empiricism, in the severe thing-to-thing universe, say, of Dr. Johnson; not in any realm of philosophical consideration, speculation, or confutation. ("Kick at the rock, Sam Johnson, break your bones" [Richard Wilbur's Berkeleyian irony].)

More precisely, we are in the thing-to-thing world of Aquinas where faith is the first and the final principle of knowledge. Faith, says Aquinas, does not eventuate in *enuntiabilia,* talk, but in *res,* the flat-out *thing* itself; or in the words of the final entry in Stevens's *Collected Poems:* "Not Ideas about the Thing but the Thing Itself." Thus Hopkins's initial statement is neither devotional nor apologetic nor hortative. The world as so conceived is a simple donnée, a given in the catalogue of common religious things which requires no auxiliary props from any other realm.

In this poem — though not in all his poems — Hopkins treats as unimpeachable fact that the basic stuff, the fundamental reality, is just *like this*. The world *is* charged with God's grandeur. Of course, we realize that from first principles flow corollaries, adjuncts, second and third principles, and so on, just as from unity flows multiplicity. In fact, for Hopkins's philosophical tradition, as noted earlier, the only way of "imitating" unity is through multiplicity. The only way of imaging the absolute oneness of deity is through its multiple refractions in creation. For Hopkins, as for the tradition, not even the most exalted mystic naturally knows Unity in its Trinitarian selfness. Hence the unvarnished, unembellished triteness of the statement. Of course, as unity is manifest only in multiplicity, we expect the statement ultimately to be diffused, to be parceled out and articulated, to be unraveled — as inevitably it will be.

But, the question almost immediately arises, Why "grandeur" and not the more biblical/ecclesial "glory," which the meters would as readily accommodate? ("Greatness" appears in one redaction, but this was simply a misreading by Bridges, and has never been defended by subsequent editors.) As to the apparently intentional avoidance of "glory," it seems not unlikely that precisely because the latter word had been so overworked in religious contexts, it had lost its "dearest freshness." It evokes public ritual and ceremony, theological and ecclesiastical stereotyping, biblical argot, even. It thus does not bespeak the kind of stark, factual power congruent with the implications of the initial sentence. If only by repeated use, it evokes the artificiality of manmade rituals and of humanly designed language. In short, it wears man's smudge.

And furthermore, for Hopkins "glory" would play off the Jesuit slogan, "Ad Maiorem Dei Gloriam," which, however unused in earlier days of the Society, was in Hopkins's time the epigraph for almost every commonplace communication, at least to fellow Catholics. I shall discuss this in greater detail when considering "Pied Beauty," though the word "glory" is also avoided in the title. Thus such avoidance must have represented on the part of the poet an almost conscious decision, another basis of which may be that "glory" entails an almost purely visual phenomenon. "Glory" is what one observes; it is a kind of refulgent object of distanciated contemplation, rather than the subject of self-engagement.

Or, as Hopkins will say in what I have already called his *ars poetica,* it suggests the realm of staring, however much in awe, or *gazing,* however worshipfully — where "a glance master more than gaze," says the poet in "To What Serves Mortal Beauty." The "glance" implies penetration, the sharp edge that gives entrance (and *entrànces*) and the *power* implicit in both notions: penetrate, enter — as when we refer to a glancing blow; that is, not merely an oblique blow, but a blow that cuts into, as subject and object cut into each other, interpenetrate and interanimate each other. In gazing, the subject is here, as over against the remote object, which is *there.* "Glory" is merely visible, "scopophiliac" — as current jargon has it. "Grandeur," however, is palpable, penetrable, penetrant, *and* visible.

I use a contemporary example relating to a quondam-Jesuit theologian who, though critical of aspects of Scotus, was also a great admirer of Hopkins. The translated title of Hans Urs von Balthasar's theological esthetics, *Herrlichkeit,* conveys the notion of the *dominus* who dominates, of the Lord who exercises *Herrschaft.* And again I note, as I shall frequently, that *dominus* is cognate of "dangerous," a term in "To What Serves Mortal Beauty," which is usually misread as entailing sexual peril — a somewhat prurient motif for those mystified by the alleged oddities of celibate Jesuit life. Whereas, I shall make the case that Hopkins is also, if not exclusively, writing about the mortal, created, friable beauty which "takes dominion everywhere." In any case, it is this notion of "Lordship" that is lost in the common English translation of *Herrlichkeit* as "Glory of the Lord."

What is needed in place of "glory" is a term that while expressing the radiantly visible — indeed the dazzlingly visible — is also expressive of a force and power ("a pressure" as Hopkins says in "The Wreck" [4]), that charges and impels: a power St. Paul refers to when he says it is "the charity of Christ that *urges* us." Moreover, this is a real urgency, a public urgency, as in "liturgy" in the primordial sense, and not in the sense of a mere spectacle which — "during the pauses in the action," Aristotle would say — one can watch in wonderment. Certainly this grandeur *is* a refulgence, a *doxa,* an illumination, a "glory," that one observes; but it is also a propulsion, a dynamism, an en*ergy* (again, as in "lit*urgy*").

If the world were charged with merely the *glory* of God, it would inadequately mirror the variegated reality of God's single unitary being. The term "glory" would be true to the poem's notion of "shining" but not to the notion of "crushing": it would be true to the notion of flaming-out but not to the notion of a rod to be reckoned with. It would be true to the visual but not to the palpable; true to contemplative detachment but not to felt and experienced action. On the other hand, "grandeur" conveys all of those multitudinous (though reductively complementary) aspects of deity, as do all those isomorphic notions introduced above: glory *and* public urgency, refulgence *and* domination, visibility *and* tangibility, contemplation *and* action — this latter, another Jesuit axiom from Ignatius's successor who defined the complementary goal of each member of the Society as *contemplativus in actione,* thus distinguishing its mission from that of an antecedent order, the Dominicans, with their goal of *tradere contemplata.* It is with this *grandeur* that the world is *charged.* God's grandeur is the *cargo* that is *held* by, that is, in "the hold" of — what is now being called — "spaceship" earth.

Here one touches on the world's participatory role in Christ's redemptive office, as Hopkins would have read of it in St. Paul, for whom creation itself "groans and travails" awaiting the day of salvation, and for whom humanity itself makes up that which is "lacking to the passion of Christ." Therefore, the world (i.e., creation itself) is also "in charge of" this grandeur, and indeed has been charged with this duty of expectation and fulfillment, just as one would charge a soldier with the performance of a mission — a military image that would be attractive to a member of the Company of Jesus.

And here, I want to allude to a notion that would be dear to

Hopkins, to Ong, and to Jesuits in general, particularly to Teilhard de Chardin — of whom Ong is one of the most responsive expositors, as, we have noted, he is also of Hopkins. If creation itself groans and travails, if humankind makes up that which is "lacking to the passion of Christ," *both* creation and humankind discover their commission in that Jesuit slogan referred to above: "To the Greater Glory of God." In any case, the world has somehow been charged with the obligation to be carrier (cognates of "charge" and "cargo") and protector of this grandeur. By fulfilling that charge, creation itself seems to complement the divine action: *le Dieu a besoin de femmes et hommes.*

Thus the religious tradition encapsulated in the maxim, "To the Greater Glory of God," is strongly voluntaristic and far removed from any Western Quietism. Hence the Jesuit — and Hopkins's (to Patmore, August 21, 1885) explicit — antagonism to Miguel de Molinos and his followers, as well as to any oriental passivity: hence, too, the sinologist Joseph Needham's reverence for Teilhard's vision of a deity with whom *we* are co-workers, and by whom *we* have been so mandated and charged. One here says "we" because what is the world's "eye, tongue, or heart else, where / Else, but in dear [the pun is on *Tier*] and dogged man?" ("Ribblesdale": the ancestral text is Henry Vaughan on Romans 8).

Change/Exchange

But "we" (and in order to speak in Hopkins's voice, I will drop the quotation marks) have not only been so mandated by the Judge whose rod of authority we must submit to, as a bishop with his crosier delivers a charge to his diocese, or as a human judge gaveling for order delivers a charge to a jury, or as a pastor is charged with care of souls: we have not only been so mandated, we will also be audited for this charge on the last day by our final Judge, as "Ribblesdale" — the more monitory companion poem to "God's Grandeur" — makes clear. The language in both poems is similar, however fittingly judgmental in "Ribblesdale," concerning the consequences of failing to live up to one's charge. Instead, we are told, man *plunders* "both our *rich* round world bare / And none reck of world after": that is, none reck of that future when the final audit will be presented, when *liber scriptus proferetur*, and the final "charges" rung up.

However, in the larger context of the entire poem, what humanity has gained on the stock exchange, it has lost on the "spirit exchange." The marital union, the *admirabile commercium* celebrated in the Christmas liturgy when heaven and earth were "charged" with the real "exchange" of divine energy, has degenerated into mere "commerce," and humankind is now engaged in nothing but "searing" "trade." But though the mintage of the human *Antwort* has been gradually devalued and its image disfigured, so as almost to become counterfeit and useful only for human cupidity, the coinage of the *Wort* continues to ring true. Defiled humanity can continue to charge against the divine account, which is "never spent," because the ultimate exchequer mines the depths of being to redeem the creaturely debt, and to revivify the bare and barren surface of the earth.

Thus humankind, though rich in "worldly plunder," is found wanting in the spiritual provisions necessary for the *admirabile commercium*. But as we have seen, this deficiency is made up by the divine merchant of whom the preconversion poem, "The Kind Betrothal," speaks in the language of "bridal mysticism":

> The handling of His hands is sweet
> And dear the footing of the Lord.

For, *commercium* is now fused with the notion both of trading and of sexual exchange or pledge: *Handel* and handling *are* acts of inter-course, and the dear "footing" is the final reckoning or accounting whereby human debts are forgiven and redeemed. In the language of our polysyllabic/monosyllabic complementarity, and writing with all due seriousness and precision, *apocatastasis* (universal salvation) occurs because Christ "foots the bill."

If I seem here to be falling into the interpretive excesses scored in chapter 1, I would plead in defense, first, that nothing by Hopkins plumbs so profoundly the reduplicative paradoxes of the mystic's apophatic way as this very early poem where he conjoins the motifs of *agere contra* and of *admirabile commercium*; and, second, that "The Kind Betrothal" has an almost unquestionable ancestral parallel, and validation, in the structure and copiousness of an another "trading" poem, Herbert's "The Pearl."

As to the parallel, both poems catalogue the totally licit enticements the world proffers the individual who nevertheless still chooses Christ. Hopkins is somewhat sparse (his range of images straitened by his youth), detailing the natural attractions of each of the senses, while Herbert details those same attractions, but in relation to the profusion of his wide public experiences of the life of learning, honor, and pleasure. The verbal and imagistic echoes are too numerous to elaborate here, save for the concluding stanzas of both poems, which explicitly focus on the *commercium* theme.

First, the whole of "The Kind Betrothal" (MacKenzie, 1990 edition):

> Elected Silence sing to me
> And beat upon my whorlèd ear,
> Pipe me to pastures still and be
> The music that I care to hear.
>
> Shape nothing lips, be lovely dumb:
> It is the check, the curfew sent
> From there where all surrenders come
> Which only makes you eloquent.
>
> Be shellèd eyes with double dark
> That brings the uncreated light:
> These pièd shows they make their mark,
> Tease, charge, and coil the simple sight.
>
> Palate, the hutch of Like and Lust,
> Wish now no tasty rinse of wine:
> The flask will be so clear, the crust
> So fresh that come in fasts divine!

> Nostrils, that dainty breathing spend
> On all the stir and keep of pride,
> What relish will the censers send
> Along the sanctuary side!
>
> O feel-of-primrose hands, O feet
> That want the yield of plushy sward,
> The handling of His hands is sweet
> And dear the footing of the Lord.
>
> And Poverty be thou the bride
> And now the wedding weeds begun
> And lily-coloured wear provide
> Your spouse not toilèd at nor spun.

Grace builds on nature. The only way to know the Creator is by contemplating creation. Yet in each stanza, the images of the created order are employed not to transcend that order but to reveal its obverse: silence sings, beats, and pipes the person to pastures *still* (i.e., to pastures of *ever deeper* silence wherein one hears some ultimate *melodìa*). The unshapen (the un-inscaped) dumbness of physical speech is lovely because it is the barrier extinguishing the interior speech of the heart's fire (curfew = *couvre feu*), which then allows the infinitely silent eloquence of the *Wort* to speak *through* the creature's mute *Antwort* — much as in Donne the creature becomes the Creator's "musique."

The closed eyes not only obscure the visible world of "simple sight" with all its "pied" attractive lures (cf. "Moonrise June 19"), but the "shelled" eyes (Keats's oyster-cloister bivalves) also extinguish the interior world (*couvre feu*) of consciousness ("double dark") so that the "uncreated light" of "dazzling darkness," the gospel's and Herbert's pearl of great price, is discovered. Dining, like the "pied shows" of verse 3, is neutrally both teasing and ensnarling, but one finds the real nurturing power in the negativity of "fasts divine" (and of "*pastures* still"). Breathing is also equally neutral (dainty = dignity) but is involuntarily spent on the malarial "stir" ("marsh air") as well as on the perfume of flowers ("keep of pride"), which here betokens the wafted remnant ("relish" = relic) of the odors of Eden Garden, and its "paradisaical" paradigm ("the sanctuary side").

In Hopkins's penultimate stanza the *admirabile commercium* emphasizes the "mercantile" exchange, or better, "inter-course" of deeper and deeper limited sensate experiences groping their separate ways for the infinite compensatory *gift* of the Lord. Then the final stanza describes the wondrously "admirable" marital bond between creature and Creator, and the wedding garment of [neg]*otium:* "not toiled at nor spun." Herbert reverses the order by symbolizing the "betrothal" of heaven and earth as a kind of Jacob's ladder — after the fashion of Dante's *strenge,* Milton's "golden Chain," or even Rossini's *Scala di Seta* — while also stressing the now-eclipsed "trade" imagery:

> I know all these, and have them in my hand;
> Therefore not sealed, but with open eyes
> I fly to thee, and fully understand
> Both *the main sale, and the commodities;*
> And at *what rate and price* I have thy love;
> With all the circumstances that may move;
> Yet through these labyrinths, not my grovelling wit,
> But thy silk twist let down from heav'n to me,
> Did both conduct and teach me, how by it
> > To climb to thee.

Electric/Eclectic

In "God's Grandeur" the images are for the most part traditional biblical commonplaces: the rod is both a "comfort" and a chastisement. But, as noted in the previous chapter, in no case could the priestly warnings of Hopkins be described as "disgust at man" or as "misanthropic broodiness" (Norman White). Such admonitions are simply what used to be called "expressions of pastoral care." "Care" is merely another word for "being in *charge* of," and "expressions" is merely another product of olives being pressed, as in Milton's "Let me express thee unblamed." For both poets, the office of conduit of God's grandeur entails the pain of the burning coal at the lips of Isaiah, to which Milton explicitly refers, and about which Hopkins prayed daily at Mass — hence such harsh language as "crushed" and "pressed."

Nevertheless, those readers who find an allusion to electricity here are certainly correct. The use of "lightning" for "shining" in another redaction, and the explanation by Hopkins that he had "fork lightning" in mind, confirm the notion of electric charge, since the word "charge" had been used in that context for over a century. The electric-charge motif and its relation to *the entire poem* is made explicit in Hopkins's oft-cited gloss on the Ignatian *Exercises:* "All things are charged ... with God, ... give off sparks and take fire, yield drops and flow." (Throughout the present treatment, I am trying to avoid repeating what I have spelled out at length in *Celestial Pantomime,* where the complementarity of this and related imagery constitutes the theme of chapter 4. Nor will I do anything more than refer to the marvellous enjambement of "the ooze of oil / Crushed," which is explicated, along with scores of parallels, in that earlier work.)

What has not been discussed elsewhere, so far as I know, is this imagery as the expression of one of Hopkins's favorite texts: Augustine's "beauty ever ancient, ever new," where it could be said that the Psalmist meets (who would have thought?) Benjamin Franklin; where in "God's Grandeur," one of the most *ancient* sexual (the Holy Ghost is "birthing" the world) figures of Western literature — children like olive plants, the olive-tree bed of Penelope and Odysseus — meets one of the most *modern:* meets, to take one example of many, Hopkins's own haunting *bête noire,* Whitman and his "body electric." And in both of his shipwreck poems Hopkins uses the terms "electrical" and "electric" for indomitable force. This dual aspect of God's grandeur is not only the fundamental *res* of *things* (I am intentionally tautologous); it is at once the most *primordial* and the most *contemporaneous,* the ever-ancient and the ever-new. Moreover, this is true not only of the images *qua* images, but of their source and substrate.

In reading Hopkins on God's grandeur one would almost think he were alluding to the major scientific controversy at the close of the last century between those who believed brain conduction to be essentially chemical and those who believed it to be essentially electrical. The proponents of the first assumption were known as "soup" people, and the proponents of the second were known as "spark" people. For "soup," one may read "ooze of oil," and for "spark," one may read "shining from shook foil." In fact, these polemical ascriptions were launched several years after the composition of the poem. But had the scientists followed the lead of the poet, they would have realized that it was in the complementarity of the two notions that truth lay: the brain is now universally recognized as an extremely complicated matrix of electrochemical circuitry.

Ratio/Generatio

Why, Hopkins then asks, do people fail to respond to this divine charge? But, of course, no one can ask a significant question without having a sense of the answer. The childish question, "Why?" is global, and therefore independent of prior knowledge. But a detailed, specific question is already somewhat self-answering. "Why do men *then now* not reck his rod?" implies that *once,* though not presently, people did attend to both the comfort and the chastisement symbolized by the shepherd's staff. The question therefore assumes a prelapsarian condition of total harmony between God and creation; and, concomitantly, between humankind and all other creatures. It was so once, implies Hopkins, why is it not so *now?*

But the "then" indicates also that we are not faced with an irresolvable issue; we are not faced with the incomprehensible "mystery of iniquity," of which St. Paul writes. "Then" is the equivalent of "therefore," with the latter's tacit and built-in assumption that the answer is attainable by the power of reason — though as Hopkins would hasten to add, reason aided by grace. "Therefore" (*ergo*) implies an answer. And such an answer is also in the *now* "fallen" present as opposed to the "heretofore" of a *then* Edenic age.

Similarly, syllogistic mediated discursive knowledge (*ratio*), as opposed to intuitive, direct knowledge (*intellectus*), is a result of humankind's created condition, just as temporal sequentiality results from the loss of pretemporal and prelapsarian immediacy. *Ratio* differs from *intellectus* as does multiplicity from unity; *ratio* differs from *intellectus,* said Boethius, as the circumference of a circle differs from its center, or as time differs from eternity. *Ratio* laboriously moves in a course, like a syllogism from beginning through middle term to conclusion: this is literally "discourse of reason," or simply discursive thought. *Intellectus* begins with a simple unified truth through which it gains knowledge of multiplicity, just as God knows in his simple essence all things that are.

"Why do men then now not reck his rod?" As the above somewhat abstruse medieval speculation indicates, the answer is implicit in the *philosophia perennis,* but it is also uniquely Hopkinsian. It is the phenomena of "generate" (active verb) and of "generations" (plural noun) that constitute the dual answer to the question. The very traditional theological answer (lurking in the historical background), which I would not dream of attributing directly to Hopkins, is the Augustinian notion that the act of sexual coitus, that is, sexual *generation,* is the medium of "original sin," and thus of our postlapsarian unresponsiveness to the divine power. However, it is not the *act* itself, but the *temporal* succession of generations, the attrition of history, that is the more plausible *and* conventional answer to the poet's question.

Unlike Augustine, who abandoned his ruminative and speculative paganism after Cassiciacum and converted to Christian rigorism, Hopkins, though understandably an almost compulsive ascetic, never overcame, at least intellectually, the "pagan" Neo-Platonism of the classical tradition embodied by, among others, Jowett and Pater. As a result, for Hopkins the answer to the question would lie in the gradual trammeling up in the temporal of each more and more self-absorbed *generation.* That answer is akin to the natural supernaturalism of Romantic Platonism. As generations ceaselessly beget (Augustine's rebarbative sexuality is totally irrelevant here), they move further and further from the primordial awareness of God's illuminating grandeur, which becomes concomitantly dimmer.

Thus Aquinas says in the *Summa* that human beings who acquire knowledge by discursive processes are called "rational." And this, he adds, "comes of the feebleness of their light." Neither angels nor God knows discursively. In Catholic thought the emphasis on the power of immediate intuition is akin to Aquinas and even more to Scotus, while the emphasis on a primordial revelation is similar to the fideism and traditionalism of J.-M. de Maistre, Louis de Bonald, and the early Félicité de Lamennais, for all of whom there was an archaic disclosure of God's existence if not of God's essence. Unlike the great ontologist Antonio Rosmini, none of this group would have said the very "nature" of the Trinitarian Godhead was also made known in this archaic disclosure. For that a special revelation was required. In any case, whatever its precise contents, this originary revelation becomes clouded with the passage of time and with evolution through space.

But it is more than this gradual diminishment which accounts for the failure to reckon with these manifestations of God's grandeur. It is also the gradual darkening of intellectual awareness through the attrition of repetitiveness as the result of actual sin; and the gradual "callousness" of the historical individual, and thus of his/her culture, that separates persons and society from the primordial Edenic "charge." The initial flash of revelation becomes a more and more fading glimmer of the original illumination: *N.B.*: have trod, have trod, have trod — with that last "have trod" fading away like a muted echo.

Or, to put it differently, the original illumination is like a *unitary* light disappearing on the horizon as humankind gets more and more fagged and fashed in the *multiplicity* of trading and treading. Both insulate (in the electrical sense) the person against the divine charge: we being shod, and shoddy. However, in the

Scholastic tradition, whether Thomist or Scotist, our intellect when it engages any created being, whether material or spiritual, can know immediately and intuitively that being, assuming of course that God cooperates in relating *our* intellect and that particular created object. This is possibly simplified, but it is "our" intellect that must be open to the "being in question": *nullam obicem ponere*. The human role is negative but not passive: "place no obstacle," and grace may flow and the immediate intuition may possess the mind. However, for Hopkins in this poem the obstacle *is in* place; humankind cannot bare itself to being, cannot keep its wits warm "to the things that are."

There is also here one of the few explicit allusions in Hopkins to a predecessor poem, Keats's "Ode to a Nightingale." On the basis of that allusion, "No hungry generations tread thee down," one could probably identify the nightingale's full-throated "ease" (*otium*) with the ever-surviving, transgenerational Holy Ghost, symbolized by the dove, brooding with bright wings. Unlike calloused humanity, caught up in the world of trade and toil (*neg-otium*), the nightingale is open to the ecstatic liberation of "easeful" death.

And beyond Keats is Herbert's play on the holy name, "Iesu," as "I ease you." Equally significant is the heavy Latinity (rare in Hopkins) of the very word embodying humanity's entropic decline: "generations." If the plain Anglo-Saxon symbolizes the untrammeled immediate insight, then the polysyllabic Latin (or Greek) is the encumbering ratiocination that obscures the originary sense of God's grandeur. One here also returns to the frustration of *being* by *doing*, of *intellectus* by *ratio*, of eternity by time. As I have noted, *ratio* is a dialectical discursive process that produces secondary, factual, "useful" knowledge; *intellectus* is the spontaneous contemplative "intuition" referred to above, and in its very exercise reaches to the immediate and insightful, but still blurred, knowledge of God's grandeur; indeed, participates indirectly in that grandeur. However, such "supernatural" knowledge, for example, of the Trinity as the "infinitely-infinite ground of the beyond," may be foreclosed. Nevertheless, the intellect in the very act of "intellecting" proceeds into the realm of God's infinite reality: *Intellectus intelligendo in infinitum procedit* (an axiom which is at the essence not only of the complementarity of creature/Creator, but of all theological speculation — however feeble and clouded).

But as, in this poem, Hopkins's "men" become more and more mired in the temporal domain, what once had been acquired without mediation becomes more and more secondhand "knowledge" by methodic reflection or dialectical technique. Ratiocination, constrained by space and time, replaces the pure spiritual immediacy of intellection. This is simply to say with Aquinas, "*quod defectus quidam intellectus est ratiocinatio.*" Or to translate into Hopkinsian, where once we flew, we now tread; where once was unself-conscious and atemporal oneness, now are time-laden, hesitant probings toward a necessarily obscure conclusion; where once was passionate and unself-conscious consummation, now is laborious syllogistic preamble — resulting in only a simulacrum of interinanimating communion with the Godhead.

Here, then, is the "hypocritical" power of that now-exotic and Latinate term, "generations." Having lost the pure simplicity of primitive "Saxon" insight, we now live in the blinkered world where layer upon layer (syllable upon syllable) of acculturation prevents us from reaching those depths, where *live* those "deep down things" to which the poet shall refer shortly. We cannot "mate ourselves with life" (Stevens, again), because we cannot feel, touch, palpably experience this *res*. We are victims of an enervated *traditio* (trod, trod, trod). And we are insulated against whatever is this strange divine electricity — we being bleared, smeared, smudged. Hopkins tells us, we are cogged and fashed by hypertrophied syllogistics and over-elaborated dialectics, by the "business" (*neg-otium*) of attritional time and space — symbolized here by fragmented, polysyllabic, ratiocinative Latinity (gen-er-a-tions): the pure, white radiance of original insight (symbolized by simple Anglo-Saxon) is obfuscated, blurred, disarticulated, and prismatized. As a sermon of Hopkins has it: "This life is night... because the truth of *things* is either dimly seen or not seen at all." In short, we cannot provide an *Antwort* to the *Wort*, a contact point to the divine battery terminal — we, "being shod."

Let me add, parenthetically, Hopkins's obsession with radical Saxon, or with noncontaminated Welsh, had little to do (*contra* Wellek and Warren) with some general Teutonizing, Saxe-Coburg-Gotha syndrome — presumably related to the marriage of Albert and Victoria. As had Thomas Gray, a century before studying Old Norse and Welsh, Hopkins was seeking in England's pleasant land a return to a lost paradise, the key to which he imagined was a kind of "prelapsarian language," a language untainted by Norman-French bastardization, a language of his imagined roots, of the childhood of his people and of his own peculiarly childlike vision: "I cannot doubt that no beauty in a language can make up for want of purity.... I am learning Anglo-Saxon and it is a vastly superior thing to what we have." And as with Gray, Hopkins's "learning" was nongeopolitical, certainly only indirectly connected with marriages in the royal family. There is nothing in Hopkins that would suggest "Chips from a German Workshop," though he had dabbled in Max Müller, and even in that work. But it was an effort to refresh the language, not unrelated to Ossian a century before, or to Francis Newman's debate with Arnold on translating the *Iliad* into a kind of primitive English, or to the general interest in purifying the language of the scribe evinced not only by Hopkins but by Swinburne and Patmore.

And/Oh/Ah

Nevertheless, after all of the repetitive and almost despairing anguish over the sad fate of humanity in the octave, there still seems to be some redemption for such losses (including the linguistic) on this postlapsarian stock exchange. Nor is this redemption entirely unexpected, a Barthian dialectic moment, or an O. Henry-like reversal in the story we call history. Nor is it even a condescending reprieve after the fashion of Eastern Orthodox theology.

Against the background of millennia of humankind's defilement of "the world," against a scene of narcissistic rape, pollution, and filth, against all of this..., we are *not* subjected to such an anticipated ecclesiastical bromide, along the lines of: "*but* nevertheless God still loves us"; nor are we proffered some other spiritual anodyne. Rather we are told in what seems a religious *non sequitur: "And* for all this...*And* though the last lights... "

"Poetry should surprise," said both Keats and Hopkins. However, it should not surprise by contradicting itself, particularly in a poem which is intended, at least consciously on the part of its author, to be a preachment of hard sayings. After having been told: "*And* all is seared with trade, bleared, smeared with toil; / *And* wears man's smudge *and* shares man's smell; the soil / Is bare now, nor can foot feel, being shod"; after having been told all of this, and anticipating a Donnean redemptive reversal, we do *not* expect a coordinating conjunction, as though each side of the equation were in balance. Nor, certainly, with so careful a craftsman as Hopkins, would one argue that the anaphoric repetitions of "and" before the turn of the sonnet dictated the fourth and the fifth repetitions in the first two clauses of the sestet. Clearly humanity is sinful, BUT where sin abounds grace does more abound. However, this "mechanical optimism" (Stevens) is precisely what the poet doesn't affirm; though in fact this is what he had originally said. An earlier recension has the expected "but," which is crossed out and replaced by "And": so obviously the correction reflects serious thought.

After this catenation of rot, fetor, and reek in the octave we are told: AND, *for* all of that defilement and corruption, the creature and the Creator, the world of nature and nature's maker, are still companioned, and can still cooperate. Only Hopkins's conviction of the power of redemptive grace would transform the expected adversative "but" into the coordinative "and." Even more surprising is the phrase, "for all this, nature is never spent." Though the surface meaning seems to be, "in spite of all this, nature is never spent," *that* is not what the poet says. Rather it is precisely *for* humanity's healing and rejuvenation that the inexhaustible wealth of the divine treasury can be drawn upon. "Dearest freshness," then, also has its root meaning of "expensive," "high-priced," and "newly minted." So, the gloriously charged surprise is that nature *and* grace, even after the fall, are not adversaries; they are co-partners, however sometimes at odds, in the redemption of their shared cosmos. And the visible warrant of this remuneration is that most ancient symbol of hope, dawn after darkness — like the biblical rainbow after the storm — as covenantal pledge of Creator to creature.

Gratia presupponit naturam: grace builds on nature, even on fallen nature — that latter being the precise word Hopkins uses here: "*nature* is never spent." Hence the startling "and." Had Hopkins retained more of his Protestant heritage, with its legacy of conflict between nature and grace (a conflict which in our time Barth has sounded and from a different but profound perspective justified), then the *coniunctio* (grammar-glamour) could only have been "*But.*" Similarly with the repetition of "and" in the sestet: "*And* though the last lights...went..." Again, it should be "*But.*" As in, to paraphrase: "But though all of this evil occurred, nevertheless, the following good things must take place."

Again, that adversative conjunction would bespeak a litany of Augustinian, Lutheran, Pascalian, Barthian, antagonist relationships between fallen creation and beneficent deity. (I intentionally ecumenize the indictment, though Hopkins would himself certainly have used his compulsive Victorian code word, "Protestant.") In any case, for the mainstream Western religious tradition, all is a continuum, however interrupted by lapses; all is an interchanging flow ("to-fro tender trambeams") of grace. No absolute breaks, only mild interruptions; no "buts" only ANDS.

In the sestet, the words "dear" and "fresh" are favorites of the poet, and though used in poem after poem to what would be in other artists the point of tedium, they never appear facilely introduced. Like the seemingly stereotypical repetitions of "happy" in Keats, such favorites precisely because so unself-consciously in-

troduced reinforce the childlike, spontaneous insight of the artist.
In that sense they are, again, an attempt to adumbrate a kind
of prelapsarian innocence. Thus they are not padding, they are
not mere ballast for the line, they are not empty exclamations
intended to muscle the reader into elation or anguish — as they
invariably appear to be in a poet like Matthew Arnold. Rather,
they are validations of a genuinely unreflective vision, of a vision
oblivious to readers' reactions or to critics' animadversions.

So, too, with the exclamations "Oh!" and "Ah!" in the sestet.
Where in a poet like Whitman these usually come off as bombast,
in an *anima naturaliter candida* like a Hopkins or a Keats, they
are spontaneous, psychologically unthematized declamations of
wonder. A plain indication of this spontaneity in Hopkins is the
complete lack of uniformity from one poem to another in these
ejaculatory outbursts: in one poem we have "*Oh,* morning," in
the next, "*O* look." The one thing a child is master of is inconsis-
tency. And with both Keats and Hopkins, what would be flaws in
other poets now become affecting strategies. As so often, Pope is
our mentor in the *Essay on Criticism:*

> Great wits sometimes may gloriously offend,
> And rise to faults true critics dare not mend;
> From vulgar bounds with brave disorder part,
> And snatch a *grace* beyond the reach of art,
> Which *without passing through the judgment, gains*
> *The heart,* and all its end *at once* attains.

"Grace" is the *mot juste,* in its sense of natural esthetic and supernatural disposition. But, it is not pedantry to point out that,
again, the very rare enjambement italicized in Pope's *Essay* is
highly functional: we experience the bypassing of the judgment
(*ratio*) as the verse rushes to take possession of the "heart" (*intellectus*), a rush that allows no pause for *dialectic* reflection as the
reader is moved *immediately* ("at once") — my language parallels
that used earlier — toward the "end" the poet ordains and attains.

A "literarily" self-conscious religious ecstatic, writing with one
eye on her audience, would have had to be consistent, if she

were going to create a mystical *Summa,* a systematic symbolic pattern of such exclamations as Hopkins's "Ohs" and "Ahs" — like the self-conscious "prelude of disparagement" of Tennyson's "The Epic": "mouthing out his hollow oes and aes..." With a poet like John of the Cross, who wrote, one suspects, with a view to his future massive glosses and commentaries, there are lengthy discussions of the emblematic import of such "grace-snatching" proclamatory enthusiasms initiated by a presumably *ex sponte* "O." But, why does one find innocence in Hopkins, and contrivance in such expressions as the following from one of John's *Canciones?*

> O noche que guiaste
> O noche amable mas que el aluorada
> O noche que juntaste

Similarly with a self-conscious naivté, Marianne Moore, preaching in Audenesque patter about the evils of war: "O shining O / firm star, O tumultuous ocean... O star of David, star of Bethlehem, / O black imperial lion of the Lord..." ("In Distrust of Merits"). So, too, with the equally self-conscious, if not ecstatic, Donne in such a triple pun as, "O more than moon," where the "O" figures the moon, then figures the tear of Anne More, and finally figures the image stamped by his own reflection in that tear — the true man in the moon.

In the poetry, Hopkins never preaches, nor does he affect the metaphysic, as do both John of the Cross, trained precisely as a metaphysician, and Donne, legatee of Scholasticism in its most "subtile" forms. As for the "Oh!" or "O" of Hopkins, it is literally a "rounder" reply, an *Antwort* that can come only from the ultimate *Wort* heard in "Hurrahing in Harvest": "what lips yet gave you a / Rapturous love's greeting..., of rounder replies?"

Returning explicitly to "God's Grandeur," we pick up another aspect of the line: "There lives the dearest freshness deep down things." I have already mentioned it in terms of the inexhaustible wealth of the divine exchequer. I would also emphasize Hopkins's use of such favored words as "dear" and "fresh," to describe here

the ultimate depths of the ultimate *residuum* of reality: "things."
But "fresh" is not only metathetically sonic kin to the "shine" of
the "shook foil" in the octave; it is also the ever-new and ever-
shocking lightning of which Hopkins had originally written. Just
as what is "dear" to us is the ever-present "beloved," the soothing
ambience in which we live, move, and have our being, the Com-
forter well-symbolized in emollient ooze of oil. And as "ooze"
and "broods" are also homophonic, and circumambiently com-
forting and dear, so too the "shining from shook foil" is akin to
"bright wings," which the ecstatic "ah!" further illuminates.

Brooding Over

I want to treat again of that structural strategy, enjambement,
which we paused over in the octave. I have written at length on
what I view as the fundamental, one might even say, as the psy-
chobiological source, of this trope. It is the preeminent figure of
transcendence, of the breaking out of limits and into the unknown
beyond — "unknown" because the future, the e-vent of the next
phase, that is, of the next phrase, cannot be understood until it is
reached — as one moves forward and reads it.

"The ooze of oil / Crushed" represents simply an overflowing,
a breaking through of the conventionally end-stopped line. The
locus classicus, as usual, is also in Pope's *Essay on Criticism,* and
the passage is unique and justly canonical:

> Then, at the last and only couplet fraught
> With some unmeaning thing they call a thought,
> A needless Alexandrine ends the song....

Of the forty or so lines that surround this passage only one is
not end-stopped. And that is because this train of *ideas* and *numbers* (they are identical) will not bear the extra freight ("couplet
fraught") with which Pope has loaded it; so it simply must be
supported by the additional carriers in the next line (on the next
track?).

One point here is to clarify Kenneth Burke's misunderstanding of my theory of enjambement; the latter need have nothing explicitly to do with transcendence in any religious or sexual sense — though in Hopkins it obviously is religiously undergirded. But unless induced by aleatory metrics, by sloppy poetics or whatever, enjambement does have to do with cargo, with a "charge," and with "transport" (a biological, a mystical, as well as a commercial exchange) — even unto that caboose we call a "coda." So, too, here in Hopkins, the enjambement in the last two lines does not fit some *a priori* recipe or method. "Morning...springs," overflows, into the next two lines:

> Because the Holy Ghost over the bent
> World broods with warm breast....

Here is where my notion of enjambement "joins" that of John Hollander in *Vision and Resonance.* All the enjambements I have proffered are connected to some dramatic/prosodic overflowing, that is, are connected to some *sonic* figure. But here the figure is literally *visible:* the first line of the couplet is quite manifestly "bent" over its following companion line. The "picture" is identical with that of Donne in an equally "holy sonnet":

> That I may rise, and stand, o'erthrow mee, and bend
> Your force...

Here too the line is visibly bent over into the succeeding line, as it is also in Milton's "When I Consider...":

> ...though my Soul more bent
> To serve therewith my Maker...

For Hopkins, the line is bent as the world is bent, and only the "brooding" *and* the "bright," the "ooze" *and* the "shine," will set "things" to right, will heal the fracture, will make the fraction an integer, and so restore the lost gift of "integrity." Lastly, it is the Holy Ghost — the supragenerational and transtemporal dove — who is symbolized by the flaming-out of Pentecostal fire

and the chrismic-anointing of strengthening and com-forting oil.
But the poem is not called, "The Grandeur of the Holy Ghost";
it is called "God's Grandeur." And clearly this is the Trinitarian God whose circumincessional unity-in-variety is central to the
religious tradition.

In that tradition the works of the Trinity *ad extra,* while at-
tributable "poetically," as it were, to the individual persons, are
really the works of "God" in his simple oneness: hence, "*God's*
Grandeur." But "poetically" we do have the judgmental deity
("reck his rod") identified with the Father. We also have the
kenotic Christ who lives *deep down* in "things" which have been
smeared and smudged — that kenotic Christ who has pitched his
tent in the black West. And, in the *final* lines, in this *last* dawn,
we have the third-mentioned person who is not identified "poetically," but is identified explicitly, by "her" proper name, the
Holy Ghost.

Now, all of what has been said of the Trinity's works *ad
extra* can also be said of the finale of Hopkins's greatest poem,
"The Wreck of the Deutschland," where the final invocation
alludes to all three persons — but here more metaphorically:
"the Father compassionate," "mid-numbered he in three," and
"*hearts' charity's* hearth's *fire.*" The reference to Father and Son
is clear enough, but that to the Holy Ghost is more oblique.
It is drawn directly from the prayer (not the hymn), "Veni,
Sancte Spiritus," which continues: "Fill the *hearts* of the faithful and kindle in them the *fire* of divine *love.*" However, unlike
"God's Grandeur," in "The Wreck" the New Testament Christ
is explicitly set in contrast to the biblical Jehovah: "A released
shower [soup], let flash to the shire, *not* a lightning [spark] of fire
hard-hurled."

But in the final three lines of "The Wreck," though the *imagery*
contrasts the cymatic (released shower) with the corpuscular
(lightning of fire), the *structural pattern* shows their complementarity. The penultimate line is corpuscular: "Pride, rose, prince,
hero of us, high priest"; whereas the climactic final statement
of the entire poem is cymatic. It is also a line that harks back

to the dominant metrics of much early Renaissance (i.e., "Catholic") verse, with one caesura, in what used to be called the "fourteener": "Our hearts' charity's hearth's fire, our thoughts' chivalry's throng's Lord."

Since "pattern" is a much-repeated and key word in Hopkins, a case could be made for it being at least as significant as imagery in assaying the nature of complementarity in his total *oeuvre* — if that is not too pretentious a word for so relatively unproductive an artist. In any case, it is to these kinds of patterns that I shall return in the next two chapters.

I conclude with a brief observation on a quite different kind of tradition than the theological and spiritual considered above. Gardner's work related to Hopkins's alleged idiosyncrasy in relation to the poetic tradition. But this is to take too narrow a view of that tradition. What Hopkins might be said to have done was scant the "high" Chaucerian strain in favor of the "native" Langlandian (though Hopkins himself was disappointed when first reading Langland). But anyone who takes seriously the pairing of nomen/numen by that authentic "Teutonizer," Max Müller, will recognize the affinities of G. H. with G. H., that is, of George Herbert with Gerard Hopkins. So in terms of the British tradition of religious poetry, as much of the discussion above indicates, Hopkins's imagery and terminology are hardly idiosyncratic. But neither are his themes, as a brief illustration here — to be elaborated later — will underline.

Virtually all of Hopkins's poems are songs of innocence *and* experience, of spring *and* fall. And one of many antecedents of "God's Grandeur" is Blake's:

> O Earth O Earth return!
> Arise from out the dewy grass;
> Night is worn,
> And the morn
> Rises from the slumberous mass.
>
> Turn away no more:
> Why wilt thou turn away

> The starry floor
> The watry shore
> Is giv'n thee till the break of day.

I will not emphasize the exclamations, nor the universal symbolism, of the daily resurrection (going back to the gospel, "the sun being now risen"); but clearly we can correlate the "shining" with the "starry floor" (spark) and the "ooze" with the "watry shore" (soup). Moreover, not only is Hopkins integral to the "poetic tradition," he is integral to the scientific tradition. As Leonard Shlain affirms in *Art & Physics* (1994), "art and physics, like wave and particle, are an integrated duality." Even more, one can say that Hopkins is integral to the cardinal principle of the Western tradition: the principle of complementarity, which is celebrated in "God's Grandeur" and in the poems that I will now take up.

THE SEA AND THE SKYLARK

On ear and ear two noises too old to end
   Trench — right, the tide that ramps against the shore;
    With a flood or a fall, low lull-off or all roar,
Frequenting there while moon shall wear and wend.

Left hand, off land, I hear the lark ascend,
   His rash-fresh re-winded new-skeinèd score
    In crisps of curl off wild winch whirl, and pour
And pelt music, till none's to spill nor spend.

How these two shame this shallow and frail town!
   How ring right out our sordid turbid time,
Being pure! We, life's pride and cared-for crown,

    Have lost that cheer and charm of earth's past prime:
Our make and making break, are breaking, down
     To man's last dust, drain fast towards man's first
      slime.

In the discussion of "God's Grandeur," I concluded with the observation that what best bespoke Hopkins's vision and that of the central Christian tradition which inspired such a vision was the notion of complementarity. Briefly, that was the basic complementarity of wave and particle in the established orthodoxies of modern physics, of soup and spark in nineteenth-century debates, of New Testament deity as comforting companion (emollient oil) and Hebrew Bible deity as awesome remote judge (hurler of lightning like Jupiter fulgur), of Thomistic *analogia entis* relating Creator and creature and Augustinian chasm between Creator and creature bridged, if at all, only by the Barthian *analogia fidei* — with Hopkins embracing both putative polarizations in what is now being called "the myth of a unified theory" (David Lindley, *The End of Physics*, 1994). I have discussed extensively in *Celestial Pantomime* (chap. 9) why this is not a "myth" in the pejorative sense Lindley intends, and so will not repeat that material here. However, in chapter 5, I will take up the application to complementarity of Hopkins's use of Aristotelian Thomism and, to a lesser degree, of Scotism in the poems.

What I want to do in this chapter and the next is discuss the influence of the notion of the complementarity of wave and corpuscle, first, on Hopkins's verbal imagery — as in the previous chapter on "God's Grandeur" — and, second, on Hopkins's structural strategies. For the imagery, I will examine "The Sea and the Skylark"; for the structures, "Pied Beauty." The penultimate chapter of the book will consider the poet's most renowned lyric, "The Windhover," because in it imagery and structure are combined in a "unified theory" that is not a "myth" in the conventional negative sense.

In the first lines of "The Sea and the Skylark," with their blatant but brilliant homophonic repetitions, the context of complementarity is defined not with regard to God's grandeur but with regard to the creature's nature:

> On ear and ear *two* noises *too* old *to* end
> Trench — ...

A creature of duality (two) experiences the transcendentally superabundant (too) which is teleologically oriented (to). The "Trench" points to the sillion of "The Windhover," and stresses by its fricative harshness the arduousness of the conjunction between what is on the right, the rise and fall of the tidal waves, and what is on the left, the pelting music.

By definition, "tide" is an undulating mass covering an extensive temporal and spatial span (like the ooze of oil crushed), while the lark's ascending song is brief and particulate (like shook foil).

But it is the confluence of both that here defines the divine/human reality: the person — a term used analogously of the divine and the human — as vector of the sequential and instantaneous, as well as of the ponderous and the lyric. The experience of the two conjoined is the very nature, the very grandeur, of God, and by strict analogy, also the very grandeur of created being.

I begin with the following from Heisenberg's *Physics and Philosophy,* where he observes that the theory of complementarity "starts with a paradox" — and we shall see, terminates in a paradox as well. Heisenberg continues:

> Bohr advocated the use of both [wave and particle] pictures, which he called "complementary" to each other. The two pictures are of course mutually exclusive, because a certain thing cannot at the same time be a particle (i.e., substance confined to a very small volume) and a wave (i.e., a field spread out over a large space), but the two complement each other. By playing with both pictures, by going from the one picture to the other and back again we finally get the right impression of the strange kind of reality behind our atomic experiments.

However, I am not at this point in the discussion concerned with poetry and the notion of complementarity in general — that has been shown to have a growing relevance to the critical enterprise in the pioneering studies of Kenneth Pike on language, in the work of Frank Kermode on fiction, and in the writing of Norman Rabkin on Shakespeare. Rather, it is the terminology of Heisenberg that I want to reflect upon.

I note, first, the use of "picture," originally intended to convey merely the provisional nature of the hypothesis, but with strong bearing on literary analysis — certainly a much stronger bearing than the more voguish (after Thomas Kuhn) and somewhat misleading "paradigm." Yeats was correct in translating literally from Plato and adding the adjective, "*ghostly* paradigm," because the word does suggest something disincarnate and skeletal — and is clearly quite remote from the poet's preoccupation with an embodied totality. I note, second, the notion of "playing with" as congruent with Hopkins's emphasis in the *Sermons* on "freedom of play, that play which is given by the use of a nature." Both senses of "play" suggest the chanciness, the unpredictability, of what may ensue in the quasi-ecstatic moment of poetic/scientific discovery and concurrence. Again, Heisenberg's is a happier rendition than Kuhn's much-abused problem- or puzzle-solving (read: *"ratio"*), with its overtones of the purely quantitative and measurable, and its unawareness of the poet's intuitive realization (read: *"intellectus"*) that the balances of opposites are not "balances / That we achieve but balances that *happen*, / As a man and woman meet and love forthwith" (Stevens, "Notes toward a Supreme Fiction").

Now, this chanciness, this unpredictable balance is precisely what Hopkins conveys in the octave of "The Sea and the Skylark," a poem originally called "Walking by the Sea" — a much more casual and (literally) pedestrian title, and also a title that evokes no notion whatever of the duality implicit in the principle of complementarity. And like the religious assertion considered in the previous chapter, "The world is charged with the grandeur of God," here too Hopkins begins with an ordinary statement of what is clearly an everyday event (Stevens: "It comes of itself"): "On ear and ear two noises too old to end / Trench." But the unexpectedness of the climactic enjambed verb indicates that it is in the quotidian that the unpredictable epiphanies take place. They "occur as they occur" (Stevens, again).

The polyphonic intermingling of the two subjects (sea and lark) expressed in the poem's final title is duplicated and emphasized in the first stanza by the chiastic structure: "With a flood or a fall, low lull-off or all roar."

| flood | fall |
| lull-off | roar |

But this chiasm also stresses how remarkably nature is "at home" with itself: "Being draws-home to Being" is how Hopkins translated a fragment of Parmenides — and hence the term "frequenting" (another verbal surprise) for the tide's relationship with the seashore. For the word suggests a kind of unexceptional, even homey ease, in what can only be regarded as a Wordsworthian nuptial moment: "That uncertain (wear *and* wend) heaven received into the bosom of the steady lake" — "steady" not in the sense of calm or placid, but in the sense of fidelity to its nature, of stability in reliably and unremittingly "doing what it does" (about which more shortly) with its own "frequency."

Doings/Twoings

Humankind is here the "unnatural," unstable, besmirched alien; while nature, as I said, is "at ease" and is "at home": *natura naturans*. Thus, again, Hopkins's poem ties into the tradition, more specifically the Anglican tradition, with its reverence for the whole of inanimate and of animate creation. In fact, the sacred character of the latter is a topos almost unique to the English poetic, and religious, tradition, as illustrated, for example, by Lancelot Andrewes's Good Friday sermon (1604) in which *"all the creatures* in Heaven and earth" attend to Jesus' death cry, "and sinful man only not moved with it." The same contrast is established in Henry Vaughan's "Man": "Weighing the steadfastness and state of some mean things...I would (said I) my God would give / The staidness of these things to man!" And *I would* emphasize how this sibilant + dental "chimes" with Hopkins's own theory of wordhoards, of verbal kinships: *st*ability; *st*eadfastness, *st*ate, and *st*aidness are all linguistic expressions of the *analogia entis*, seeking to express gematraically (cognate of grammar/glamour) the ultimate logological "*st*ate" of the Creator and the *st*atus of creation.

One may extend this even further. "These two," the sea and the skylark, shame mankind not only by "being pure," and not only by "pouring" out their very being — like Christ on the cross, Andrewes, Vaughan, and Hopkins would have said — and "spending" themselves. They shame mankind by doing what is enjoined upon mankind exclusively: to be images of God.

Evil is *Deus inversus.* So, too, here the condition of the human person is inverted (no longer *imago Dei*) to the condition of the animal (conventionally relegated to mere *vestigium Dei*). The traditional "Catholic" as opposed to "Anglican" theological view was set forth by Hopkins himself in a reflection on the Foundation of the Ignatian *Exercises* when he wrote denigratingly of animals in relation to God: "[T]hey make him known, they tell of him, they give him glory. . . . This then is poor praise, faint reverence, slight service, dull glory." And it stands in contrast to Henry Vaughan's question which might well be addressed to Hopkins:

> And do they so? have they a Sense
> Of ought but influence?
> Can they their heads lift, and expect,
> And grone too? why th'Elect
> Can do no more; my volumes sed
>
> They were all dull, and dead,
> They judg'd them senselesse, and their state
> Wholly Inanimate.
> Go, go; Seal up thy looks,
>   And burn thy books.

There is no doubt that Vaughan, like Hopkins, like the entire tradition, recognized the distinction between *imago Dei* (humankind) and *vestigium Dei* (the rest of creation), and both poets are regretful that humanity, abusing its gift of freedom, fails to do what animals do by "instinct," or by their very nature. But the Anglican tradition has a greater sense of the mystery of animal existence, as represented not only by its emphasis on the texts of St. Paul in Romans alluded to by Hopkins and explicitly referred to by Vaughan, "expect and groan,"* but also by its emphasis on

---

*In what Father Devlin designates as chapter 3 in the *Spiritual Writings*, "On Personality, Grace and Free Will," Hopkins refers to Romans 8 (December 30, 1881), and finds in the groaning and travailing of creation the latter's very definition. Using the word "sigh" for "groan," he observes: "[A]nd this least sigh of desire, this one aspiration, is the life and spirit of man. . . . And even the sigh or aspiration itself is in answer to an inspiration of God's spirit and is followed by the continuance and expiration of that same breath which lifts it, through the gulf and void . . . , to do or be what God wishes his creature

the centrality of "brutes" in the divine economy, as when Mark's gospel says of Jesus that at the beginning of his ministry he lived among wild beasts and was ministered to by angels.

Thus Vaughan may be thought of as proleptically refuting the Catholic Hopkins — but it is Hopkins the Ignatian retreatant, not Hopkins the illuminated poet. And so Vaughan's play on "ought"/"aught" is particularly effective: the "aught" indicates there is a deeper mystery to animal existence than the Continental religious tradition ("my volumes") embodies. Indeed, that tradition is in error: "burn thy books." The play on "ought" is more subtle, since animals seemingly lack a sense of duty, of what is "owed"; and nature is apparently nothing but an ensemble of physical/chemical/"magnetic"/mechanical responses to its surroundings — nevertheless animal nature's responsiveness to this supernatural "alchemic" influence is more in tune with the Creator than is fribbling humanity in its condition of lapsed indifference. ("Influence" is here translated as in the modality of Vaughan's own esotericism, as "response to *berākā*," cognate of BRK = blessing.) It is a theme underlying that frustrate inanition of Donne in "A Nocturnall upon S. Lucies Day," where he cries out: "I should preferre, / If I were any beast, / Some ends, some means; Yea plants, yea stones detest, / And love... / But I am None." Here, too, in Donne, but in an erotic setting, animals and inanimate creation are envisaged as superior to humankind.

But even Hopkins obliquely recognizes in his Ignatian meditation that animal nature in its innocence, as *vestigium* aspiring ("longing") to become *imago,* does have a "sense of ought," since the animal fulfills another central Jesuit axiom: *Age quod agis* (Do what you are doing). And so, after dismissing "brute things" for providing only "poor praise, faint reverence, slight service, dull glory," Hopkins observes: "Nevertheless what they can *they always do*" (italics in original).

to do or be." This is a remarkable refinement of the *Wort/Antwort* theme. Fallen creation sighs in aspiration, responding to God's inspiration, until creation's expiration of that same indwelling breath deifies the New Creation.

Nature *does* what it is doing, and so achieves and fulfills its proper *telos;* whereas mankind violates its destiny by breaking things down, frustrates its God-given vocation as collaborator in carrying on that work of redemption I referred to earlier. This is why I have "translated" the heavily Latinate "frequenting" as "being at home." Nature, I repeat, does what it is doing; it is therefore the "homing nature" of "The Handsome Heart," where the allusion is to birds that know instinctively where they are going. "Homing nature knows the rest" tells us that nature knows both its final *"oughtness,"* and where it shall be "at rest." This is indeed its only mission: to do what it does, "its own fine *function,"* and to be what it is: utterly free in responding to the basic drive (inscape) of its nature, "wild and self-instressed."

Hopkins here is also introducing what is probably the most ancient motif in British Christian thought, the lessons of the homing bird (first narrated in Bede's *Ecclesiastical History* and recast in Hopkins's era by Wordsworth's *Ecclesiastical Sonnets*) that symbolizes the mystery and the ultimate fate of humanity. Hopkins was to use, with equal latitude, the Venerable Bede in "To What Serves Mortal Beauty" when describing Pope Gregory's decision to send missionaries to England — a description that would have appealed to Hopkins, among other reasons, because of its expression by the Pope in triple puns. The missionaries themselves with their gospel faith concerning the future of redeemed mankind convert their listeners by the narrative of the homing bird that knows its final destination.

And, again, the Anglican Vaughan is exemplary not only in describing the bird's instinctive awareness of home but also in illustrating the symbolic lesson the *imago Dei* learns from the mere *vestigium Dei:*

> Their eyes watch for the morning hue,
> Their little grain expelling night
> So shines and sings, as if it knew
> The path unto the house of light.
> . . . .

> If such a tincture, such a touch,
> So firm a longing can impower
> Shall Thy own *image* think it much
> To watch for Thy appearing hour?
>
> ·
>
> If joys, and hopes, and earnest throes,
> And hearts, whose pulse beats still for light
> Are given to birds; who, but Thee, knows
> A love-sick soul's exalted flight?
>
> ("Cock-crowing")

But in "Ribblesdale," the companion poem to "The Sea and the Skylark," Hopkins may be said to combine the Ignatian with the Anglican tradition:

> Earth, sweet Earth, sweet landscape, with leaves throng
> And louchèd low grass, heaven that dost appeal
> To with no tongue to plead, no heart to feel;
> That *canst but only be, but dost that long* —
>
> Thou *canst but be, but that thou well dost. . . .*

There are three remarkable touches here: first, nature as imputed *imago Dei* replaces fallen man in being the faithful servant to whom are addressed the gospel words: "well done." Second, there is the pun on "dost that *long*," with its play on endurance, and on St. Paul's "creation [by which all commentators understood "nature"] *longing* for the revelation of the sons of God" (Romans 8:19: the very title of Vaughan's poem, and the Latin text Hopkins attached to "Ribblesdale"). Third, there is the allusion, remarked above, to *age quod agis,* but here combined with the philosophical axiom: *Agere sequitur esse,* that is, "Doing flows from being." So by contrast to human narcissistic perversion ("self-bent"), created nature by *doing* good ("well dost"), proves it *is* good ("canst but *be*").

And it should be noted that this multiplicity of meaning in a single word — similar to the pun — is analogous to Hopkins's notion of "chiming," whereby language itself points back to that prelapsarian condition when all words — like all creation — were implicit in the one Word. Hence also the fascination of the threefold play in "Ribblesdale" on "dear" ("precious" as well as *Tier* = deer: cf. Marvell, "Nymph Complaining..." [32]) and "dogged" man, when all animate creation, animals and human-kind, were implicitly unified and innocent. Whereas, now in the fallen condition, sinful man selfishly and perversely hunts down the innocent animal that, ironically, becomes — as Martin Buber indicates in *I and Thou,* and Franz Marc in his paintings — a reminder of "earth's past prime."

And this triple *Wortspiel* may also evoke what might be thought of as Joyce's *Antwortspiel* on the per-verse or re-verse word of "god" in the mirror of fallen creatures. As Hopkins says, "Hope holds to Christ the mind's own mirror out" but fails to reflect him. And, again (now echoing Sor Juana Inés de la Cruz, on *Il Divino Narcisso*), the world is "a glass he [God] looks in" where he does not see his glorious reflection, this because of "us" sinful creatures who "are deep in dust ['down to man's last dust' of 'The Sea and the Skylark'] or our silver gone or we are broken or, worst of all, we misshape his face and make God's image hideous" ("Notes on the Foundation"). Now, Joyce's pun was that "god" reversed is "dog," and just as evil is *deus inversus,* so sinful man is not "the image of God," he is merely the "dogged" misshapen creature.

But the poem is neither "ominous" nor "hope-denying" (Ellis, *Gerard Manley Hopkins and the Language of Mystery*), because though "hideous," humanity is still "dear" and is still dogged by what a contemporary of Hopkins called "the hound of heaven." The paradox is that to the degree the creature is steadfast and animal-like, to that degree she is no longer a "broken" being, but one who is open to the gift of integrity who can "but only be" — again, Donne's "If I were any beast [I should have] some ends, some means." Drawing on his Anglican tradition, Hopkins wonders in an early journal entry (May 2, 1866): "What would be the just statement of the effects of cruelty to animals, cruel sports, etc." And there are from the same period self-criticism for killing insects and the famous incident of Hopkins seeking to protect a rat from its human tormentors.

In another aspect of this same tradition of natural supernaturalism as it relates to inanimate creation, the tide of Hopkins's "The Sea and the Skylark" can be identified with that of Keats in "The Bright Star" sonnet. "The moving waters" respond to higher "influence"; they *do* what they are doing; that is, they do their "priestlike task of pure ablution" (Hopkins's "being pure") "round earth's *hum*an shores," round "man's last dust" (*hum*ous). And Keats suggests in another sonnet, "The Sea," that it is the "cloying" "din," the "sordid, turbid time," that prevents us from hearing the corpuscular "whisperings" in the wavelike "mighty swell." But, Keats continues, if we could escape the "uproar rude," we would hear "sea-nymphs' choirs," pouring and pelting music — as did the youthful Hopkins himself in "A Vision of the Mermaids."

Hence, also, in "The Sea and the Skylark," the punning on "ringing right out," what Hopkins called the "shallowness" and others have called the "one-dimensionality" of "our time" — for there is no depth without the experience of point meeting line and generating volume, much like the juncture of two images in a vectograph: the kerygmatic "ring out" is also the tortuous "wring out" (a pun more commonly recognized in the "wring" and "rung" of "Spring" and "The Windhover," respectively). In the first instance, the verb is proclamatory, as in Milton's "ring out ye crystal spheres"; in the second instance, the verb bespeaks torment, as in Shelley's "wring the truth out of these nerves and sinews." And as I have noted, we have not only a marriage of heaven and earth (moon and tides, as in John Donne's moon and seas), but also, as in "God's Grandeur," a conjoining of that most *ancient* ("too old") tidal imagery with — from the poet's perspective — the most *novel* and electrifying, the most recent rash-*fresh*, *new*-skeined songs of the lark, which also join earth and heaven.

Among the scores of lark poems in English, Wordsworth's "To a Skylark" is the most Hopkinsian (while Hardy's "Shelley's

Skylark" is the least). Not only does Wordsworth's bird reflect
the grandeur of God; not only is the bird "true to the kindred
points of Heaven and Home," but it literally conjoins the "flood"
of Hopkins's first stanza and the "pouring" music of his second in a single "complementary" utterance — which also has a
foreshadowing of Hopkins's enjambement:

> A privacy of glorious light is thine;
> Whence thou dost *pour* upon the world a *flood*
> Of harmony, with instinct more *divine. . . .*

Every integrated work of art is made up of isomorphic structures, as the upward soaring facade of the Gothic cathedral
contains ogival niches, with vertically aspiring statues, all culminating in the overall ascendant tower. It is this congruency within
congruency that Hopkins describes in a letter to Bridges explaining "The Sea and the Skylark." The principle of complementarity
not only is evident in sea and bird, but permeates the song of the
latter: "a thing both new *and* old . . . tricklingly *or* wavingly," that
is, corpuscularly *or* cymatically.

Instressed Nest

And here there is need for a clarifying excursus more characteristically Hopkinsian than that from Heisenberg at the beginning
of this chapter. There is a problem in evaluating Hopkins's more
or less permanent, definitive views on any given subject because
of the relative brevity of his life. Thus it may be distorting, in
the context of any particular interpretive crux, to treat judgments
made as an undergraduate with the same seriousness as his more
mature observations fifteen or twenty years later — and with what
would certainly have been his further revisionary views had he
lived another two or three decades after that.

While it is obvious, as with most undergraduates, that his opinions of painters and poets changed radically with the passage
of time, it is sometimes implicitly assumed that his philosophical or postconversion theological opinions were fairly stable and

consistent (just as it is tendentiously assumed that his affective inclinations as a student colored the whole of his adult life). Thus what I have described as two of the most creative studies on Hopkins, J. Hillis Miller's treatment of the poet in *The Disappearance of God,* and Walter J. Ong's in *Hopkins, the Self, and God,* though separated by about two decades, both seem to be marred by this assumption of the continuity of Hopkins's views — though it would be ungracious to extend the indictment of two such magisterial books beyond that precise point. As I noted in chapter 1, these works (along with Hartman's "Dialectic of Sense Perception") not only are among the most original treatments, but are also, from the viewpoint of the reader, among the most fruitful.

But concerning the alleged continuity, I proffer two quotations, both basically centered on texts dating from Hopkins's Oxford period, and both subject to the kind of distortion I noted above: "It might seem...that Hopkins means by 'inscape' uniqueness of pattern, what Duns Scotus calls the *haecceitas* of a thing, its ultimate principle of individuality.... This is not really the case, nor does inscape here mean anything like Scotus' *haecceitas*" (Miller). Second: "[I]nscape can refer to an individual existent, to *haecceitas,...* a Scotist term, the 'thisness' of any being.... Inscape, with its corresponding instress, refers to distinctiveness of being not as simply analysed but as intuited in an insight deeper than analysis can go" (Ong). That the issue is moot if not utterly otiose is evident in the fact that another Jesuit, W. A. M. Peters (1948), had affirmed Ong's view, only to be vigorously "refuted" by another Jesuit, Christopher Devlin (1959), editor of Hopkins's *Sermons.* The whole business evokes Swift on big-enders vs. little-enders, and gives the lie to Pope's observation: "Scotists and Thomists, now, in peace remain." *Haecceitas* is important, particularly in the prose theological speculations, but Hopkins's slippery and even sloppy use of language — he elsewhere has a reference to "outscape" — should not be taken by his admirers as indicative of deeply thought-out and permanently held reflections. And in fact Ong observes, in agreement with

Miller, that Hopkins's "theorizing, though always interesting," is "not always watertight."

All philosophy, said Kierkegaard, is tautology. The problem is only partially the imprecision of Hopkins's use of these coinages to express his own unique vision; it is also, again only partially, his application of them to a contradictory range of ideas and experiences. But it is primarily that in any attempt to define the inexpressible or the ineffable, pleonasms and circumlocutions with their inevitable collusions and collisions will abound. After all, we have only finite words with finite definitions to express the undefinable — to express, stammeringly, that activity which was traditionally the consequence of "inspiration." Finally, there is the fact that this most haphazard of thinkers (if that is even the appropriate designation), but most meticulously precise of poets, is often read as the systematic developer of some kind of harmonious intellectual organon, as the rigorous creator of a gradually unfolding, spiraling, evolutionary synthesis. Unfortunately, it must be acknowledged that such a reading does more credit to the ingenuity and creativity of his commentators than to the synthesizing prowess of the poet.

Hopkins, though fascinated by philosophical speculation, is his own worst prophet of future development. A year after Oxford and conversion, Hopkins with the self-deluding grandiosity of the newly gowned writes to a friend, "An interest in philosophy is almost the only one I can feel myself quite free to indulge in still." "Indulgence" is probably the precise term, since this interest is only clumsily and amateurishly put into the service of some very great poems and some occasionally enlightening poetic aperçus. Here a parallel would be with Stevens's formal philosophical pronouncements, which are often embarrassingly trite in contrast to his letters and poems.

With Hopkins, perhaps more than any poet of his time, the intense temptation to reflect, to rationalize, to self-thematize, was overcome by the even more intensely spontaneous drive simply to utter, to outer his selfness: myself I speak and spell. Whence also on Hopkins's part, the subsequent quasi-pathological obsession with Whitman — no homosexual affinities whatever here since Burns and Goethe were also characterized as "scoundrels" — and his seemingly unpremeditated outblurtings; and, also on Hopkins's part, the equally vehement, and canonically unforgettable, excoriation of Browning: " . . . a man bouncing up from table with his mouth full of bread and cheese and saying that he meant to stand no blasted nonsense." That this comes in with the Chartist Parson, "Kingsley and the Broad Church school," only underlines the anxiety of influence at play here. Hopkins, apart from his Catholic asceticism, is the most Browning-like of Victorian poets, as Edith Sitwell recognized; and in many ways "Inversnaid" is Hopkins's "Childe Roland."

But my point in deprecating these Oxford philosophical speculations — if they can be so described — is not flatly to identify Hopkins with the typical undergraduate's cosmic or universalist effusions (though such an identification sometimes seems valid), but to suggest that like most such talk their consequences are usually vacuous and pretentious, and therefore hardly the foundation-stones for the seamless philosophical edifice his creative critics have erected.

For an example pertinent to this central matter of complementarity, both Ong and Miller focus on what Hopkins called "A Platonic Dialogue" (1865, *aetat* 21), in which Hopkins sets up the distinction or conflict, alluded to earlier, between diatonic and chromatic notions of beauty. The language is traditional and the concept is banal: in prose the "distinction" is between the pulsodic, aphoristic Senecan, and the polyclausal, multiconditional Ciceronian — Hopkins suggests Carlyle vis-à-vis Newman, or anyone might as readily suggest Emerson vis-à-vis Henry James. The distinction is banal because in all instances we are contrasting the language of moral certitude with that of speculative probing.

But Hopkins, with extremely limited musical skills, attempts to construct on this slight stylistic convention — its relations and its analogies — a large-scale theory of beauty. His expressed option is for the diatonic, because it invests — or so he *appears* to ar-

gue since this *is* an undergraduate debate — more import in what
we have called the "corpuscular" rather than in what we have
called the "cymatic." And this investment seems to fit more harmoniously with Hopkins's burgeoning preference for singularities,
oddities, uniquenesses as opposed to universals, commonalities,
and so on. The diatonic is the "nodal" (Hopkins's term) exception
to the general flow of things — that flow, however, *is* celebrated
in "That Nature Is a Heraclitean Fire . . . " — and by its very al-
lowance of the exceptional and the eruptive seems better able to
express the uniqueness of Incarnation, and the "inscape" of the
individual. For Hopkins, the diatonic is, as it were, "like Giesek-
ing playing Scarlatti" (M. Moore, whom I now exalt by pairing
with Milton); whereas the chromatic is "notes, with many a wind-
ing bout / Of linked sweetness long drawn out . . . untwisting all
the chains that tie / The hidden soul of harmony." (Milton's enjambements also suggest the undulations of our original image
of complementarity.) The chromatic is the flowing evolutionary
wave ("Thy creatures leap not," says Herbert in "Providence")
progressively engendering more and more homologous forms of
life that will ultimately conjoin with the original blueprint, the
Logos, at what the religious tradition called "the end-time," "the
eschaton." But — and for Hopkins this seems to be the nub — the
conjunction will not entail the explosive brilliance that would illuminate adequately another facet of the "eternal diamond" (here
I amend): Christ.

Why one is to be preferred to another is not clear in Hopkins's
theory. I emphasize "theory" because in practice, as illustrated in
the poems, there is no preference for the diatonic over the chromatic, the quantum over the wave. In fact, the whole point of
all this discussion is that the chromatic and the diatonic must be
complementary. So far as any theoretical adversarial relationship,
it can be viewed only as a contradiction of what Hopkins intuitively affirmed in practice, that is, in the actual composition of
his poems. Here the very *raison d'être* of creation is to image
forth in finite form the traits of the infinite being, the being whose
grandeur is manifest in the diatonic quanta (spark/shook foil) and

the chromatic waves (soup/ooze of oil). Similarly, in the actual execution of poems, in the emergence of their imagery, and in what Hopkins called their all-important "patterns," both waves *and* particles are seen to be in harmony.

In fact, it was a musical analogy (without spatial metaphoric villains like Hopkins's) that Max Planck's disciples employed in explaining that celebrated "black box" experiment which gave birth to the notion of complementarity well before Niels Bohr actually used the term. That analogy is of listening to a piece of music, say, Beethoven's Second Symphony, with all its tremolos and glissandos on a mass of instruments, strings, horns, and so on, which generate waves of music sonically contiguous. One then listens to Beethoven's piano trio arrangement of the Second and hears particulate notes generated discretely.

So, what is the "grandeur of the Second Symphony"? It is the converging, the "trenching," the continuum of glissandos and stacattos, of waves and particles, of chromatic and diatonic: all as Hopkins manifested in his mature *poems* — if not in his undergraduate *essais*.

The conclusion must be that, regardless of Hopkins's flying headers into speculative "philosophy," his poetic practice is quite detached from what Ong would have called the leaky "theorizing." Like their innumerable analogues, "diatonic" and "chromatic" are terms aspiring quite directly to the condition of music, but their differences cannot be transmuted into gauges of excellence, any more than could one establish the superiority, say, of a piano over a fiddle. Each is simply a different but dovetailing mode of expression. To cite a poet whom Hopkins described as "most rich and nervous":

> Some to the lute, some to the viol went,
> And others chose the cornet eloquent,
> These practising the wind, and those the wire,
> To sing men's triumphs; or in heaven's choir.
>
> (Marvell, "Music's Empire")

Tonic/Chthonic

Since "The Sea and the Skylark" was originally called "Walking by the Sea," one might extrapolate from the musical imagery
above, and supply as subtitle or notation on the "new-skeined
score," *andante cantabile.* In any case, I am now concerned directly with the chromatic "tide" and the diatonic "crisps." And,
as in the previous chapter, it may be noted that here we also have
two heavily Latinate terms (cf. "grandeur" and "generations"):
"frequenting" and "ascend," both being the dominant verbs in
their stanzas, and both affirming the complementarity, first, of the
congregating oozing, brooding waves and, second, of the momentous and momentary bright-winged song. Again, I am conflating
the images of "God's Grandeur" with those of "The Sea and the
Skylark."

Also, for reasons of historical comprehensiveness, I reemphasize the complementarity of the Chaucerian and Langlandian
lineage — though, as always in Hopkins, it is the sparse (cognate of "spark") Anglo-Saxon which predominates. Hopkins, I
have already suggested, remains on what may be thought of as
the "left" of the poetic/politic tradition. He has more in common
poetically and even politically with Langland, Skelton, Herbert,
Vaughan, Milton ("[A]ll English verse, except Milton's almost,
offends me as 'licentious' "), Bunyan, Smart, Watts, the Wesleys,
Blake, Browning (with his skewed metrics and asymmetric cadences), and even (at least *religiously*) the Tractarians of *Lyra
Apostolica* and *The Christian Year.*

For a contemporary expression of this "leftist" heritage, one
need merely look at that Clapham-chapel manual of Donald
Davie, *The New Oxford Book of Christian Verse,* where the
catholic and the Catholic are almost ludicrously eschewed: for
example, Crashaw has two poems, Hopkins, four; while Watts
and Charles Wesley have eleven each. (The really ambidextrous
faux pas de deux is the presence here of Wordsworth's "Resolution and Independence," included explicitly because of its
reference to "grave livers in Scotland" — grave, no doubt from

too much single malt.) But given Davie's low-church bias, the fact that Hopkins is included at all points up an authentic aspect of his nonconformist roots, for he has more in common with this semirepressed tradition than with Chaucer, Shakespeare, Spenser, Catholic Pope, Wordsworth, and the later Tennyson, to say nothing of any future Anglo-Catholic monarchists.

Here also is the link between Leavis's vigorous defense of Lawrence and advocacy of Hopkins's verse against the assaults on both writers by Eliot. For Eliot, Lawrence and Hopkins were unconstrained by "a living and central tradition," which for Eliot meant Puseyite Anglo-Catholicism, American-émigré adulation of royalty, and "classicism" of the Poundian and Maurassian (i.e., Action Française) fascist variety. Leavis's response concerning Lawrence is relevant to Hopkins as well: "That Lawrence was brought up in a living and central tradition — there, it seems to me, is where to lay the stress." And equally so with Hopkins. It just didn't happen to be the tradition being endorsed and enforced by Eliot.

Politically Hopkins has more in common with the dissenting tradition from John Ball on through the parliamentarians, again including Milton — up to his whimsically serious vaunt about "communist" sympathies, and to writing a poem "on the unemployed." But all of these entail primarily matters of emphasis: though inclined to the "left hand," he will occasionally allow it to "trench" with the "right." And hence the Catholic Romanticism and those rare Latinisms I have pointed out above in "The Sea and the Skylark."

However, in that poem, not only do the tide and the song complement one another in their *pure* merger in the "trenches" of existence, but both are willing to be sacrificed that humankind may benefit. That is the office of the twofold "grandeur" of God: to "spend" itself so that foot can feel "the yield of plushy sward" ("The Habit of Perfection"), so that sordidness can be wrung out and cleansed. And this is why nature shames humanity: like the Creator from whose infinite depths goodness flows — *bonum est diffusivum sui* is how theodicy rationalizes a perfect Being *want-*

ing to manifest itself beyond itself — nature too is willing to pour out *its* very *esse* for the *bene-esse* of un-deserving, "shallow and frail" humanity.

It is from the juncture of wave and quantum that depth ensues, and this juncture comes only from death to self for the well-being of the other. The cymatic tide depends on the moon's "wearing and wending," while the corpuscular notations on the unraveling score "*pour* / And pelt music" (a wonderful kenotic enjambement reminiscent of Keats's nymph in "Lamia": "At whose white feet the languid Tritons poured / Pearls"), until they too have exhausted themselves for the good of humankind. And as we have looked back to Keats, we can look forward to Louis Mac-Neice, an early Hopkins devoté, in "Sunday Morning," where the musical "notes...vanish with a wink [cognate of 'winch'] of tails."

Nature has cheer and charm, "being pure": as "men" in "God's Grandeur" are literally senseless, "being shod." And this discrepancy opens up a polarization which is perennial throughout the history of Western thought from the pre-Socratics to J.-P. Sartre and Gabriel Marcel, the polarization — which we have examined briefly in the previous chapter — of *"being"* and of *"doing"*: here, the latter term is identical with "make and breaking." Again, the ontology is essential. "Being" is the realm of harmony and unity, as when one says, "I *am* happy": I-ness and happy-ness are identical. But on the plane of "making," the first term and the third are separated: "I *make* things." Here subject and object are opposed: the one is acting on the other and therefore cannot be identified with it.

"Cheer" is etymologically *cara*: hence, attitude or mood (again, "the way one is"); while "charm" is *carmen*. The two then relate back to the undular tide which "does what it does" (*literally*, from the moment of creation) and to the corpuscular pelting music which jets forth from the skylark. But "cheer" more radically is "face," so the poem relates again to "God's Grandeur," where the Holy Ghost — as the hymn affirms — *renovabis faciem terrae*, where the Holy Ghost will renew, cleanse, and wring out the soilure on the *face* of the earth. Furthermore, if the tide, like the ooze of oil, introduces the most ancient of images, and the electrifying *carmen* (charm) of the lark introduces the most *"new*-skeined" music, then it will only be by the complementarity of old and new, of "earth's *past* prime" and of our present making and breaking, that the entropic deterioration to dust and slime will be halted.

But mankind's sin is more than "impurity," more than infidelity to its originary mission. *Caritas aedificat,* says St. Paul, by which he means that supernatural charity literally "builds up" into cosmos; it does not "break down" into chaos. On the "natural" plane, that "edifying" mission — I have already noted — is defined by another Jesuit, Teilhard de Chardin, as *"construire la terre."* But this is mankind's mission in the *natural* order of things, and so the evil is less grievous than mankind's violation of the supernatural hierarchy of existence.

It is this violation of the divinely ordained structure of the cosmos that accounts for that strange — and to the twentieth-century reader, almost unbelievable — trio forever crunched by the three mouths of Satan, himself the arch-principle of disorder, in Dante's *Inferno.* Imagery of evil is, by definition, incomprehensible; though once again Eliot got it wrong. In his essay on Dante's conception of Satan, he wrote: "I can only say that Dante made the best of a bad job. In putting Brutus, the noble Brutus, and Cassius with Judas Iscariot he will also disturb at first the English reader, for whom Brutus and Cassius must always be the Brutus and Cassius of Shakespeare." Hopkins, too, had his objections to Dante's hell (but on esthetic not historical grounds) in that it seemed a strained allegory not unlike the anthropomorphic myths attached to the Greek gods.

But why, except as proleptic (so to speak) parody of Milton's inversion of the celestial Trinity, does Dante introduce a tricephalic Satan who appears and, indeed, is depicted as a grotesquerie out of Bosch, Breughel, or Bakhtin? The answer is in the Pauline texts that are also implicit in Hopkins's poem. On the surface level it is, as with Milton's self-inflated Satan or Herbert's Death "puffing at the door" (*inflat* is paired by St. Paul with *aedificat*), a mockery of his actual metaphysical impotence, and of humanity's self-deluding terror. More profoundly, it is because Dante's Satan has sought to "break down" that eternally established order and harmony, to "break down" that ultimate hierarchy which is the structure of the universe.

Thus the killing of Jesus violates the "spiritual" laws, as the killing of Caesar violates the "material" laws, that build up the edifice of the cosmos. And in Hopkins's poem this is also true. The tradition — which Hopkins embraces in the sermons — had it that mankind was created to replace the angels whom Lucifer led in the original rebellion against divine order. Of these "new" beings it was said, they are "a little less than the angels," they are "crowned with glory and honor." However, they are now described as violating that sacred order. Humanity, "life's pride [*superbia* = loftiness] and cared-for crown," has abdicated not only its natural office, but its supernatural role. The "shame" is that humanity is now not only less than the angels, but less than inanimate creation itself, as the three Vaughan poems attest. And the opposite of *superbia,* as we have noted, is *humus,* the lowliness of "dust" and "slime."

At the conclusion of these two chapters and these two analyses, two critical observations are called for — as I "chimingly" circle back to our original "two"/"too"/"to." First, any reader must be struck by the enormously wide-ranging allusiveness of these poems. It is also clear that, however compact the poems, they are also literally superabounding with ideas, images, even patterns, from the whole of the Western cultural tradition. In this, Hopkins is comparable only to his much-admired and great model, George Herbert. Second, these analyses give, incontrovertibly I would hope, the lie to another of those Olympian opinings of T. S. Eliot, who wrote in 1934, at the very moment of Hopkins's entering into the canon (a threat to the ever-watchful hegemonic compositor of "The Waste Land" — possums be it noted are omnivorous scavengers): "[A] whole poem [of Hopkins] will give us *more* of the same thing, an accumulation, rather than a real development of thought and feeling." Since the Eliot cultus has been progressively declining decade by decade since the 1950s — an undertaking definitively validated in the 1990s by his cinematic entombment — it is perhaps an exercise in smugness to emphasize how manifestly flawed such a judgment is. This will become even clearer in my consideration of our next two poems, "Pied Beauty" and "The Windhover."

V: *Visual Complementarity*

"Couple Colour"

PIED BEAUTY

Glory be to God for dappled things —
    For skies of couple-colour as a brinded cow;
      For rose-moles all in stipple upon trout that swim;
Fresh-firecoal chestnut-falls; finches' wings;
    Landscape plotted and pieced — fold, fallow, and
        plough;
    And all trades, their gear and tackle and trim.

All things counter, original, spare, strange;
    Whatever is fickle, freckled (who knows how?)
    With swift, slow; sweet, sour; adazzle, dim;
He fathers-forth whose beauty is past change:
          Praise him.

I want to focus this chapter on the poem that seems to bear out Eliot's criticism of Hopkins that concluded the preceding chapter. ("I know even less [of course anyone knows even less / Than T. S.]" [Reed Whittemore].) But even theoretically the gravamen of the indictment, like the burden of most of Eliot's memorably phrased arguments, cannot be sustained since the basic distinction between lyric and dramatic is that the former is essentially constituted by the presenting or re-presenting of images and emotions, whereas the latter is "developmental," with a plot that goes from beginning through middle to end. Obviously, these are shorthand definitions, but they circumscribe the essential difference between the two "genres."

Contra Eliot, I proffer a lyric that will figure significantly in my later discussion, Wordsworth's "Lucy" poem, "She dwelt..." Nothing could be less developmental; it is simply a catalogue of contradictory qualities and states, like any traditional *descriptio puellae*, though the latter usually went from forehead to feet, just as Wordsworth may be said to go from life to death; but I hardly imagine that kind of sequence would be described by Eliot as a development. Similarly, with the litanic delineation of attributes and subjects in "Pied Beauty" until — as in Wordsworth — the coda introduces an element of climax. But, again, precisely because it does come as a surprise, it can hardly be thought of as "developmental."

Eliot's opinion was taken up three decades later by Paul Fussell (1966) in his treatment of "Pied Beauty." In Hopkins's lingo the poem is a "curtal" sonnet with the traditional ratio of octave and sestet here shrunk to sestet and quartet. Fussell observes that "the two parts...are pretty much of a piece in substance," and the poem is criticized for not performing (*sic*) "the fundamental Petrarchan action...of complication and resolution." This all seems a trifling issue of definition, since Hopkins says nothing about Petrarch, and the literature abounds in sonnets of widely varying lengths, in many of which the "turn" is merely a visual phenomenon. "Curtal sonnet" means, literally, "abbreviated little song."

But my purpose, regardless of nomenclature, is to show that the poem cannot be faulted on any grounds, whether taxonomic or generic, and is indeed extraordinarily rich — with a richness directly dependent on our basic principle of complementarity. "Pied Beauty" is explicitly about glory, not grandeur, and is the only poem discussed thus far that explicitly alludes to the Jesuit A.M.D.G., with all its acronymic, tradition-sanctioned, and problematic theological implications, which I referred to in previous chapters and which I will now briefly take up.

Doxa/Paradox

The very concept of the creature contributing to "the greater glory" of the Creator entails a seeming contradiction we have examined in the relation of animal innocence to human evil. Not merely the use of the phrase "Ad Maiorem Dei Gloriam" would have been dear to Hopkins, to Ong, and to Jesuits in general, particularly to Teilhard de Chardin, but its theological implications would have been part of the religious agenda of these genial, congenial, and "developmentally" very interrelated Jesuits. For if creation itself groans and travails, if humankind makes up that which is "lacking to the passion of Christ," both creation and humankind receive their religious commission, indeed their mandate and their purpose, in this Jesuit charism.

But there is a theological contradiction, relating to Hopkins, which demands resolution. If the glory of God is infinite, as *ex definitione* it is, how then can finite actions make it "greater"? Interestingly, in another reflection on the Foundation, Hopkins broaches then burkes the issue of creation's "contribution" to God's glory: "In other words *he does not need it*. He has infinite glory without it and what is infinite can be made no bigger." Then in a curious *non sequitur*, he adds: "Nevertheless he takes it: he wishes it, asks it, he commands it, he enforces it, he gets it."

The parallel Benedictine slogan, "That in All Things God May Be Glorified," by its neutrality and its more seemingly passive acquiescence in providence, succeeds in evading the contradiction implicit in "To the Greater Glory of God." Similarly, in Whiteheadean process theology — and on a different basis, in Teilhard — one of the "dipolar" aspects of God can be enriched by human progress and development. Unfortunately, this sounds very much like anthropocentric complacency of the sort that Pascal saw in the Jesuits, and which Karl Barth, on similar grounds, also condemned in Catholic theology for most of his career. However, opposition to such creaturely "enrichment" of the Creator is not only very Augustinian, as were Catholic Pascal and Protestant Barth, but also theologically incompatible with the mainstream of the entire Christian tradition, where God is envisaged as the "immutable other" who, in the words of Milton's sonnet, "doth not need either man's work or his own gifts."

Nevertheless, in the light of those cryptic texts from St. Paul, alluded to above and cited in the previous chapter, there is a case to be made that creation can achieve — no doubt introducing Wordsworth's "auxiliar light" (read: "Grace" as in the Jesuit-Dominican *De Auxiliis* debates) — something which does make God's glory and concomitantly God's grandeur "greater." It is the Dominican translator of Karl Rahner's *Theological Investigations* who observes (there is clearly a Dominican/Jesuit complementarity here as well): "We are not merely the spectators of a cosmic play, with God behind the scenes as stage-manager and producer; we are also the actors and God is our author." Such a judgment historically is questionable, but it may be noted that this is also a leitmotif of what Hans Urs von Balthasar calls "theodramatics."

Hopkins seemed to recognize both sides of the issue in a personal, near-despairing Dublin meditation where converge Barth's gaps (creature and Creator are infinitely separated) and Whitehead's synapses (creature and Creator co-engage in "constructing the earth"). On the one hand, Hopkins observed: "[T]he work [of salvation] goes on in a great system which even drags me on with the collar round my neck though I could and do neglect my duty in it." The allusion is not to Herbert's "The Collar," with its play on "choler" — since it is clear Hopkins never wavered in his clerical vocation — but is, again, to Milton's sonnet on the need to bear God's "mild yoke." And therefore Hopkins adds: "But...I am only too willing to...help on the knowledge of the Incarnation." The remainder of the reflection is not pertinent here since it goes on to lament the kinds of failure that engendered the devastating "terrible" sonnets.

Returning now to the point of departure in Eliot's and Fussell's criticism of the failure of Hopkins's "curtal" sonnet, I would point out that in the prototypical Romantic sonnet by the poet who virtually reestablished the form after a century of abandonment, that is, Wordsworth's "Upon Westminster Bridge" (of which Hopkins was not fond), there is no complication and resolution. In fact, the poem is, like Hopkins's, merely another mélange, with Wordsworth's "turn" evident only in a couple of very brief, almost casual allusions to a shift from objectivity to subjectivity, "Ne'er saw I, never felt..." Once again Hopkins's penchant for creative coinage ("curtal") has misled critics. However, if that kind of argot proves attractive, one may emulate by denominating "Pied Beauty" — again like "She dwelt..." — as a "decile descant with a coda of reversal." But that coda, as Keats discerned in Wordsworth, is what gives the poem its final touch of "perfection."

I repeat: what the present-day reader first expects in Hopkins's poem after the title is the implicit A.M.D.G. — as analyzed above. But the expectation is not fulfilled, since the first line of the poem is: "Glory be to God...," with its anticipated New Testament conclusion, "in the highest." But Hopkins's complete line is almost as familiar to educated readers as the song of the angelic choir, so we are in danger of being inured to the delightful surprise Hopkins has perpetrated as we are pulled up short by the startling: "Glory be to God...for *dappled* things." It is as though one were to hear the solemn repetitions of "Gloria" in Beethoven's "Missa Solemnis," flowing immediately, and then intermingling, with some punk rock grungey cacophony: "Glory, Glory, Glory to God in the highest": no, Glory, Glory, Glory...for *dappled things!* Nor shall we close the circle of the angelic choir by returning *in excelsis* until the very end of the poem.

For now, we have been hurled *in terra:* out of the realm of triune unity into the realm of utter multiplicity. "Dappled" can be described in this context only as a kind of startling, childlike prattle — almost certainly it is onomatopoeic — though there is nothing particularly shocking about the word in "The Windhover," since in medieval and much subsequent usage "dapple" was descriptive of animals, particularly horses; and so it is integral to the equine imagery running through that poem. But then one encounters the triteness of dappled *"things!"* — another esthetic embarrassment, indeed a blush-inducing banality: these platitudinous seas incarnadine, or at least they should. And yet here, in fact, they don't. They are winsome, again, almost childlike, in their unself-consciousness (like the repeated, "Look, Look," of "The Starlight Night").

"Glory be to God for dappled things": but we are still haunted or possessed, as certainly was Hopkins also, by echoes and expectations of the New Testament and the Mass: *Gloria in excelsis Deo, et in terra pax.* For this *pax* is defined by St. Augustine and the tradition as the orderly fusion of colliding and contrasting opposites. And as everyone recognizes, the poem is nothing other than a celebration of these harmoniously related contrasts, initiated in the next line with "couple-colour" and "brinded cow." The whole poem is a commentary, first, on the mystical insight that the world is the shadow of God; second, on the philosophical insight as worded by Aquinas that unity (God) can only be imitated by multiplicity (things); and, third, on the poetic insight of Hopkins's nemesis, Browning, in "Abt Vogler": "Why rushed the discords in, but that harmony should be prized?" And this, precisely, is the "development" of the poem: the classic *ingressus, progressus, regressus* — out of unity, through multiplicity, and then back to unity ("who fathers forth," unlike the "mothering forth" of the Holy Ghost at the end of "God's Grandeur").

But this reference makes even clearer my original observation that for Hopkins the Gloria of the Roman Mass must have echoed in his mind at the initial "Glory be to God" in the poem. For the last line of the Gloria is also an invocation, but not as in the first, of God as so denominated, but of God under the title "Father." And thus the concluding phrase, "who fathers forth," parallels the Mass's concluding *"in gloria Dei Patris."*

But, again, as noted earlier, the works of the Trinity *ad extra* (i.e., with respect to creatures) are only "metaphorically" attributed to the individual Persons, and hence the actual conclusion to the poem, like A.M.D.G. at the beginning, is in the letters L.D.S.: *laus Deo semper.* And as A.M.D.G. was a paraphrase of the first words of the poem, L.D.S. paraphrases the sharp imperative of Hopkins's last words: "Praise him." Finally, as further indication of the influence of the Gloria, or more precisely of the doctrine of the Trinity, I point to the Trinitarian structure evident in the two poems examined earlier, where are embodied the last words of the Gloria: "Jesus Christ, with the Holy Ghost, in the glory of God the Father." And for what it is worth, it may be noted that this, too, is a "developmental" pattern.

But there is also a historical development to be considered here. For what Hopkins is doing is simply what poets have done from the beginning: from Adam naming the animals, through Psalms, and the Song of the Three Children, through the great medieval "lists" of birds, plants, and so on, up to the present century with the underrated Rupert Brooke's "The Great Lover," to Howard Nemerov's punning on his office as "namer of." And, I stress again, that for anyone who, like Hopkins, would instinctively take the nomen/numen syzygy with the seriousness it deserves, what seems like mere cataloguing would in fact be a sacred mission. At the core of Hopkins's "theopoetics" is the assumption that all words are seeking to rejoin and to recall the ultimate Word which is their source.

One final observation on the overshadowing influence of the Gloria on this poem, particularly its brief coda: "Praise him." As indicated in the discussion of "Ribblesdale" and Henry Vaughan's poems, nonhuman creation *does* participate in celebrating God's grandeur and glory, even though Hopkins did make a homiletic point of disparaging "brute" creation. But in "Pied Beauty," the assumption must be that since nothing directly relating to human-kind has been mentioned in the poem, the injunction, "Praise him," refers most immediately to *all* those dappled *things* the poet has catalogued.

And the mode of their participation is also best explained by re-turning to the Gloria of the Mass. The initial clause introduces the angelic choir praising "God in the highest," and then moves down to "men on earth." So, in the graduated hierarchy of the tradi-tion, the imperative, "Praise him," goes from the highest choir of angels, down through the lower choirs, then to "men" (including those reading the poem) who have been made a little less than the angels, and then to all the spare, strange "things" named in the poem. (I shall return to the coda at the conclusion of this chapter.)

The leitmotif of complementarity is evident, first, through the *analogia entis* joining "God" to "things" in the beginning line; second, through the juncture of seemingly conflicting contrasts (couple, brinded) in the next line; third, through enlisting again our soup and spark imagery, in the "swim" and "firecoal" of the next two lines; and lastly, through the fusion of concrete and universal, as the reader moves from the first to the second part of the entire poem. And in that second part there is an obvious complementarity between the polysyllabic, "counter, original," and the immediately following monosyllabic: "spare, strange."

In Excelsis/In Terra

One may then define "Pied Beauty," as I suggested earlier, as a complex ten-line lyric — arbitrarily divided perhaps out of homage to some Petrarchan ratio — with the addition of a simple coda. Viewing it straightforwardly in this hard Husserlian light, we will find nothing to criticize, but much to commend, certainly much more, in terms of interesting relationships, than would be suggested by an imaginary Italian sonnet structure.

I have already alluded to these relationships above, but I now look at them in the perspective of the poem as a closely integrated structure. There is first of all the specificity of the named entries in lines 1 through 4: cow, trout, chestnut, finch, and so on; and the generality in the next four lines: landscape, trades, things, whatever, and so on. The complementarity — to use the language of our overridng figure — parallels that of the kinetic pulsating images of those first four lines; "skies," etymologically and radically "clouds *in motion*"; "swimming," "falling," etc., with the static, immobility of the images in the next four lines: "landscape," "fold," "plough" (here meaning ploughed field), "gear," and so on.

It is the complementarity that I am stressing. No one questions that beauty entails some interplay of unity and multiplicity, and if one wants to cite in support of this commonplace Burke, Lovejoy, assorted impressionists (no diatonic pointillists, however) as the commentaries do, fine. It is perhaps a greater distraction to set off, as they also do, Scotists against Thomists by observing that the former "recognized diversity even among individuals in a species," since this is a truism throughout the Scholastic tradition. But all such talk is the kind of irrelevant critical litter that I have scored in my first chapter as obscuring the poetry of the poems — and about which I will say no more, except to animadvert to Sulloway's curious definition of "Pied Beauty" as "a Ruskinian document"! (Though this kind of far-fetched source hunting does make one wonder whatever happened to Coleridge's Preface to "Christabel" with its indictment of those who would "derive every rill they behold flowing, from a perforation made in some other man's tank"?)

Returning definitively to the Gloria and "Pied Beauty," I want to note another aspect of the *in excelsis et in terra* juncture referred to above — and again with the same jarring combination of the sublime and the banal. I have already underlined the startling collision of "Glory be to God" with the bathos of *"for dappled things,"* which now parallels: "For skies of couple-colour" and again the descent to the comparably banal *"as a brinded cow"* — with the latter also eliciting Hopkins's almost instinctive "chiming": couple/colour/cow. But this chiming is not the facile poetaster's device condemned by Pope:

> While they ring round the same unvaried chimes,
> With sure returns of still expected rhymes.

Rather Hopkins's "chiming," like alliteration and assonance, is simply an effort to bring the vast range of earthbound words into harmony with some single transtemporal *logos,* even as the whole of "Pied Beauty," celebrating multiplicity, finds its engendering (Hopkins says, "fathering") principle in the single and simple concluding phrase: "Praise him."

If it is only through multiplicity that one can know unity, it should be noted that it is equally only through the refracted prismatic colors (Blake's and Shelley's "staining") that one can come to know the single white radiance of eternity from which they originate. Or, rather more esoterically, it could be said that the four elements (Empedocles) of fire, air, earth, and water — all of which are introduced here — are the material manifestations of the archetypal "more divine" (Aristotle) quintessence from which they flow.

Finally. there is the chiastic structure, the hermeneutical "X," of the first line in each of the two sections of the poem:

> "dappled things"
> "things counter."

And even more cryptically, it should be noted that the *chi*asm is followed by the only sequence of words in the poem each of which stresses the letter *rho:* "counte*r*, o*r*iginal, spa*r*e, st*r*ange" — in short, one may discern here the age-old symbol of Christ, the *chi-rho*. Probably, this would sound even more exaggerated had it not been preceded by James Finn Cotter's extraordinary and creative "kabbalistic" analysis. But when one realizes how packed are these poems — and even more their author's mind — with the collective wisdom, conscious and unconscious, of the tradition, any conceivable interinanimations, any intersections and *coniunctiones,* have to be taken very seriously. Indeed, it is the purpose of this book to illustrate how in a very small body of poetry, there is compressed an immense corpus of traditional lore from the whole cycle of learning. Each is a poem where sweets *compacted* lie.

The christological allusion, *chi-rho*, is intensified by the third line that follows immediately in "Pied Beauty." After the reference to fire and falls, we have what seems an arbitrary entry in the catalogue: "finches' wings." And this brings us back to the lark of the previous chapter, and possibly forward to another of the various *coniunctiones* referred to above, to the *chi-rho,* the Christ Our Lord of "The Windhover."

In folk-iconography, finches, because they found their food among thistles, were identified with the thorn-crown of Jesus, and hence with his passion and death. Thus art historians and mythographers, perhaps of naive-aviary tendencies, have explained the presence of these birds (auspices, so to speak, of the bleeding wounds of Jesus) in such lovely paintings as the *Belle Jardinière,* the *Solly* and the *Gran'duca* and the *Cardellino* madonnas. This may seem like a lot of Bulfinch, since one can explain the presence in the paintings of these birds by the fact that they were the most docile, the most beautiful, and most melodious of fieldbirds. (And there are several varieties of finches in that loveliest of late medieval paintings, *The Little Paradise Garden.*) But as the historians Jean Delumeau and Piero Camporesi have both shown, frequently folklore and allegorical conceptions did in the Middle Ages often supplant ordinary lived experience, prosaic observation, and what we laud as "common sense." It happened with the so-called Judas Tree, and one might think, for a pertinent illustration from the British poetic tradition, of the "alphabet mysticism" found in Herbert and Milton.

In any case, it is possible, as with Hopkins's interest in the Bleeding-Heart flower, in the Sacred Heart, and in his devotion to the five wounds ("Stigma, signal, cinquefoil token" ["The Wreck"]), he was responding to two centuries of folkloric myth by wittingly or unwittingly identifying finches with Jesus' bloody death. Though it is noteworthy, parenthetically, that the first translation of this poem into French correctly translates "finch" as *pinson:* for example, *gai comme pinson;* or as we would say, "happy as a lark." Clearly by the latter reading, one is quite remote from thorns and wounds.

But that would hardly cancel the interpretation above since Hopkins was, even as an undergraduate, receptive to those excesses of Italianate devotion which Newman never ceased to deplore. Moreover, for all its joyousness, the fragment "The Woodlark" is akin to "Pied Beauty" in both heavenly and earthly setting:

> To-day the sky is two and two
> With white strokes and strains of the blue.

Then in lines reminiscent of "Easter" (his first foreshadowing of the blue-bleak embers theme — "beauty now for ashes wear"), he continues:

> ... lush the sash
> And crush-silk poppies aflash,
> The blood-gush blade-gash
> Flame-rash rudred ...

So, these are more or less foundational images, as Romano Guardini suggested, which will recur in "The Windhover." They are not necessarily derivative from other poets or religious writers, but merely the instinctive figurations of an intensely Christian devotional writer.

Mystique/Mistake

Before returning to the structural format, complementarity, there is one final teasing phrase to be considered in "Pied Beauty." This is the brief, detached parenthetic question: "(who knows how?)" — which, it may be noted, also embodies its own chiming pattern. I will consider the responses to this apparently arbitrary question, in their likely order of probability, recognizing as one must with so creative and self-inscaped an artist as Hopkins that esthetic "probabiliorism" really offers here no sure guide. What seems "more probable" to the reader might have seemed absurd or at least diametrically opposed to what the poet himself imagined. Nevertheless the question "who knows how?" remains puzzling.

First, the possibly indifferent or even blatant gratuitousness of the poet's question is evident in the fact that there is no preparation or sequentiality to this brief interjection. I have written elsewhere on the function of parenthetic insertions as indicators of the undisclosed private or secret attitude, mood, feeling, and so on, of a given persona as glimpsed against the background of the public *situs:* for example, the song that found a path through the heart of Ruth when, *sick for home,* she stood ... Without the parenthetic "inburst" (or suddenly disclosed outburst), there is in Keats's description simply a kind of Barbizon stereotype, of the sort depicted in "The Song of the Lark" (not unlike Hopkins,

with his finches and falcons), or some kind of Wordsworthian
solitary reaper who can be invested with whatever "sorrow, loss,
or pain" the reader may want to supply. But the function of the
parenthesis, semantically *and* visually, is to break open the public
scene and disclose (perhaps as with Hopkins in "The Windhover," returning circuitously to the exposed bleeding heart of
Jesus?) the hitherto concealed mysterious interior.

For Keats, Ruth is not just a girl standing in a field; she is a
girl, with a broken heart, standing alone in a field — as a believing Christian would see Jesus hanging from the cross; or, as with
Matthew's gospel, parenthetically crying out (it is his only utterance): "Why have you forsaken me?" So, too, here the question
(who knows how?) may be read as a straightforward expression
of doubt over the perennially debatable issue at the core of "Pied
Beauty" concerning the relation of the one and the many; or in
its Christianized form, over the homologous issue of *"Cur Deus
Homo?"*

The very brevity ("who knows how?") may suggest the sheer
unanswerability of the question. If "I" believe because the matter
is absurd (*credo quia absurdum*), what is the point of spelling out
at length an answer? Such detail would involve one in what Hopkins called "the dense algebra of the Schoolmen" — though it was
a Schoolman, Duns Scotus, who, in 1872, five years before writing "Pied Beauty," had provided the poet with if not an answer
at least a tentative assuagement of the question's strain. But the
strain may have been personal as well, and the brief question may
be a passing effort to attenuate the latent Scotism of the poem by
the suggestion that its author was not in fact as committed to Scotus as his occasionally provocative defenses of the latter had led
his Jesuit brethren to believe. Hopkins was, as observed earlier, a
square peg in a round hole, that is, was, by instinct and rearing,
a "contrarian." Or, arguing along these same lines, this "curtal"
question may have been merely a sop to his own conscience at
being so at odds with the official Thomist "manualism" prevalent
in all Jesuit schools of the time.

But it is the apparent unanswerability and pointlessness of the question that lead one to think it does have some deeper meaning than — though aware of the futility of the effort — merely *appearing* to plumb the depths of impenetrable mystery. In short, why bother to raise the issue at all, if it is to be so immediately dismissed?

My suggestion is that by this time in his career, in contrast to his undergraduate philosophical phase, the kinds of questions assayed in the previous chapter, and summarized in this brief, "who knows how?" — those kinds of questions were simply of less and less interest to Hopkins *qua* poet. It is the esthetic, broadly defined, and ultimately the suprarational, that preoccupied him. In fact, the two are one, since in Scholasticism, the transcendental manifestations of "being" are ultimately rooted in unity; thus, *pulchrum et bonum convertuntur*: the esthetic is the suprarational (though not necessarily the supernatural).

Even in the relatively early "Pied Beauty," Hopkins is moving, again perhaps unknowingly, toward the "fell of dark" and toward the last tragic-haunted sonnets. Thus one might profitably weigh the allusiveness of "Pied Beauty" with its unanswered question ("who knows how?") to one of those later sonnets of despair, "My own heart...," where in the second stanza he says:

> I cast for comfort I can no more get
> By groping round my comfortless than blind
> Eyes in their dark can day...find.

John Hollander in an exegesis of A. E. Housman's "The chestnut casts his flambeaux..." points out the paranomastic relationship of "chestnut" (genus: *castanea*) and "cast." Similarly, in Hopkins's poem "cast for comfort" readily evokes the martyrial "chestnut falls" of "Pied Beauty," and brings us back to that unanswered question, "who knows how?"

As I shall detail shortly, the question has to do with philosophical doubts only in the sense that Hopkins is on the way to rejecting all such inconclusive, theoretical ventures. In its octave, "My own heart..." twice refers to his "tormented *mind*"; but then in the sestet the poet immediately rejects any possibility of allaying such torment by mere speculation. Instead he insists, "call off *thoughts* awhile / Elsewhere." But what is to replace "mind" and "thoughts"? What is to put the quietus to theoretical questions like, "who knows how?" Again, in "My own heart...," it is the contemplation of beauty, here defined as God's "smile" which "lights a lovely mile" — and so dispels the "dark" hovering over this and the other terrible sonnets. This link between "Pied Beauty" with its spurning of philosophical speculation is even more emphatically brought out in "My own heart..." by its description of the transcendent esthetic experience as similar to the glimpse of "skies / Betweenpie mountains": the very language expresses the entire point of the earlier poem. By this reading, the "dark" in the terrible sonnets represents, certainly among other disillusionments, the futility of abstract thinking to penetrate the mystery of existence: "call off thoughts."

Thus I question the utility of introducing any kind of purgative, *via-negativa,* night-of-the-soul conjectures into interpreting the terrible sonnets. This "mystical" escape-valve has been too often employed in clarification of any obscurities among religious writers of the most varied persuasion. But precisely because mystics are stammering over the ineffable, virtually anything they say can be justified by excerpting assorted and disparate fragments out of the tradition from Pseudo-Dionysius onward. It was the now-venerated Evelyn Underhill who first lent credence to the notion of Hopkins-as-mystic when including him in a collection of devotional poetry, and observing (1920) that Hopkins "was perhaps the greatest mystical poet of the Victorian period."

But here "mystical" is obviously being identified with merely heightened spirituality. Such misattribution is, however, too complicated a matter of definition to go into now, since it entails the "pragmatic" mysticism defined by Cuthbert Butler in *Western Mysticism,* vis-à-vis the "oriental," apophatic mysticism of the Rhennish-Hispanic school, with its curiously chromatic experiences, eulalaic utterances, stigmata, levitations, and so on. But for present purposes it suffices to agree with one of the earliest and one of the latest Jesuit admirers of Hopkins, André Bremond

and Walter Ong. Anticipating M. H. Abrams, André Bremond
(1934), who is here explicitly speaking for the great historian and
ex-Jesuit, Abbé Henri Bremond, remarks that Hopkins represents
a "kind of sacramental naturalism which is...the true mystery —
not mystical but poetical." And Ong in his *Hopkins, the Self, and
God* remarks that "the various 'dark nights' which the soul can
go through are much worse...than they appear in T. S. Eliot's
genteel assessment of St. John of the Cross." Not all who cry
negativa shall enter into the mansions of the soul.*

The mere invocation of *apophasis* by dabblers in Catholic culture too often blankets over virtually every unresolved issue in
the life of anyone even tinctured with religiosity, much less spirituality, much, much less mysticism. (I proffer the title to one
such tractate, *The Dark Night of Samuel Taylor Coleridge*, or the
facile repetition of *nada* in a tawdry Hemingway parody, as pal-
mary instances of what I am indicting.) Or one could as readily
adduce those present-day *prix fixe*, hippety-hop, techniques for
anything from Zen housekeeping to Sufi diets. If Hopkins had
"mystical" inclinations (and what poet does not?), they were of
that solidly British style that Newman extolled: no psychophysical
concomitants such as visions, voices, elevations. Instead, this non-
Dionysian mysticism (of which St. Augustine or St. Bernard are
exemplars) is identified with concern for active cure of souls,
self-abnegation, rebellious acceptance of suffering, reliance on a
sacramental spirituality and on good works; in short, with *praxis,*
a word Scotus favored. (There is also the instance of Hopkins
delightedly — though unecumenically! — narrating a hilarious
"mystical" vision of Swedenborg.)

---

*The most discriminating treatment of poetry and mysticism is William T. Noon's *Poetry
and Prayer* (1967), a title indebted to Abbé Bremond, of whom Noon is excessively critical. But on Underhill, Noon is delicately perceptive: "[O]ne might possibly wonder if Miss
Underhill has not so much broadened her definitions of mysticism as to claim very little for
it specifically either as a way of poetry or a way of prayer.... Few readers care to contest
the merits of Miss Underhill's widely received account of mysticism. It is one, nevertheless,
that might understandably leave the commentator on one or another poet, Hopkins, for
example, in doubt as to the senses in which his poetry might be spoken of as a poetry
of the mystical way." But this does not contradict my earlier contention that "The Kind
Betrothal" is a profound analysis of mystical themes.

Thus by "fell of dark" above, I merely understand that for Hopkins, traditional philosophical theorizing is more and more supplanted by simple esthetic experience. What the terrible sonnets commemorate are no first steps on a Ruysbroekian "ladder of love" to the chamber of union, with all its attendant agonizings — though Hopkins certainly suffered his own characteristically unique vastation of mind and body — but simply depression, despair, and probably, in the end, a longing for death comparable among major English poets only to that of Keats: "I wish then for death.... O my God, look down on me." Still what can be said of the original point of departure? that is, Hopkins's curt and immediately disposed-of question: *"who knows how?"*

The very brief, implicit, and *intentionally* pointless answer could only be: *"And who cares?"* The poet is clearly affirming in all the poems considered above: sufficient for the day is the beauty thereof. His almost contemptuously dismissed question suggests that the antepenultimate vanity, prelude to the penultimate futility, is the pursuit of ultimate answers. In confirmation of this, I would draw two parallels from poems quite removed in tone and content from the gloomy agonies of the terrible sonnets.

But before considering those two poems, I must at least advert to one other possible explanation of the unanswered question: "who knows how?" — an explanation supplied by Michael Lynch's homosexualist analysis of this and other poems (1979). After identifying Hopkins's obsession with spareness, strangeness, and so on, with "queerness" in general, on the curious grounds that "counter" is "closely related to the *peccatum CONTRA naturam*" (caps supplied), Lynch observes: "The parenthetical '(who knows how?)' is a wondering, in both senses; an awe-full exclamation, but also a question about the etiology of variance. And the poem shrinks from an answer" — as would the present writer. And this, simply because to "counter" such an argument would take one back to the overarching thesis of Martin's biography, and to the homosexualist reading of all the poems which no one, certainly not Martin or Lynch, has ever developed. In short, it would require a leap of faith in the *a priori* assumption of homosexuality — the latter being precisely what must be demonstrated and not merely asserted. But no leap of faith is required for my argument above concerning the pithy question — who knows how? — and none is required for the two supportive textual arguments that follow.

In "The Leaden Echo and the Golden Echo" there is a parenthetic insertion even more enigmatic and brief than that in "Pied Beauty." The poet, speaking as a single voice, exclaims in part 2 at his initial recognition of the divine alchemy:

> Spare!
> There is one, yes I have one (*hush there!*),
> Only not within seeing of the sun.

But to whom is *this* particular jussive phrase which I have italicized addressed? Who knows whom? The entire "song" is chanted entirely in the first-person singular, and is in effect a choral ode. So, who is being hushed? Again, it can only be those questioning voices within the poet himself; those dreamers who venom all their days (Keats); those undergraduate doubters, like young Hopkins himself, who raise the eternally unanswerable questions — whether atheist, agnostic, *or* Scotist and Thomist — about the unfathomable mystery of being.

Consider the two situations. In the first instance the poet is totally absorbed in the splendor of the prismatic contrarieties which are the colorful epiphanies of the pure radiance of unity — when, suddenly, the hectoring *quaestiones disputatae* interrupt: "But who knows how?" And all the dreary orthodox, conventional etceteras drone on: though now totally ignored by the poet whose implied — and one would hope, disdainful — rejoinder is, again, in effect: "During this ecstatic moment, *who cares?*" Similarly, in the second instance, as the vision accelerates, as the despair reaches its anguished repetitive breaking point, and the redemptive "spare" is echoed back, what does the ever-upward-spiraling poet hear? He hears: "fashionable madmen raise / Their pedantic boring cry" (Auden). And heterosexual or homosexual: who knows how? and who cares? It is to these metaphysicians

and moralists that Hopkins says with the curtness of certitude:
"Hush there!"

For we are now in the realm where all *logoi* become the lovely
Logos; where "God's utterance of himself in himself is God the
Word, outside himself is this world. *This world then is word*,
expression, news of God," said Hopkins in "Further Notes on
the Foundation" in 1882. For we are now in the realm where
appears "the wimpled-water-dimpled, not-by-morning-matched
face"; where appears (as in the preceding chapter) in that water-
dimpled pool Sor Juana's Divine Narcissus: creation and Creator
mirrored in one another — a theme related to Donne's "Batter my
heart" sonnet and echoed, as noted, in Hopkins's poem beginning
"Hope holds to Christ the mind's own mirror out."

"The Starlight Night" is my third illustration of Hopkins's esthetic vision eclipsing his ecclesiastical, philosophical, and clerical
considerations — a transcendent eclipse Hopkins almost failed to
recognize in the sacerdotal pharisaism (using the word in its conventional, not historical, sense) of "The Candle Indoors." But it
must strike even the most obtuse or the most fanatic ideologi-
cally "orthodox" co-opter (and Hopkins, like Chesterton, C. S.
Lewis, Charles Williams, *and* Evelyn Underhill, is now a *"projet"*
for religious fundamentalists and academic evangelists) that in
"The Starlight Night," with the saints and Mary and the heavens
themselves all hand-in-hand, there are only *two* lines devoted to
how we bruised and broken creatures can attain this presumably
longed-for blissful state where, as Hopkins's text has it, we might
all dwell within the "piece-bright paling" alongside of *"Christ
and his mother and all his hallows."*

However, here another theological conundrum emerges. It
must be noted, first, how the lack of punctuation in that dox-
ological concluding phrase (which I have italicized) points up
the absence of barriers within this heavenly community. Second,
it should be noted about this *Communio sanctorum* that that
phrase is invariably translated "Communion of Saints." However,
sanctorum is not only a personal — alas, we have been instructed,
not gender-inclusive — plural possessive; it is also a neuter plu-

ral possessive, meaning that the communion of which the Creed speaks refers not only to humankind but also to animate *and* inanimate creation in general — as attested uniquely by all those wondrous texts cited in the previous chapter from the English religious/poetic tradition. Thus we are not talking only about the "reign of the saints," meaning holy *persons,* but about the communion of all holy *things* — including the "brute" creation emphasized earlier.

But now back to "The Starlight Night" and the "dazzling darkness" it sheds on "Pied Beauty." In the first of these poems, one reads seven complete lines beginning with the ecstatic, quadruple insistence, "Look" (at all this beauty); then, after a momentary break in the thought, one reads the last six lines repeating trebly, with the same ecstatic insistence, that same imperative: "Look." Astonishingly, during that "momentary" interruption of less than two lines (reduced to their proper caducity, even negligibility, in the light of all this astral splendor), almost as negligible as "Hush there!" or as "Who knows how? — astonishingly, during that break there are only two (very slight) moralizing admonitions; only two sermonic exhortations by this priest-poet to the grace-seeking, spiritually anxious virtuosi who presumably constitute his avid listeners, and who — in short — are there to find out "how to get to heaven."

Two parenthetic observations: first, I have already rejected the notion that the underlying motif of the poem is an "auction." Herbert, maybe; Hopkins, never. The repetitions are those of an excited childlike visionary, and express one of Hopkins's most attractive traits, as in the song-of-innocence, "stirred for a bird," or the reference to *(the)* thrush in "Spring." For in this latter poem there is no article and its absence means the poet, like a child, refers to this bird with a personal name, as in a personal relationship with another person: "and thrush does so rinse and wring / The ear...," just as a child would say something like "and bird, come here," or "bird, fly away." Again, this is the voice of Hopkins as the *anima naturaliter candida.* Second, I suggest the reader contrast Hopkins's indifference to "methodism" — that is, "How do I get it?" and his quickly dismissed, "buy then, bid then" — with Herbert's fully spelled-out "applications of the meditation," where for all his endearing piety, Herbert can not put off the preacher's robes and feels obligated to detail in virtually every poem "what the sinner must do" to attain the spiritual goal.

In Hopkins, even these dutiful pastoral warnings are fragmentary, tentative, and uncertain; they are almost ad hoc improvisations or afterthoughts. It is as though the poet is saying, "All [is] a purchase: *but,* no, that can't be right [as he has a second thought]: that's pawnshop soteriology." And so he corrects himself: "*no,* all is a prize"; all is a matter of divine benevolence in the grace-filled gratuity of existence. One doesn't bargain with God; there are no "indulgences" assuring salvation. Similarly, with his next very brief, and again seemingly more-or-less obligatory advertence *to* his self-centered listeners' (i.e., *to* us, his readers') problem of: "How can we get ours?" The priest-homilist's first answer is a hesitant: "Buy then" — and, again, there is a second thought, another correction — "*No,*" emphatically implies this slowly discerning Jonah. Instead, all must be left to providence — "*Bid* then."

It is rare that a poet lets us enter into the process of his compositional thinking. But it occurred in stanza 28 of "The Wreck" (built on Browning's discovery of the dark tower), and it occurs here as Hopkins reveals his doubts, his self-corrections. In each case with Hopkins, the questioning, the thinking, the pursuit of intellectual *se-curitas* must be put in brackets, must be erased, so that beauty may possess one's being. All the creature can do is let all this self-searching remain in parentheses, let life itself be a parenthesis between the beauty of past and present: "as skies / Betweenpie mountains." Hopkins knew from his sacramental theological training that all the creature can do is be open to beauty. Consider, again, his sacramentally seven-times repeated, "look" of "The Starlight Night." *This* is a naive enthusiast, *not* an auctioneer. All the creature can do is place no obstacle to beauty. This was the sacramental formula he memorized in his not altogether successful theology courses: again, *nullam obicem ponere.*

De-undevelopmentalizing

At the beginning of this chapter I drew a parallel between one of Wordsworth's "Lucy" poems and Hopkins's "Pied Beauty." And though we have seen analogies in the two "lark" poems, at first glance such parallels do seem an exaggeration since few poets (Wordsworth *and* Hopkins) appear more different in choice of subject, genre, and language — not to speak of personalities and what we would today call "lifestyles." But I also affirmed in the first chapter that the best keys to interpreting any poem are kindred poems. Moreover, I am attempting a structural analysis; and here the isomorphism of the Wordsworth and the Hopkins is truly amazing. Both poems, I noted as a commonplace, contain ten lines of disparate ("undeveloped," the Eliot would say) imagery, followed by short codas. In both cases the imagery is highly paradoxic, not to say self-evidently riddled with contradictions. It would be redundant with two such well-known poems to repeat all the separate instances. But the codas bear closer scrutiny.

In Wordsworth, after the construction of a catalogue almost baroquely artificial (again, I will not itemize), the coda startles the reader by its expression of the most unadorned emotion which, in one reader at least, engendered a sense of "perfect pathos":

> But she is in her grave, and, oh,
> The difference to me!

The pathos derives not from the exclamatory tone of the statement — we have encountered that earlier, "Half-hidden from the eye!"; rather, it derives from the sudden dissolution of the elaborate intricacies of the first ten lines with their exaggerated oxymoronic quality — literally a pre-posterous aggregate of contra-dictions: the sudden dissolution of this whole world of artifice in favor of the world of seemingly simple and spontaneous declaration. It is a break *away* from the esthetic narrowly defined and *toward* the ethical, also narrowly defined — both definitions supplied by Kierkegaard. And it is the collision of these two rival realms, rival as Keats said, "from Plato to Wesley," with the resultant triumph of the second that arouses this sense of pathos. More banally, it is the conflict of art and life, with life suddenly emerging as victor.

In Hopkins, the sudden shattering of the heavily paradoxic first ten lines also entails a startling shift from the esthetic to the ethical — but with something more. In Wordsworth the body of the poem is entirely descriptive of Lucy, either "historically" or metaphorically, so that the shift in the coda is merely from description of Lucy to description of the speaker's egotistical bathetic: "oh, the difference to me!" And the mood of the whole poem remains in the relatively abstracted and neutral indicative. But in Hopkins the shift is much more radical, *from* the matter-of-fact, purely observational, and clinical indicative *to* the action-demanding, *engagé*, imperative. Hopkins's coda, totally unlike Wordsworth's, is comparable to the controverted coda of Blake's first "Holy Thursday" poem. But Blake's coda is almost irredeemably attenuated by its sheer ponderousness: "Then cherish pity, lest you drive an angel from your door." One does *not* give effectual commands — any drill sergeant would know — in a statement that, like a wounded snake, drags its slow length along. Hopkins's coda, on the other hand, is intensified by its Senecan — or rather, its Mosaic — brevity and utter irreversibility: "Right arm's rod-sweep, tongue's imperial fiat" (Browning).

Hopkins's sermons could not be described as Ciceronian, however polyclausal; rather they were, all commentators have noted, a jumble of maundering and incomprehensible oddities. For one brief instance, from his sermon on the Magdalen, which he records with characteristic self-irony a critical parishioner confessed to "sleeping for parts of it":

She not only loved because she was forgiven, she was also forgiven because she loved: both things are true. When she came she came as a sinner, she had heard no forgiveness spoken, she came to get it, and to get it she shewed all that love: in this way then she was forgiven because she loved. On the other hand she knew of Christ's love, she knew he *offered* mercy to the sinner, to the great sinner great mercy, this love of his was first, mercy, forgiveness, *offered* forgiveness, on Christ's part came first and because he forgave her, that is offered to forgive her she loved: So then she loved because she was forgiven.

Kingsley's comment about F. D. Maurice could have been made of Hopkins: "What shall be done with a prophet who prophesies into his waist-coat pocket!" But in "Pied Beauty," for once Hopkins is the unflinching prophet, brief and unyielding: "Praise him."

To this discussion, I add a coda of my own. The first French critic of Hopkins (André Bremond, whom I have already cited), writing in 1934, translated "Praise him" by using the indicative "Louange à Dieu." Similarly, the otherwise quite excellent translator, Gérard Leyris, followed his predecessor with "Louange au Père," rather than in both cases with what one would expect: the imperative, "Louez Dieu," the standard translation of the psalm, "Laudate Dominum."

There is a pedagogical lesson in *explication de texte* here which confirms Valéry's and Mallarmé's observations critical of French poetry and of methods of teaching it in contrast to the British: complete indifference to the musical element. (Better to have said complete preoccupation with the elements of order and consistency.) Similarly, it is the French sense of order, or more precisely of propriety, that led Leyris to transform the enthusiastically childlike exaggeration "a *billion* / Times" of "The Windhover" into "un *million* / de fois": a transformation presumably based on the hieratic ground that "billion" is dismissible as mere *enfantillage*. It seems very likely that it was the presumably *proper* "development" in "Pied Beauty" and "The Windhover" that governed these mistranslations into the French. Whereas, it has always been recognized that the strength of British poetry lay precisely in its capacity to exorcise Francophonic *ordre et clarté,* and embrace the irregular, the deviant, the rebellious — in short, to embrace the native *roots* of English.

Insulation/Insufflation

This radicalism (taken literally) is a point worth detailing if one is to get a sense of Hopkins's real place in the tradition. A *catena aurea* is called for. One might consider what was viewed by his contemporaries as the achievement of Donne:

> ... whose imperious wit
> Our stubborne language bends, made only fit
> With her tough-thick-rib'd hoopes to gird about
> Thy Giant phansie, which had prov'd too stout
> For their soft melting Phrases.

Thomas Carew in his elegy had in mind not only the commonly assumed inferiority of Anglo-Saxon to Latin languages in general, but more particularly the language of those whom Donne himself called, "Men of France, ... shops of fashions" ("Elegie: On His Mistris") — a sentiment echoed by Marvell on a translation *into* English (by Robert Witty) to be read by a "Celia" whose,

> ... native beauty's not Italianated,
> Nor her chaste mind into the French translated:
> Her thoughts are English. ...

More specifically relevant to Hopkins's poetic concerns is Christopher Smart on Henry Purcell, both poets admiring the composer for avoiding continental canons and rubrics: "mellifluous yet manly too," says Smart of Purcell; and then continues:

> Not like the soft *Italian* swains
> ·
> His vigorous notes with meaning teem
> With fire, with force, explain the theme,
> And sing the subject into life.

Hopkins picks up the teem/theme:

> Not mood in him nor meaning, proud fire or sacred
>   fear,
> Or love, or pity, or all that sweet notes not his might
>   nursle:
> It is the forgèd feature finds me; it is the rehearsal
> Of own, of abrupt self there....

And here the forgèd feature, the abrupt self, may be accurately denominated inscape/thisness, even as Christopher Devlin In *Poor Kit Smart* views the latter's epistemology "very much the same as Gerard Manley Hopkins's 'inscape.'"

But back to Hopkins and the "native" tradition. Since everyone knows Milton's strengths as defined by Marvell, and Shakespeare's strengths as defined by the young Milton, I once again invoke our great model:

> Thence arts o'er all the northern world advance,
> But critic-learning flourished most in France.
> . . . .
>
> But we, brave Britons, foreign laws despised,
> And kept unconquered, and uncivilized....
>
> > ("An Essay on Criticism")

Precisely the point of the whole of "Pied Beauty" is to overcome Augustan and mid-Victorian uniformity ("Louange au Père," indeed!) and to exalt the malformed, the unfashionable, the uncivilized — both in language and in structure. (And perhaps the point for readers is to recognize, again, the bond with Browning that marks both poets as pioneers of twentieth-century modernity.)

Thus one might observe that it was Eliot, true Arnoldian, who was hankering "after strange gods" and engaged in continental congress across the channel. In 1923 he wrote that if everything "derived from Norman-French society,...direct and indirect, were withdrawn, what would be left? A few Teutonic roots and husks... ": but roots and husks that nourished Hopkins and that nurtured all poetry subsequent to his. Similarly, nothing could be more un-English (or more linguistically fascistic) than Eliot's ukase: "[T]he existence of a *right* tradition, simply by its influence upon the environment in which the poet develops, will tend to *restrict* eccentricity to *manageable* limits: but it is not even by the lack of this *restraining* influence that the absence of tradition is most deplorable. *What is disastrous* is that the writer should deliberately give rein to his 'individuality,' that he should even cultivate his *differences* from others" (emphasis added).

To this Hopkins *and* the whole English poetic tradition up to Theodore Roethke — who begins a poem with the clarion with which Hopkins concludes his poem — would reply: "Long live the weeds and the wilderness yet."

I close this treatment of "Pied Beauty" with a passage that lexically, visually, and audibly embodies the complementarity which is the focus of so much of this discussion. As already noted, "Pied Beauty" ends with the brief command, "Praise him," and it is from that simple *laudate* that the entire poem emerges.

As with much of Herbert we have a *carmen figuratum,* in this instance, a verbal image expressing two of the most ancient symbols for the relation of the "one and the many," of the Logos and the *logoi:* the single jet that fountains forth multitudinous rays, streams, and droplets; and the single bole that flourishes through innumerable branches, leaves, and blossoms. (And, again, we are near to Hopkins's chestnut falls.)

But the text I am focusing mind, eye, and ear upon is the couplet:

> With swift, slow; sweet, sour; adazzle, dim;
> He fathers-forth whose beauty is past change...

In the introduction to the next chapter, I proffer several passages illustrating the wave-particle motif, but I do not know of any that express so fully as does that of Hopkins the complementarity of the corpuscular and the cymatic. If anyone were to hear and see these two lines of Hopkins, and were to respond to them bodily, the chironomic action *could only take* the form of a sequence of sharply punctuated downward beats (cf. letter to Patmore, November 10, 1883, on *thesis* as fall "of the conductor's arm"), followed by an irrepressibly flowing undular movement. In fact, one would be moving both arms — diatonically and chromatically, to use Hopkins's language here — as the body sways to the music of this structure with its pulsating arabesques. Anyone who "reads with the ears" experiences in the first line the percussive diastolic-systolic forces that hang upon the beatings of the heart followed, in the second line, by the melismatic unambiguous undulations of the fathering-forth passage. Then a breath upon the hand: a cymbal crashes — "Praise him."

Two allusions to Stevens are enough, but I cannot resist a quotation that will introduce Hopkins's own omnipresent complementarity. From "A Rabbit as King of the Ghosts," we have "brute" creation also facing the polarities and contrarieties of existence:

> There was the cat slopping its milk all day,
> Fat cat, red tongue, green mind, white milk.

Hopkins's colors and themes are less whimsical but no less serious. In his most extended treatment of the wave motif in "The May Magnificat" (not unrelated to Stevens's magnifi-cat, a word play introduced by Smart on his "Jeffrey") Hopkins writes:

> When drop-of-blood-and-foam-dapple
> Bloom lights the orchard apple
>   And thicket and thorp are merry
>   With silver-surfed cherry
>
> And azuring-over greybell makes
> Wood banks and brakes wash wet like lakes...

Clearly, we have one flowing *wave* without breaks (though, brakes); and in a moment, as everyone remembers, we shall have the *corpuscular* "magic cuckoocall" that "caps, clears, and clinches all."

But I want to gloss this in terms of our recurring musical motif. When Pater made his celebrated comment about all art aspiring toward the condition of music, he was not merely thinking of musicians as such, but of such artists as those of the Venetian school (including early El Greco), for whom the "silver-surfing" red and blue was almost their painterly, coloristic signature. So in this passage of Hopkins we have the unbroken flow conjoined to the quantum. We also have the spectrum of colors from cool blues to hot reds of the "black box" that gave rise to such neologisms for complementarity as "photons" and "wavicles." We have, in short, that combination of all the arts which was the goal of every major painter, musician, and poet at the end of the nineteenth century, along with that combination of the principles of the new physics which has been the goal of early twentieth-century science, as well as that combination of digital and analog which continues to be the goal of late twentieth-century communication theory; and finally the possibility of the combination of Stephen Jay Gould's novel evolutionary theory of "punctuated equilibrium" (Hopkins's "diatonic" and "nodal") with the more conventional hypothesis of incremental gradualism (Hopkins's "chromatic") which may come to be acknowledged in the twenty-first century.

VI: *Personal Complementarity*

"Here Buckle"

THE WINDHOVER
to Christ our Lord

I caught this morning morning's minion, king-
    dom of daylight's dauphin, dapple-dawn-drawn Fal-
        con, in his riding
    Of the rolling level underneath him steady air, and
        striding
High there, how he rung upon the rein of a wimpling
        wing
In his ecstacy! then off, off forth on swing,
    As a skate's heel sweeps smooth on a bow-bend: the
        hurl and gliding
    Rebuffed the big wind. My heart in hiding
Stirred for a bird, — the achieve of, the mastery of
        the thing!

Brute beauty and valour and act, oh, air, pride, plume
        here
    Buckle! AND the fire that breaks from thee then, a
        billion
Times told lovelier, more dangerous, O my chevalier!

    No wonder of it: sheer plod makes plough down
        sillion
Shine, and blue-bleak embers, ah my dear,
    Fall, gall themselves, and gash gold-vermilion.

As we approach what is at once Hopkins's most famous
and most controverted poem, I again suggest to the reader the
more detailed discussion and illustration of complementarity in
Celestial Pantomime.

Repeatedly I have indicated that because Hopkins like all true
poets was writing unprogrammatically and more out of his personal vision than out of any prescribed convention, whether
philosophical, scientific, or theological, this motif of complementarity constantly and more or less spontaneously recurs. Thus in a
passage from "The Wreck of the Deutschland," he again indicates
that it is by the wavelike and the corpuscular that the absolute
affects the contingent:

> With an anvil-ding
> And with fire in him forge thy will
> Or rather, rather then, stealing as Spring
> Through him, melt him but master him still:
> Whether at once, as once at a crash Paul,
> Or as Austin, a lingering-out sweet skill,
> Make mercy in all of us, out of us all
> Mastery, but be adored, but be adored King.

We have the "fire" (spark) and the "melting" (soup), along with
the corpuscular "crash" and the cymatic "lingering-out." And
elsewhere in the poem, the mystery of suffering in a world of
grace entails "Stroke and a stress that stars and storms deliver"
(6), while God is "lightning and love..., a winter and warm" (9),
whose adorers will "bathe in his fall-gold mercies..., breathe in
his all-fire glances" (24). Similarly with the "dim woods" and the
"diamond delves," the "grey lawns" and the "quickgold" (while
the latter plays back to quicksilver, the hermetic medium), of
"The Starlight Night"; the "yellow moisture" and "trambeams"
(these latter cognate to "ooze of oil" and "shook foil") of "The
Candle Indoors"; the "lift me, lay me" of "Henry Purcell"; and
finally the "glide" and "hurl" of "The Windhover."

Since, as I have also been emphasizing, ultimately all figures are
homologous, and all patterns are congruent one with the other, it

is hardly surprising that in this context of waves and particles, and in this penultimate chapter, I will draw upon some of the most celebrated passages in the literature.

Thus in Herbert's "Redemption":

> I straight return'd and knowing his great birth,
> Sought him accordingly in great resorts;
> In cities, theatres, gardens, parks, and courts;
> At length I heard a ragged noise and mirth
>
> Of theeves and murderers: there I him espied,
> Who straight, *Your suit is granted,* said, & died.

I have elaborated elsewhere on the striking enjambement here which signals the discovery of the transcendent; I want only to point out that the overflowing and unpunctuated line, "At length I heard a ragged noise and mirth of theeves and murderers," is structurally undular while the heavily punctuated line which precedes it is structurally corpuscular. The pattern thus exemplifies my present focus: the delight experienced in conjoining the broken and fragmented with the harmonious and unified. "Dramatically," one might say that the poet is indicating here that Jesus is to be found not in the chaos of the discrete and particulate but in the harmony of the unified and tranquil; or, better, that Jesus — word become flesh, spirit become matter — is the nexus of both; and it is the realization, the experience of this structural nexus, that engenders theological insight and esthetic delight.

It is difficult to read the lines from Herbert without thinking of a similarly organized passage in a sonnet of Wordsworth which, we noted earlier, Hopkins rather severely criticized:

> Ships, towers, domes, theatres, and temples lie
> Open unto the fields and to the sky.

The enjambement needs no emphasis, nor does the fact that the poet is describing the merger of heaven and earth. In the context of this discussion, I want to stress primarily that the corpuscular fragments find their complement in the cymatic unity of the second line — all not unlike the transcendently beautiful opening to "Vertue":

> Sweet day, so cool, so calm, so bright,
> The bridall of the earth and sky.

Again, one is witnessing the marriage of heaven and earth, and experiencing the "chord" of multiplicity-unity, of matter-spirit.

One of many ancestors of Herbert's "Vertue" is Edmund Bolton's "A Palinode," in which the first four lines are cymatic and the next four corpuscular; and the entire poem follows the circular pattern we have seen in several works by Hopkins:

> As withereth the primrose by the river,
> As fadeth summer's sun from gliding fountains,
> As vanisheth the light-blown bubble ever,
> As melteth snow upon the mossy mountains:
> So melts, so vanisheth, so fades, so withers
> The rose, the shine, the bubble, and the snow
> Of praise, pomp, glory, joy (which short life gathers),
> Fair praise, vain pomp, sweet glory, brittle joy.

The overall paradoxic complementarity is brilliantly intensified, as it will be also in "The Windhover," by the fact that the wave-like lines are all end-stopped, while the corpuscular lines are enjambed.

And certainly one of the immediate heirs of "Vertue" is Keats's "The Day Is Gone," with its many direct verbal echoes of Herbert:

> The day is gone, and all its sweets are gone!
> Sweet voice, sweet lips, soft hand, and softer breast,
> Warm breath, light whisper, tender semi-tone,
> Bright eyes, accomplish'd shape, and lang'rous waist!
> Faded the flower and all its budded charms,
> Faded the sight of beauty from my eyes,
> Faded the shape of beauty from my arms,
> Faded the voice, warmth, whiteness, paradise —

> Vanish'd unseasonably at shut of eve,
> When the dusk holiday — or holinight
> Of fragrant-curtain'd love begins to weave
> The woof of darkness thick, for hid delight;
> But, as I've read love's missal through to-day,
> He'll let me sleep, seeing I fast and pray.

The poem is almost the perfect exemplification of this basic structural format of complementarity. The first and last lines of the octave are respectively cymatic and corpuscular, while the six central lines, in chiastic pattern, reverse the preceding order and are respectively corpuscular and cymatic. One might say, further, that the fragmented lines in the first quatrain symbolize the spasmodically attained experiential reality, while the unbroken and flowing lines of the second quatrain evoke the now unattainable, remembered ideal. The entire octave is heavily charged and explosive; the chiasm hints at not yet attained union, and the polarization of waves and particles manifests an unrealized complementarity on the personal and the ontological, the sexual and the metaphysical, levels. And as in a number of major poems, the attainment of that complementarity, of that ecstasy of transcendence, is signaled by the heavily enjambed lines of the third quatrain, which stand in marked contrast to the bluntly end-stopped lines of all that goes before:

> When the dusk holiday — or holinight
> Of fragrant-curtain'd love begins to weave
> The woof of darkness thick...

The actual resolution of this straining vigil will come, as all true lovers know, on the good-morrow of their waking souls. Then they shall no longer kiss by the mass book but in their sexual sacrament shall share in the *individual* kiss of Milton's *admirabile commercium* ("On Time"), which the climactic coda-couplet clearly anticipates.

Since matter, body, is traditionally described as "part outside of part," as the principle of the discrete and fragmented, while spirit, soul, is traditionally defined as the principle of unity and harmony, the following from Donne should not startle us since he is explicitly and precisely contrasting "spirit" and "matter," soul and body, and *pari passu,* wave and corpuscle:

> Inter-assured of the mind,
> Care lesse, eyes, lips, and hands to misse.

Nor is it startling that the density, ponderousness, and particulate nature of the classic definition of matter is brought out in Pope's "When Ajax strives, some rock's vast weight to throw" — as it is also brought out in the heavy and the weary weight of what Hopkins calls "mould." And such is the quasi-subliminal power of these complementarities that Pope's companion line on spiritual Camilla introduces oceanic and cymatic "waves": "Flies o'er the th'unbending corn, and skims along *the main.*"

A similar relation between the particle and the wave is drawn by Shelley in the renowned fifty-second stanza of *Adonais,* on multiplicity and unity:

> Flowers, ruins, statues, music, words, are weak
> The glory they transfuse with fitting truth to speak.

My two final examples are both quite telling because they involve a dualism emphatically underlined by the poet himself. In Marvell's "The Gallery," the paradoxic fascination of Clora is described in terms of several portraits, with the first two described here. On one are depicted her purely physical charms, her seductive sensuality, with the concluding line heavily corpuscular:

> Here thou art painted in the Dress
> Of an Inhumane murtheress;
> Examining upon our Hearts
> Thy fertile Shop of cruel Arts:
> Engines more keen than ever yet
> Adorned Tyrants Cabinet;
> Of which the most tormenting are:
> Black Eyes, red Lips, and curled Hair.

This last line recalls in its structure the predatory feline of Stevens. But the other portrait is the "spiritual" Clora, displayed in all her cymatic allure — as again the concluding line brings out:

> But, on the other side, th'art drawn
> Like to Aurora in the Dawn;
> When in the East she slumb'ring lyes,
> And stretches out her milky Thighs;
> While all the morning Quire does sing,
> And manna falls, and Roses spring;
> And, at thy Feet, the wooing Doves
> Sit pefecting their harmless Loves.

But, of course, it is the particles *and* the waves that trace out what — Marvell would certainly agree with Heisenberg — is the delight of "playing with both pictures."

So, too, with Tennyson's "The Sisters," where Evelyn, who is intended to be the less "spiritual" of the two, sings the following:

> O diviner light,
> Thro' the heat, the drowth, the dust, the glare . . . ;

while her sister, "the paler and the graver, Edith," sings:

> O diviner light,
> Thro' the cloud that roofs our moon with night.

The narrator, their father, remarks at the end of the songs on the complementarity of both: "Marvellously like, their voices — and themselves!": that is, in these moments of union, polarities are fused, and we marvel at the experience.

Cycle/Circle

Tennyson, whose poetic prowess the young Hopkins had confessed to doubting, brings us to the poem that is central to this chapter, "The Windhover," my reading of which I want to briefly rehearse. As with the various examples above, there is the undular-corpuscular paradox of the "level underneath him steady air" *and* the "striding high there"; the gliding *and* the hurling previously mentioned; the sheer plod *and* the shine; and finally "the Sunday puzzle" of the Hopkins guild: "*Brute* beauty and valour and act, oh, air, pride, plume, here / *Buckle*" — no historiographical allusion here.

As to the initial adjective, it is not clear to me why "brute" has disturbed some readers. We have already examined Hopkins's contrasting the innocence of brute creation with bleared, smeared humanity. In this poem "thing" is appropriately the word immediately preceding "brute," since both terms express an utterly natural and instinctive phenomenon: "doing what one does," without any external influence or mediation. Though of two different orders — the material and the sensate — they achieve mastery simply by "being true," simply by being in tune with the sheer structure of their being. More specifically, concerning "brute beauty," a medieval hunting expression for a worthy prey was "the beauty of its wildness"; and finally "brute" chimes with "beaut[y]."

As to "buckle," considering the heap of critical lumber piled around the word, it would be rash (though certainly not fresh) to profess to having gleaned the definitive interpretation; but following the hermeneutic being pursued here, "buckle" meaning "to clasp," "to join together," seems to be the preferable reading. "Left hand" there is brute beauty and valor and act — all lexically synonymous with the instantaneous and the particulate; "right," air, pride, and plume, all synonymous with the tremulously undular and sigmoid. Air and pride are here parallel, since pride is to be read primarily as *superbia,* loftiness — and plumes, if they do anything at all, "wave."

But what I would want to emphasize now even beyond this first-level reading is the presence of a further *dédoublement,* which may be compared to a kind of mathematical "squaring" of the paradox. It is noteworthy that those terms that literally relate to the corpuscular, to the fragmented and broken, are structurally cymatic, that is, have no punctuation to interrupt their flow: "brute beauty *and* valour *and* act"; whereas the terms lexically related to the wavelike ("oh, air, pride, plume,...") are structurally particulate, that is, are broken off from each other by the four commas. Lastly, the two separate segments are shown to be complementary by their juncture at the outburst "oh," which visually buckles together the two parts of the line. It is also, as noted earlier, a "realer and rounder reply," an outburst that is circular. In fact, other recensions have the more direct and more graphic, "O."

That figural utterance is more precisely related to two images which we have already sounded: "rung upon the rein," and "smooth on a bow-bend." Such circularity expresses the classic mystical, poetic, and sexual imagery of fulfillment, as evidenced in the "not overmuch nor over little" of the mystic Richard Rolle, the structure of the nature poems of Wordsworth, and that of the love poems of Donne. The flight of Hopkins's windhover is thus entirely different from the flight of that ominous falcon of Yeats which circles out beyond all limitations and into oblivion. Hopkins's image might therefore be better compared to the spiraling contemplation (the finite meditating the infinite) symbolized by a self-restraining, hovering hawk, lauded by Pseudo-Dionysius, and studied assiduously by all his commentators, including Hopkins's own Duns Scotus.

Admittedly, this is a very preliminary sketch which demands, first, a more detailed analysis of the entire poem; second, the validation of the structural and esthetic centrality of the initial tercet in its relation to the body of the poem; and, third, in this chapter, a demonstration of the "origin" and the *raison d'être* of the recurrent, almost willfully self-indulgent Francophonic imagery and language of "The Windhover" — so at odds, as we have already seen, with everything Hopkins affirms in his letters and displays in all his other poems. Fourth, in the final chapter I will develop what I say here about complementarity, and show its connection with that other overriding structural pattern in Hopkins's *oeuvre*, the concept of inscape, instress — which all commentators agree is related to *haecceitas*, though the precise nature of the relation is obviously debated.

The first two requirements are fairly conventional regarding this poem, though my readings will be less conventional. But the third has never, so far as I know, been previously pursued, since no other writer has drawn on the historical sources I will tap. As to the final chapter (and my fourth "demand") I think it can be shown that in Hopkins's poems the principle of complementarity and its clear analogies with traditional "hylomorphism" are further enriched by that *tertium quid* called "inscape." But, as I have said, I reserve this treatment for the last chapter.

Since I shall subsequently discuss the hitherto undiscerned significance of the date of the poem, I will begin at the very beginning ("so be beginning") with title and dedication. As is well known, the latter, "To Christ our Lord," was added after the poem was completed. The reason for this seemingly tardy but explicitly religious note is that without it, the poem would be just another sonnet descriptive in much of the octave of a not unusual natural phenomenon; and, in the sestet, of the observer's response to that phenomenon.

In the body of the poem, as noted, what first startles a reader of Hopkins is the unexpected and almost ubiquitous French imagery. That imagery is flaunted in "minion," used in its modern sense of petite and pretty (with faint echoes of "follower" or "servant"), and like the Anglo-French, "falcon" is also a word that can be feminine or masculine — and hence "minion" had in an earlier era overtones of homoerotic subservience — though it is clear that etymologically if not grammatically, both words *are* feminine. The male hawk was technically called a "tiercel" or "tercel" that is, third born, and thus smaller and (*contra* Browning's conclusion to "Count Gismond") less suitable for hunting — the runt of the litter, as one might colloquially say. This cross-designation will prove to be important, even though clearly Hopkins will, like any nineteenth-century writer, use masculine pronouns where the neuter (as noted: he refers to the bird as "thing") or feminine would be more "gender inclusive." In Hopkins's prose contributions to the journal *Nature*, the sun is referred to as "he."

Along those same lines, there is in French a direct translation of "windhover," "la *crécerelle*," and it is surprising that the French translators of the poem intentionally avoid this term which is related to our "kestrel," even as Hopkins simply referred to his "falcon" poem. Two other clues from the French may as well be introduced here. The bird is described as *Faucon-phaéton* — the latter an arbitrary insertion, but an allusion to Phaethon's flaming fall to earth, preparatory to the falling embers at the end of the poem. Also in the French, the "dappled dawn" becomes "*l'aube miroitée*," a remarkably precise translation since this adjective, like "dappled" (as noted earlier) was usually applied to horses, and so prepares the reader (as also already noted) for the equine imagery running through the poem, including the subsequent reference to "chevalier," which, of course, is the same word in both the original and the translation.

It is also of note that "dapple" was used two years later in the sonnet on Duns Scotus (who "*fired* France for Mary without spot": that is, defended the doctrine of the Immaculate Conception) to describe "the dapple-eared lily," or what was called the fleur-de-lis. This not only was for centuries the French national emblem, but was figured forth as the dove symbolic of the country's being protected by the Holy Ghost. On banners and shields this lily was colored gold against a blue background: blue-bleak gashes gold.

But all of these *coniunctiones* make only more pointed the question as to what would have prompted Hopkins in "The Windhover" to employ so ubiquitously, and so echoically and resonantly, not only French imagery, but the very language itself. Something must have inspired such (for him) singularly unique notions as that a bird denominated, in the most picturesque Anglo-Saxon, a "windhover" would be transmuted into a "minion"; that dawn would be transmuted into the "dauphin"; that a furrow would be translated into a "sillion"; and that a "chevalier" would represent..., a what? a heart, a bird, a Hopkins? The answer remains to be determined, but in any case the determination will not resolve the oddity of each of those starkly

Anglo-Saxon nouns being denominated by an archaic French *substantif.*

Returning to the beginning of the poem, it is to be noted that "caught" in the first line has nothing to do with the verb in "as kingfishers catch fire." In the latter, this is the very nature, the selfness, of that very Britishly designated bird (a name which Hopkins would have delighted in playing with both for its Anglo-Saxon roots and its Catholic affinities, since it is a type of martin — after the saint of that name). But here "caught" is used as in that treatise on contemplation, *The Compleat Angler,* and tells us that we are in the domain of the unpredictable, as fish — even "skates" — are caught by "dear chance." This is, of course, the domain of freedom and spirit — as matter is traditionally the domain of predictability. Again, the complementarity of the two, particulate matter and unitary spirit, will be the key to interpreting the whole poem, as in the wavelike "riding of the rolling level" and "gliding," conjoined to the corpuscular "striding high" and "hurl."

That the bird is flying toward the eastern dawn relates back to the final stanza of "The Wreck" with its prayer that Christ will "easter in us" in the "crimson-cresseted east." That we are preparing for a resurrection of sorts is also evident in reverberations of the very early fragment, "During the eastering of untainted morns." Ong's ingenious introduction of the Pegasus motif, with all its implications for poetic creativity (Pope's "Muse's steed" and Keats's "true Hippocrene"), indicates not only that *pulchrum et bonum convertuntur,* but also that "mortal beauty" is the complement of "God's better beauty," and that in this poem we are talking about both. Similarly, the correlation of "lovelier" and "dangerous" in "The Windhover" with "mortal beauty" and "dangerous" in "To What Serves" should not necessarily be taken *au pied de la lettre.* Neither the "fire" of the chevalier nor the "tune" of Purcell can accurately be described in the commonly accepted sense of "dangerous." Rather, as previously noted, that word has roots in *dominus* (after all, Hopkins did add "our Lord" to the dedication "To Christ"), as in Stevens's jarring "dominion" and Keats's Homeric *demesne*. But Hopkins's use of equine imagery to describe the flight of the falcon is also deeply embedded in the medieval hunting tradition, as John Cummins shows in *The Hound and the Hawk* (1988), with a score of examples of the association of falconry and chivalry.

Moreover, there is in Hopkins and in the poetic tradition a close parallel, if not lamination, of flying bird and flying *cheval*: Hopkins himself tells us of the falcon: "how he rung upon the rein of a wimpling wing in his *ecstacy!*" And in the tradition — Pope's "Essay," again — one reads:

> The winged courser, like a *generous* horse,
> Shows most true mettle when you check his course.

("Generous" is, etymologically, "of noble birth" — like a dauphin.) As to the ambiguous "rung," it chimes *literally* by "ringing the changes" on various racing, soaring, skimming patterns. And, of *course*, it also plays on all the paranomastic cognates relating to bells, ladders, "wringing and rinsing." But most significantly, this language relates to the meditation in the *Exercises* on the Ascension, referred to in the discussion of "God's Grandeur": "give off sparks and take fire, yield drops and flow, *ring and tell* [toll] of him." Here I anticipate my treatment of inscape/*haecceitas*, since the complementary "sparks" and "flow" reveal that *tertium quid* I mentioned above.

I have difficulty sympathizing with the finicky casuistry brought to bear on what is the poem's only simile, and one that would come instinctively to so boyish a spirit (cf., in a moment: "stirred for a bird") as that of Hopkins: "As a skate's heel sweeps smooth on a bow-bend." We have earlier encountered some quirky readings of this clause in chapter 1. The image would also come instinctively to mind, in the context of reins, horses, and so on, if the skaters were playing that "dangerous" game known as "crack the whip," to which I have also referred earlier.

Mastery/Mystery

But in fact all soaring "things" (interestingly, in the passage I
am about to cite, they are not masculine as with Hopkins, but
feminine — a Wordsworthian trait as Coleridge suggested?) tend
to elicit similar images and similar emotions. Again, from *The
Prelude* (it is now autumn):

> The *heart* is almost mine with which I *felt,*
> From some hill-top on sunny afternoons,
> The paper kite high among fleecy clouds
> Pull at *her rein* like an impetuous *courser;*
> Or, from the meadows sent on gusty days,
> *Beheld her breast the wind,* then suddenly
> Dashed headlong . . . (I, 492ff.)

But Hopkins's "courser" is not a mere simile; it has an underside,
an underneath, an inscape, a subtext, so to speak, which is about
to be revealed. It does not merely "breast the wind," and so is
"dashed headlong." It is the very complementarity of the windhover's hurl *and* gliding that rebuffed the big wind: the fact that,
like all "brutes," it can only be true to its very nature, that it does
what it is doing (*age quod agis,* again), is what makes it triumph
over "the powers of the air." Thus Claude Colleer Abbott, editor
of Hopkins's letters, was correct in his judgment of more than six
decades ago: "Yet the dedication of *The Windhover* ["To Christ
our Lord"] does not hinder the poem from being first of all a
magnificent tribute to *a natural thing perfectly done*" (emphasis
added).

Bird-watchers are hidden behind "blinds." Suddenly not only
does this observer *see* — but he *feels* ("Ne'er saw I, never felt . . . ,"
Wordsworth again). What he had *watched* as a wondrous spectacle, he now *experiences* through a mode of "knowing" for
which the Scholastics had a score of names — so many because
it is a multidimensional, quasi-infinite type of cognitive apprehension. It is an immediate experience, they would say, *per modum
inclinationis; per quandam unionen; per amorem; propter connat-*

uralitatem. And the result is literally heart-stirring, is literally a *sursum corda* because it is not rational discursive knowledge but "affective" insight.

In this startling moment of unmediated intuition, the disguised and hidden, closed and calloused (nor can heart feel, being recalcitrant), self-imprisoned, mind-manacled core of the poet's very being experiences utter shock — as shocked as the reader is by so unexpected, so unpredictable (we *are* in the realm of total freedom/spirit) an e-vent as *"stirred for a bird"*! And this *is* the realm of the Spirit who, in a Hopkins sermon on John 16, is described as "one who en*cour*ages [*heartens*] men, *stirs* them up." But who could have anticipated such a violation of the conventional, such an affront to all *l'art poétique?* It is such a scandal to sophisticates that some have read it as intentionally ironic. A nursery rhyme! Here we have a heart no longer in hiding, but rather a heart exposed in all its boyish enthusiasm — and we, too, become as little children. All of this exemplifying, once again, Hopkins as the *anima naturaliter candida.*

And what has the bird become? Well, first of all, it is no longer *the* bird: my heart in hiding stirred for *a* bird. It is no longer *that* bird on *that* horizon with its proper name, "windhover," but a "symbol" of the fulfillment that comes from "being what one is," and "doing what one does." It has the perfection of *age quod agis,* and is thus the purely natural, "brute" manifestation of the ultimate substrate of all existents, *res* — "the achieve of, the mastery of *the thing!*" The balance of the bird's "hurl" and "gliding" is the sign of its perfection, as is the harmony of "fall" and "flight" in Herbert's "Easter Wings," and the "stooped so low" and "soared so high" of John of the Cross where the soul pursuing God is compared to a falcon seeking its prey.

But there is more to be said about "my heart in hiding stirred for *a* bird." It is not merely, as I indicated, that this particular bird has become a symbol (though it has): but, "My heart…stirred for *a* bird" suggests not only that my heart was moved by *this* bird, but that my heart itself stirred *to be as a* bird, stirred itself up to want to possess the very qualities the bird manifests in its fusion of striding *and* riding, of hurling *and* gliding. In this moment the poet stirs himself up to seek, also, the perfect unifying of his nature, the harmonizing in himself of his *interior,* graciously resplendent core (heart) and his *exterior,* unadornedly, even "brutally," visible and public state (the priesthood).

In what Ong perceptively calls a "Jesuit meditative moment" where contemplation *is* action, reality *is* appearance, the bird with its transcendence of dualities reminds the viewer of the Keatsian "ancient days" when emperor *and* clown, chevalier *and* ploughman, redream the prelapsarian unity where in Eden Garden "Adam delved," where the person is (like the bird) no longer a fraction, but an integer; no longer the divided schizophrenic image where "inside" is in conflict with "outside"; reality, in conflict with appearance; but where the person is a totally whole and holy *res.* Ong's meditative moment of the *contemplativus in actione* is confirmed by John Cummins, who describes a St. Gorgonius depicted with a missal in one hand and a falcon on the other: thus suggesting the delicate (and dangerous) balance of the contemplative and the active life.

I have stressed "thing" and *res* above because what the poet wants to bring out most emphatically is the moderately Scotist notion of the universality of what begins as a singular contingent experience. I say "moderate" because Hopkins's Scotus is, as we shall see, more Hopkinsian than Scotist. This is merely to suggest that *first* came Hopkins's sense of his own unique selfness, his "pitch," his instress; and *second,* his vague and generalized confirmation of that sense in the discovery of Scotus on *haecceitas:* first, the experience; second, the theoretical confirmation.

That each unique creature reflects in its own individuality the absolute and ultimate is a Scholastic truism. But for the Thomist tradition the proper object of the act of knowing is the universal essence (*here,* birdness) which comes from a kind of regressive mediation from knowledge of the singular bird (*here,* falcon); and subsequently, *this* windhover. Or, more conventionally put, the "agent intellect" plays upon the sense image (the phantasm) of the materially individuated thing, so that the universal essence is

known. But with Scotus, whom in this instance at least Hopkins
is following fairly accurately, the process is, as it were, reversed.
One begins with the unmediated sensible knowledge of a uniquely
individual (*haecceitas*) bird, this windhover, which by extension is
recognized as belonging to the species "falcon," and by the same
process is recognized as belonging to the genus "bird." If one followed this same epistemological trajectory, as does Hopkins, one
would also end up with "the thing." For the analogous theological reason, a similar evolution occurs in language and imagery.
We move from the rich exoticism of "dauphin," "falcon," "ecstacy," and "minion" (the latter a term of affection which hints
at the familiar relationship of object and speaker), then through
the traditional poetic image of "rein" (no "manège" here), to the
boyish "skating" simile, which then terminates in the homeliness
of "big wind," "stirred/bird" — and, climactically, in the utterly
commonplace "thing." But what is it about this mere "thing,"
in all its instinctive, brutish action (in all its unself-consciousness,
we would say) that is so stirring? Given Hopkins's preoccupation
with "chiming," and the fact that "mastery" is a favorite word,
there is little doubt that beyond its surface meaning of "lord" (as
in the second part of the dedication), there is an obvious play here
on "mystery." The supreme natural mystery, as evident in the two
preceding chapters, is the relation of contingent particularity to
ultimate absolute. And this is precisely what the bird in its perfect
balance both symbolizes and achieves.

Chevalier/Chevelure

"Achieve," of course, adds an entirely new dimension, again beyond its surface meaning of "enactment" or "fulfillment." Its
most obvious cognate is another French word, *chef*, related to
caput (and to the French regal family name Capet), which immediately evokes, first, various New Testament images for Christ, for
example, this conflation of English and French from Colossians
1:18: "And he is the head of the body the church, *le chef*...";
and, second, Hopkins's repeated references to Christ, in the med-

itation on the Two Standards, as "Captain-General," "supreme and true Captain," and so on. But I do not think the *primary* reference in this extended meaning of "achieve" is to Christ (the delayed dedication suggests *that* to be a somewhat explanatory afterthought); though of course the whole poem is laced, as was the poet's life, with christological reflections, allusions, and so on. Nor would it make sense in so rich a poem to insist doctrinairely on univocal, exact, irrefutable meanings. Everything that enhances the overall impact of the poem, everything that does not violate the overall structure of the poem — all that is to be embraced. Nevertheless, the kind of fuzzy vagaries I scored in chapter 1 are still off-limits.

By my reading, "achieve" relates obviously to the bird, but *primarily* back to "heart." It is an ancillary support of this notion that the bird is always referred to as masculine, so that speaking precisely, the neuter "thing" is more applicable to "heart." And I seriously doubt that so conscientious an artist as Hopkins would have let his thought be dictated merely by the demands of rhyme; *sic:* swing/thing. Again, it seems at least plausible that a bird referred to throughout the poem by "his" and "he" is less likely than a physical organ, whatever *it* symbolizes, to be called "thing."

This is not a quibble; for in a moment, an analogously radical reading will probe another interpretive crux. But, first, let me summarize. The bird seems to have instinctively made manifest that complementarity the observer is seeking: the healing of the primordial wound, the making holy and whole of that divided image which is responsible for the conflict of appearance and reality, of exterior and interior; which is responsible for the living lie resulting from the original sin, so that what Adam believes interiorly differs from what he expresses exteriorly when responding to the "Lord God." So, the poet — though devoted to St. François de Sales but orthodox in believing there is no "*pure* love of God" — wants *for himself* what the bird manifests: the achievement and perfection of this *coincidentia oppositorum,* and concomitantly the mastery of this mysterious schism at the very core of things.

The "thee" of the sestet is, then, his own healed heart, and the "chevalier" being addressed is himself, now heart-eased, and in full Jesuit panoply like the Christ he described as marching "before his troops." What might confirm this, and the reason for the seemingly picayune dissection of "achieve" above, would be if some relation could be established between "chevalier" and "achieve." Alas, though one plays with *chef,* chevalier, *caput* (even cabbage), *caballus,* and every cognate of the two, in strict etymological analysis there is no connection. One might speculate over a connection between chevalier and chevelure because, as every schoolboy used to know, the cavaliers wore their hair long, and that is the meaning of chevelure (but, alas, derived from *capillus,* again as in *caput,* as in chief, etc.).

But all poets, not just Hopkins, are "chimers," as Pope noted, and it was Spenser and his imitators who made the chiming connection and then the semantic one of chevaliers and achievers; so here the achieving "thing" is the heart no longer in hiding, but the Jesuit *contemplativus in actione,* balancing the hidden spiritual "contemplative" life with the manifestly valorous "active" life — and so fulfilling the Christian chivalrous mission.

That mission, which "The Windhover" encapsulates, is paradigmatic from Paul to Augustine, even to Loyola, and I parenthetically introduce its structure here to help better understand the oscillatory "up/down" spirals of Hopkins's spiritual life, from his enthusiastic conversion to his bleak Dublin disenchantment, and Keatsian death.

Heavens/Havens/Stevens

I employ to that end a cartographer of the religious psyche who mapped, in his own un-Hopkinsian way, the varieties of conversional experience. When discussing in chapter 4 Hopkins's rejection of traditional religious anodynes — the theodicies of "mechanical optimism" — in the use of "and" not "but" in "God's Grandeur," I was explicitly referring to Stevens's "A Thought Revolved," the thought in question being that of religious belief. The "revolving" and evolving of that thought are from religion as refined superstition ("The Mechanical Optimist," part I), where one might take as example the newly converted Hopkins's fears of damnation for his "Protestant" parents, or subsequently for his loved but, alas, also "Protestant," Henry Purcell. Then in part II come acceptance into the Roman communion and entrance into the religious life with their joys *and* inevitable familial, communal, and ecclesial disillusionments: here are situated the splendid, but dialogical, poems of his *annus mirabilis* (Stevens's "Mystic Garden & Middling Beast").

The third phase, of which "The Windhover" is the monument, resolves the *middling* conflicts by way of the paradox of contemplative in action — the whole denominated by Stevens, "Romanesque Affabulation," with its allusive Catholicism, its windhoveresque Latinity, and its "coincidental" Loyolan and Spanish biographical emphasis:*

> He sought an earthly leader who could stand
> Without panache, without cockade,
> Son only of man and sun of men,
> The outer captain, the inner saint,
>
> The pine, the pillar and the priest,
> The voice, the book, the hidden well,
> The faster's feast and heavy-fruited star,
> The father, the beater of the rigid drum....

The final section (part IV, "The Leader") is more predictive of Stevens's own courageous acquiescence in the "Evening Sacrifice"; but still relates to Hopkins's barren Irish exile: "Behold the moralist hidalgo.... In how severe a book he read.... And knowledge

---

*This is not the only fortuitous coincidence of Stevens and Hopkins. Though Joseph Miller, writing on Stevens in the *Dictionary of Literary Biography* (54), explicitly connects his use of the phrase "gold-vermilion" in "Le Monocle de Mon Oncle" with Hopkins's use of it in "The Windhover," there is no basis in fact for such a connection. Miller after citing the passage says that the persona in "Le Monocle" is asserting that he has nothing in common "with the Christianity of Gerard Manley Hopkins." But the duplication of the phrase is pure coincidence: both poems were published for the first time not only in the same year, 1918, but in the same month, December. Stevens could not have had Hopkins in mind.

dropped upon his heart / Its pitting poison." All this, not to suggest influences, direct or indirect, from "The Windhover" to "A Thought Revolved," but to point to recurrent and converging configurations of religious experiences.

Rein/Reign

In any case, *in* "The Windhover," the sestet indicates that if the poem is not a *débat*, or *conflictus* (like that between "heart" and "body" in Donne's "The Blossome"), it is at least a dialogue (like Marvell's "Between the Soul and Body," or like Yeats's "Of Self and Soul"), or a paradoxic harmonization (like Stevens's "Mystic Garden & Middling Beast").

In a well-known letter to Dixon, Hopkins clarified the strain entailed in his failure to publish as intrinsic to the Jesuit "hidden life." He then added, "but when one mixes with the world and meets on every side its secret solicitations, to live by faith is harder, is very hard; nevertheless by God's help I shall always do so." Four pages later, after having referred to various Jesuits, including Ignatius ("the outer captain, the inner saint"), as living virtually unknown ("without panache"), he adds: "I quote these cases to prove that show and brilliancy do not suit us, that we cultivate the commonplace outwardly ['the hidden hidalgo'] and wish the beauty of the king's daughter the soul to be from within."

But all of this language suggests a struggle, or at least a dialogue, between the lure of poetic fame and "show" (of physical, public — and publishing — beauty and valor and act) and the demands of living by faith the "unworldly" spiritual ("air, pride, plume") Jesuit vocation. Moreover, in the context of the prevalent Francophonic diction, and also in the context of Hopkins's failure to publish, that phrase, "plume here buckle[s]," certainly implies that that "plume" (meaning also *instrument pour écrire*) is in danger of breaking under the weight of Hopkins's Jesuit vocation.

And this language also reflects the struggle, "the war within," of the poem on Alphonsus Rodriguez, another martyr to the hidden life. Writing to Dixon, Hopkins seems to resolve the conflict by choosing the "outwardly commonplace" — however "very hard" that may be — over the "beauty...from within." But in "The Windhover," he takes the more difficult and more dangerous path of seeking, like the balanced flight of the falcon, to be true both to the "outward" and to the "within." Thus I have no difficulty with the word "buckle," and find attractive the seasoned judgment of W. A. M. Peters in a 1984 "Tribute" to Hopkins: "I do not think that the word *buckle* would cause any great difficulty to a child." Indeed, as noted, this is only one of many childlike elements in the poems.

The external "brute [meaning, again, the utterly unselfconscious, instinctual, physical] beauty and valour and act" are to be clasped together with the interior ("king's daughter the soul") spiritual elements, "air, pride [meaning *superbia* = 'high there'], plume ['wimpling wing,' and as noted, ink pen, i.e., 'poems']": but such a parlous effort at achieving the balance of, roughly speaking, matter and form is "harder, is very hard."

Thus one reads the "oh" at the juncture of external and internal as a cry of fear, shock, *and* supplication — all quite different from the "O" preceding "my chevalier," which is a cry of exultation and of self-encouragement to his own heart at its victory in wedding the public demands of body to the "hidden" demands of soul. The "oh" of fright and longing at the prospect of buckling together these two extremes is followed by the "O" of triumph at the success of this *coniunctio* that breaks open to reveal the poet's very selfness, symbolized by the fiery heart which is akin to that *tertium quid* denominated *"inscape."*

So what begins as a dialogue, or possibly even a *débat,* between body and soul concludes with their sublation — Max Müller might have said *Aufhebung* — by and in the third reality: the unveiled, no-longer-hiding, triumphant heart/Ignatian/chevalier who is *also* an unknown, unpublished poet priest. Nor is it unfitting, first, that the initial "catching" or physical sighting of the paradoxically hurling and gliding bird should be in the royal domain of the *roi soleil*'s son, the flashing *dauphin,* and, second, that the silent spiritual beauty of the soul is in the "from-within" realm of the *infante* (nonspeaking) "king's daughter."

Hopkins's "buckle" is, then, hurled like a challenge to his critics and to the *conventional* Aristotelian principle that "matter is the principle of individuation." That exaggerated "AND," like the equally exaggerated (but childlike) "billion times," emphasizes that when matter and the generic and specific form are in balance, *are* buckled, then the real inshaping, the utterly singular "thisness," of individual being is revealed. But the opening of the sestet with its controverted "buckle" is what Hopkins in a letter to Bridges (October 8, 1879) calls "dark": "One of two kinds of clearness one shd. have — either the meaning to be felt without effort as fast as one reads or else, if dark at first reading, when once made out *to explode.*" That upper-case "AND" signals such an explosion.

Scotching Scotism

I have italicized "conventional" above because the Aristotelian denigration of body and exaltation of soul underwent revision by Aquinas. Aristotle, partially following Plato, never quite overcame his disdain for the physical and the bodily. Though retaining Aristotle's language, Aquinas elevates the body to a co-principle with the soul, so that body is not merely the principle of individuation; it is the "hinge of salvation" or, as we would say, the interface between "personness" and the whole of the external world. Hence even the manuals Hopkins used as a student pointed out that Aquinas's revision of Aristotle's *De Anima* is entitled *De Homine,* to bring out the co-principality of body and soul. What Hopkins's textbooks would not have emphasized is that body is the substantial expression of soul, and the medium whereby soul first achieves its concrete reality. As corollary, the more human being becomes its true self, the more soul becomes body, and conversely the more mute poet becomes triumphant chevalier.

Thus Hopkins could as readily have regarded the physical or the "corpuscular" (brute beauty and valour and act) and the spiritual or the "cymatic" (air, pride, plume) as co-principles of the substantial unity which constitutes the human person as a compound that both *is* and *acts*. And Hopkins, then, could as readily have said that in this "buckling" of being/action, "the fire that breaks from thee . . . , etc." In short, Aristotelianism/Thomism offers as clear an explanation of the central idea of the poem as does what purports to be Scotism, even though the substantive terms of the poem (windhover > falcon > bird > thing) are organized Scotistically.

The fuzziness of Hopkins's categories is brought out in another letter to Bridges (October 22, 1879), two years after writing "The Windhover." Here Hopkins does employ Thomistic language: "For though even bodily beauty, even the beauty of blooming health, is from the soul, in the sense, as we Aristotelian Catholics say, that the soul is the form of the body, yet the soul may have no other beauty, so to speak, than that which it expresses in the symmetry of the body." Thus, body and soul are seen as co-principles of the substantial unity which constitutes the uniqueness of each human being.

Although this letter was written well after Hopkins's discovery of Duns Scotus, and even after Hopkins's poem honoring Scotus, that Hopkins adopts an Aristotelian/Thomistic position is another indication of the fluidity of his own notions of the principle of individuation — at least as represented *in the poems;* whereas, in the sermons and meditations, as I have noted, the Scotism is frequently an animating and ingenious interpretive principle. But, on the other hand, it may be that to have explained Scotist terms to Bridges would have entailed more clarifications than a chatty communication allowed for, and would have entailed Hopkins's discussing a personal preoccupation, from childhood on, a principle of selfness, or a uniqueness in his own being which he intuited was neither mould nor mind, neither body nor soul, but something "else" ("The Lantern out of Doors"), and which he only gradually came to identify with something "rare": Scotus's inscape/thisness.

But what is important *in reading the poems* is that the structure is recognized as triadic, whether it be conceived as body, soul, and self; or as signate matter, form, and substantial compound; or generic, specific, and individual. In each instance, Hopkins recognized what he had adumbrated in his youth and early years as a Jesuit, a principle which by its very nature is intensely individuated, or in Hopkins's language is "self-instressed."

This raises, as I have said, another issue not directly related to the poems but to the sermons and meditations where Hopkins's Scotism is often the acknowledged inspiration. However, I am not addressing that issue. What is not in question is the fact that Scotism was embraced simply because it provided a foundation that would justify Hopkins's own congenital and well-attested sense of the uniqueness of the individual self. But since "feeling is first," that sense preceded his discovery of Scotus's "syntax of things." Scotist doctrine, discovered in 1872 and well before the major poems had been written, is not their key, much less their paradigm or schema. Rather, Scotism confirmed and supported Hopkins's conviction tested, first, in his own experience of unique and singular selfness; second, in his mature esthetic; and, third, in his theological reflections on the nature of the self and its relation to God. Nevertheless, for an appreciation of the poems, an understanding of the subtle refinements of Scotism remains a luxury — and maybe a distraction.

In confirmation of that somewhat sweeping judgment, I would adduce the hybrid Scholasticism entailed in Hopkins's notion of the "true poet" who — it turns out — has more in common with the angels as envisaged by Aquinas than as envisaged by Scotus. If, for Aquinas, signate matter is the principle of individuation, and the angels are immaterial, then each angel differs from the other as species differs from species, precisely because each angel, being a purely spiritual being, lacks this material principle of individuation. Each angel is, as it were, a species of its own. Whereas Hopkins in a letter to Coventry Patmore (October 6, 1886) observed that "originality [is] a condition of poetic genius; so that each poet is like a species in nature (not an *individuum genericum* or *specificum*) and can never recur." On the other hand, Scotus, consistent with his larger vision, emphatically affirms that there can be several angels in the same species: "Simpliciter possible est plures angelos esse in eadem specie." The "lesson" is, again, that the philosophical views of the poet, however biographically important, are not necessarily the basis or substructure of the poems, including "The Windhover" — to which I now explicitly return.

Plume/Plough

It is immediately after the "buckling" that we read: "AND the fire that breaks from thee then, a billion / Times told lovelier . . . ": but "lovelier" than what? Certainly, *lovelier* than the union of matter and form as conventionally understood, since that union does not seem to fully clarify the unique beauty of the particular being as does that "super-educed" individualizing entity, "inscape/ instress"; and more precisely, in the prior context of Hopkins's letter to Dixon, *lovelier* than either "show and brilliancy" alone, or the beauty "from within" alone. But to fuse them entails a "dangerous," a literally acrobatic, achievement.

Nor, we are told, is this surprising, since the intensest, straining effort (sheer plod) beats and transforms the knight's physical sword into the spiritual ploughshare which, by the equilibrial "trenching" (sillion) action of the two (loosely, "matter and form"), engenders the unique third element, "thisness" — here identified by the immediately visible, sensible "shine." And this, in turn, corresponds to the equally visible and sensible, "fire that breaks" from the heart/chevalier revealed in the preceding tercet.

Though Hopkins used the plough image to affirm vocational commitment — "my hand upon the plough" — in a letter to Dixon (October 29, 1881) expressing regrets at seeking fame, I do not think Hopkins's "sheer plod" reference owes much to that kind of stereotyped biblical homiletics. For, one, that would contradict Hopkins's axiom above that originality is a condition of *poetic* genius. And, for two, much more relevant to the plough

image, in this setting of the *conflictus* of Hopkins's Jesuit "hidden
life" and the religiously legitimate desire to publicly proclaim his
poetic vision, is the elision of the seemingly antagonist elements
in Hopkins's sermon for May 30, 1880 (three years to the day
after the poem was dated), on the gospel parable of the guests
who refused the invitation to the wedding (Luke 14), where are
joined together the same themes: "[S]ome in pursuit of wealth
and power [*read:* brute beauty and valour and act],...some in
love with learning or name and fame and honour [*read:* air, pride,
plume], like that other [invited guest] that went to try his ploughing oxen...taught to bear the yoke, draw the plough, and tread
straight the furrow...."

But in the overall, it is most likely that it was merely a city-
dweller's obsession with tillage ("fold, fallow, and *plough*") that
explains the ubiquity of the image. But the plough is the im-
plement that allows "the corn of wheat" (analyzed in detail in
a journal note of September 24, 1863) to fall into the ground,
die, and be resurrected. Hopkins himself had experimented (and
failed) with trying to plough an even furrow, and (*Journal*, July 9,
1868) described a "noble scape of stars — the Plough *all golden
falling*...," making use of a term for the seven stars in Ursa
Major as common in England as "Big Dipper" is in North
America.

And for one as steeped in British folklore as Hopkins, the
mention of "plough" would certainly have elicited its even more
ancient designation, originally "Arthur's Wain," to commemorate King Arthur, and later — probably after the conquest —
"Charles's Wain," to commemorate Charlemagne. ("Churl's
Wain" seems to have been dismissed by the philologists, though
I will suggest shortly it may link "The Windhover" to "Harry
Ploughman.") The "Little Dipper" was then identified with
Arthur, perhaps on the basis of legend or as a "political" sop
to the Saxons, but most probably because of sonic affinities
with Arcturus. In any case, there is no doubt that King Arthur
and Charlemagne are among "the fire-folk sitting in the air" in
"The Starlight Night" — all of which may be confirmed by the

close parallel between that poem and "Penmaen Pool" of the previous year:

> And Charles's Wain, the wondrous seven,
> And sheep-flock clouds like worlds of wool,
> For all they shine so, high in heaven,
> Shew brighter shaken in Penmaen Pool.*

But more importantly, if the Plough, knowingly or unknowingly, suggested Charles the Great's Wain, we have an additional explanation for the otherwise odd allusion to "dauphin," possibly as "Lesser Wain" or "Little Dipper." And if the "fire-folk" include both constellations, it is no more surprising ("no wonder of it") that in "The Windhover" the plough shines than that, in "The Starlight Night," the dim woods contain diamonds or that the grey lawns contain quickgold — even as the blue-bleak embers, like "falling stars," "gash gold-vermilion"; or as the "noble scape of stars — the Plough," of his journal entry, is described as "all golden falling."

It is not clear why "Churl's Wain" has been rejected by etymologists, except that being among the astroclerisy, they would have sought a more sophisticated, less folksy derivation. Certainly it is more likely for a churl to be ploughing than for a king. In any case, Hopkins's "Harry Ploughman" possesses "churls-grace" and he "features, in flesh, what deed he each must do"

---

*It might be a fruitful line of speculation to suggest that the fragment "Denis" has a similar framework — though here in religious-ethnic terms. Denis, martyred patron saint of France, was identified throughout medieval Europe with Denys the Areopagite, author of a treatise on the celestial hierarchy and music of the spheres ("caps occasion with an intellectual fit" [a musical strain being called a "fit"]), and of another work on mysticism ("motionable, alert, most vaulting [i.e., 'ecstatic'] wit") — this Denis is contrasted with Arthur, a very down-to-earth pragmatic Briton (Bowman, not Archer) who, nevertheless, is right on target, both ethnically and religiously. As Newman wrote of Hurrell Froude in the *Apologia:* "He had a keen insight into abstract truth; but he was an Englishman to the backbone [bowman] in his severe adherence to the real and the concrete." Moreover, the language describing Denis is Norman-French (motionable, vault, occasion, intellectual), while Arthur is cunningly and kenningly Anglo-Saxon (three-heeled timber, bald and bold blinking gold, right-rooting in the bare butt). I leave to future critical theorists — heirs of Johnson and Arnold *vs.* Montesquieu and Taine — whether there could be a greater contrast between the ratiocinative Norman-French, and these husky kernels of Anglo-Saxon.

(*age quod agis*) with *crimson* cheeks and *goldish* curls, while from his cragiron plough, *shining "flame* furls." Again, I am not suggesting that this later poem is indebted to "The Windhover," but merely that these are the themes, the hues, and the images most deeply engraved in the poet's imagination. But that the language of "Harry Ploughman" seems almost compulsively Anglo-Saxon raises, again, the puzzle of the Francophonic exaggerations in the earlier poem.

Returning to those themes, again, no wonder of it, since embers gall themselves *and* gash gold-vermilion. But here the italicized "and" is not parallel with the "AND" in the previous tercet. The latter conjunction introduces a clause of result: that happens AND this is the startling consequence. In the final tercet, the two clauses are joined by a coordinating conjunction: this happens *and* that also happens in the quotidian linkage of life's events. There is no explosion, there is no darkness, there is no wonder, since the poet realizes that what he has discovered is a rudimentary religious truism: unless the corn of wheat fall into the ground and die, itself remaineth alone.

But before considering the personal, that is, the implications for Hopkins of this final tercet, the parenthetic phrase, "ah my dear," needs to be accounted for. The received reading is that the exclamation follows Herbert's use of it as one of his familiar references to Christ. The phrase is a conventional ejaculation in the devotional literature, but its tone is unprecedented in Hopkins save for the slightly familiar, but very deferential, "sir" and "my friend" in "Thou art indeed just." So, again, given Hopkins's passion for unique and original images (apart from some biblical tags in his prose writings), the probability of a Herbartian allusion to Christ appears less and less likely. Moreover, since *the* parallel in *this* poem is "O my chevalier" and "ah my dear," and it has been established that the former is a reference to Hopkins/heart as no longer straitened by the conflict between his presumably polarized vocations (the Jesuit hidden life vs. the poet's show and brilliancy), but as reconciled and at ease with both — then the "ah my dear" may be seen as Hopkins/heart, again, in dialogue: but here with a Hopkins confirmed and strengthened in his now-unified religious mission.*

As to the second clause in the final tercet, the blue-bleak embers represent both the "commonplaces" of Jesuit life and the external "material principle," while the interior "fire that breaks" forth in a spiritual holocaust engenders, again, the knightly "honor that is flashed off exploit," the unique selfness that "flashes off frame and face," and which we witness visibly as the inscape: gold-vermilion, which Hopkins the Jesuit identified with "that inmost self of mine."

Jean/Jeanne

The final element I wish to rejoin in this poem — its uniquely Francophonic diction — is linked to the undergirding imagery of

---

*I think such an exclamation as "ah my dear" is conventional in self-sacrificial love poems. I proffer the fifth of the *Sonnets from the Portuguese,* not as a parallel, but as an analogy — in the strict sense of that term: "*simpliciter* different; *secundum quid* the same":

> I lift my heavy heart up solemnly,
> As once Electra her sepulchral urn,
> And, looking in thine eyes, I overturn
> The *ashes* at thy feet. Behold and see
> What a great heap of grief lay hid in me,
> And how the *red wild* sparkles dimly burn
> Through the *ashen* greyness. If thy foot in scorn
> Could tread them out to darkness utterly,
> It might be well perhaps. But if instead
> Thou wait beside me for the winds to blow
> The grey dust up,... those laurels on thy head,
> O *my Beloved,* will not shield thee so,
> That none of all the fires shall scorch and shred
> The hair beneath. Stand farther off then! go.

The passion and pathos are not the links between the two poems, nor even the ardent outburst to the dearly beloved, however important; nor, finally the use of similar imagery. One draws closer to the thematic continuity in the truncated biblical allusion to Lamentations 1:12: "Behold and see" ("if there be any sorrow like my sorrow, which has been brought on me, which the Lord has inflicted..."). Both poets are torn by the conflict engendered by their poetic calling and their "religious" ("which the Lord has inflicted") vocation. Elizabeth Barrett is fearful that her marriage to Robert may founder on the shoals of her greater fame as an artist; the irony being that the very passion he has aroused in her may inspire her, may ignite her heart to poetry that will "scorch and shred" the laurels of her beloved. Hopkins's "ah my dear" bespeaks the same dilemma: will publishing his poems, inspired explicitly by "Christ our Lord," violate his vocation as a Jesuit, and tempt him to the prideful fame that would seemingly outweigh his master's (and his own chosen) crown of thorns?

the heart that, I have suggested, is the "thee" from which the fire breaks, and the "chevalier" addressed in the first tercet and the "dear" in the second. Concerning diction, there is, as we have repeatedly seen exemplified and expressed, Hopkins's commitment to "Anglo-Saxon," and his puzzling disregard of that commitment in "The Windhover."

Hopkins's views may be juxtaposed with Stevens's "Two or Three Ideas," where he wrote: "[T]he prejudice in favor of plain English...comes to nothing. I have never been able to see why what is called Anglo-Saxon should have the right to higgle and haggle all over the page....If a poem seems to require a hierophantic phrase, the phrase should pass." But if ever there were such a phrase it is "gold-vermilion" in "The Windhover," and the same phrase in "Le Monocle de Mon Oncle"—a coincidence I have already discussed. Though Stevens had written (May 12, 1954) the year before he died: "I have not read Hopkins," it is difficult to believe that at that late date in his career he did not know what Hopkins and his many followers and imitators professed, and therefore equally difficult to believe that this criticism of "what is called Anglo-Saxon" *is not* directed at Hopkins.

But, as I have been noting, it is precisely the relative paucity of "plain English" and of Eliot's "Teutonic roots and husks" in "The Windhover" that is so mystifying. In what might be regarded as the *fons et origo* of all Hopkins's verse, "A Vision of the Mermaids," there is no such mystification. A flight of winged Nereids shake

> From wings swan-fledged a wheel of watery light
> Flickering with sunny spokes, and left and right
> Plunge orb'd in rainbow arcs, and trample and tread
> The satin-purfled smooth to foam, and spread
> Slim-pointed sea-gull plumes, and droop behind
> One scarlet feather trailing to the wind;
> Then, like a flock of sea-fowl mounting higher,
> Thro' *crimson-golden* floods pass *swallow'd into fire.*
> (76–83)

This passage makes clear, again, that Hopkins's "native" poetic language was an Anglo-Saxon strain that had nothing to do with Teutonic influences; but it also makes unclear his deviation from this almost congenital tendency in "The Windhover."

Whence this singular usage of such undisguised Latinity, and its relation to this poem and to its ubiquitous Norman-French imagery? The bird, we have seen, is the minion of the morning; the morning itself is as the dauphin is to the *roi soleil* of noon. The Anglo-Saxon "windhover" itself becomes the French *Falcon*, the only upper-case noun in the entire poem. And when the reader compares this minion to a dare-gale skylark, to kingfishers catching fire, to thrush rinsing and wringing the ear, to wild wooddove, shy wings shut — to all of Hopkins's other birds, anyone could easily be convinced that one is here reading the work of a different poet.

And there is also "spiritual" Latinity as the heart breaks out in fierce and gaudy splendor similar to the depiction of the "Sacred Heart of Jesus" in Franco-Italian popular religious art. That Hopkins, a dedicated Jesuit, was devoted to the Sacred Heart is evident throughout Christopher Devlin's collection of sermons and spiritual reflections. The cultus would have had for Hopkins a special meaning since it had been promoted in England by another Jesuit, Claude de la Colombière two centuries earlier — in fact exactly two hundred years almost to the day of the dating of "The Windhover" — who had been spiritual director and confessor of Margaret Mary Alacoque, to whom the initial vision of the Sacred Heart had been revealed.

For Hopkins the devotion was to the total humanity of Jesus, and was thus entirely orthodox in being centered not on an abstract symbol much less on a physical organ, though often depicted as the latter in ostentatious oleographs from the period. As Hopkins said in his sermon on the Sacred Heart: "Christ's heart is lodged within his sacred frame and there alone is worshipped. ... [W]hen we worship Christ's heart it is a great deal more than the heart of flesh we mean, it is after all Christ himself that we worship." This sentiment had been expressed by Claude de la

Colombière on the feast of Corpus Christi two hundred years before in imagery pertinent to that of "The Windhover": "Come heart of Jesus into my breast. Ignite there a love capable, if it were possible, of fulfilling my duty to love my Saviour."

Nevertheless, the heart to which Hopkins refers in his poetry has little in common — except the yellow-red colors — with the Sacred Heart of traditional iconography or spiritual writings. The imagery of the heart Hopkins coined usually entailed such elements as that it "rears wings"; is "heaven-flung"; is in a "close vault"; is "wild and self-instressed"; is "mother of being in me" as well as "father"; is "dove-winged" and "carrier-witted"; is "handsome" and "mannerly" — all Anglo-Saxon figurative language not contradictory to that of "The Windhover"; but, on the other hand, not particularly congenial to the flamboyant, "Continental" heart-imagery in this poem with its relation to the martyrial, the chivalrous, the fiery, the wounded, the pierced, and the galled.

Some of this language may be derived from Margaret Mary Alacoque and Claude de la Colombière, whose lives, according to Alfred Thomas's *Hopkins the Jesuit* (1969), were standard refectory-reading in Hopkins's time. But with their emphasis on the nature of the revelation, on the diffusion of the devotion, and on the careers of the two protagonists, there is little that is echoed in Hopkins's poem except that Margaret Mary's vision showed the Christ-figure with heart exposed and "surrounded by a circle of flaming seraphim." So, is there another source — or better, "influence" — for Hopkins's "Franco-Latinate" heart-imagery? In a sermon on the Sacred Heart, Hopkins acknowledged that there "would no doubt be something revolting in seeing the heart alone, all naked and bleeding, torn from the breast." But in the poem this seems to be precisely the heart envisioned, the heart torn from the bodily mould, galled, and then gashed.

I think that there may be two such "sources," and I begin with the less probative, while admitting that it is not so much a matter of direct proof or even of direct influence as it is of elements and fragments of the tradition, and particularly of the Jesuit tradition, that may have knowingly or unwittingly affected the imagery and the language of the poem. In a number of poems cited earlier and that clearly relate to "The Windhover," particularly "St Alphonsus Rodriguez," a contrast had been drawn between the hidden, quiet life of those Jesuits who struggle "within," whose heroic breasts are unarmored, and whose fiercest frays are unheard (obviously including Hopkins among those whose "brand *we,* wield" unseen) — a contrast had been drawn between this former group and those other followers of Ignatius with gashed flesh and galled shield, who are described as fighters and martyrs, whose honor is flashed off exploit, and who forge the glorious day.

But what appears to be a sharp contrast is seen as dissolved by the end of "The Windhover" in a kind of penumbral state where the hidden, the quiet, the interior are blended with the gashed, the galled, the flashed exploit. Clearly, then, both kinds of Jesuit contribute equally to the Ignatian mission. Whether "with trickling increments" or "with conquest," both shall have the portals of the kingdom opened to them whether by the "brand yielded" or by merely "watching the door." The conclusion of Hopkins's dialogue with himself — and with the reader — is that regardless of one's office, whether public or private, both are celebrations of the Jesuit vocation, celebrations of the sheer plod *and* of the shine; both are celebrations of the blue-bleak embers *and* of the gold vermilion. In short, and once again, they are both expressions of the ideal of *contemplativus in actione.*

But my concern here at this final stage of analysis is not with the common themes of two interrelated poems, but with their imagery, and in this case, primarily with the atypical heart-imagery of "The Windhover." The heart as such is not mentioned in "St Alphonsus Rodriguez," and is described conventionally in the passages I have cited above. Why is it so uniquely and distinctively introduced into this poem? This heart is "in hiding"; fire breaks from it in an event or deed which is described as immeasurably lovely *and* dangerous. This heart is addressed in warlike chivalrous epithets, and it is encased in a blue, bleak vault which when broken open reveals a core, now surrounded by flames of red and yellow.

The first hint of *such* a heart, as noted in the preceding chapter, is "Easter" of a decade before:

> Beauty now for ashes wear
>
> . . . .
>
> Open wide your hearts that they
> Let in joy this Easter Day.

But this is merely a standard post-Lenten poem. The second prescient note is in "The Wreck" (23), with its conjunction, already cited above in full, of gold and fire — but this is also a commonplace as adduced in, among several *loci,* the biblical "gold [silver] tried in the fire." Usually cited is the third stanza of "Morning, Midday, and Evening Sacrifice: "In silk-ash kept from cooling / And ripest under rind," with commentators quoting Hopkins to Bridges: "I meant to compare grey hairs to the flakes of silky ash which may be seen round wood embers burnt in a clear fire and covering a 'core of heat,' as Tennyson calls it." What the commentators have ignored is the immediately subsequent statement from the letter: "But *core* there is very ambiguous." However, it would be in no way ambiguous if read in light of "The Windhover" of two years earlier, in which the *heart* (translate: "core") "of heat" refers to the fire "that breaks from" the "heart in hiding" about to be revealed as the "contemplative-in-action" Ignatian chevalier.

Again, familiarity with the images may callous the present-day reader (as it might have calloused Hopkins's contemporaries accustomed to popular Catholic depictions of the Sacred Heart) to their iconically shocking nature. That nature has nothing to do with the Christian death/resurrection *locus communis* of the fiery Phoenix born from its own ashes. The shock here is that a *human heart* in concealment bursts forth in fearsome yet seductive flames, analogous to the manner in which smoldering ashen coals *fall, gall themselves, and gash* open. It is this actual physical shock, induced among readers either unfamiliar with Catholic devotionalism or coming afresh and unprepared to the bloody display of such a spectacle, that may be an additional explanation for what could be seen as the poet's otherwise redundant protestation — "No wonder of it." For surely it *is* something to wonder at, particularly in the context of the poet's inspiration: the mere flight of a small predatory bird. How does one get from this matutinal Wordsworthian setting to brute beauty, valor, heart bursting into fire, danger, ploughed furrows, plumage, knights, and embers that fall, gall, and gash?

Indeed, the sestet evokes imagery that would seem more appropriate to William Prescott's detailed descriptions of battles and human sacrifice in his works on the conquest of Mexico and of Peru — the same Prescott who had strongly influenced Hopkins's first poem, "The Escorial." The question, Whence comes *that* imagery?, demands an answer. For we are treating of the flight of a bird that symbolizes, to this poet, both aspects of Jesuit life, the hidden uneventful porter in Majorca *and* the flesh-gashed martyr..., in..., well, I am going to suggest, two possible places, the first being Canada in 1649.

Among the refectory/retreat readings mentioned in Alfred Thomas's *Hopkins the Jesuit* is John Gilmary Shea's *History of the Catholic Missions among the Indian Tribes of the United States: 1529–1854* (New York, 1855), in which the story of the Jesuits in New France figures largely, particularly the bloody martyrdom of Jean de Brébeuf. His own letters were read avidly in France; the annals of missionary work known as *The Jesuit Relations,* containing letters and reports from the New World, were published in over forty volumes beginning in 1632; were reprinted by the Canadian government in 1848; and lastly, were read in abridged translations in Jesuit houses throughout the nineteenth century.

The records of the death of de Brébeuf and his young companion Gabriel Lalemant, all derived from unimpeachable sources, are almost unbearably vivid. Eyes were gouged out and burning coals inserted in the sockets; white-hot iron hatchets were draped

over de Brébeuf's torso so that if he leaned forward they seared
his shoulder; if he leaned backward they ate into his breast; if he
stood upright "these burning blades, touching on all sides were a
double torture"; resinous bark wrapped around his body was set
afire so that his flesh could be eaten; finally his skull was crushed
and a horde of Indians assaulted him, tearing a gaping hole in
his chest and wrenching out his bleeding heart. Lalemant was literally roasted alive from sunset until sunrise; his skull was then
crushed, and finally he was shot. The narrator in the *Relations*
states that Lalemant "had come late to this war, and gained the
victory among the first": a statement that could have been para-
phrased, "a billion times told lovelier, more dangerous, O my
chevalier."

This history — the accuracy of which was attested to by Francis Parkman — may give a new "source" to the fire that breaks
from the heart and to the embers that gash gold-vermilion. It may
also give a new meaning to "the burning ['shine'] blades" and
"the double torture" of de Brébeuf: "The plowers plowed on my
back; they made their furrows long" (Psalm 129); or as a French
translation of the time worded it: "Des laboureurs ont labouré
sur mon dos; ils y ont tiré tout au long leurs sillons." As to his
"embered" body, it did fall, and his galled chest did yield up his
gashed blood-red heart.

But as I have tried to indicate, it is not a question of a direct
"source" of Hopkins's images and language. For one reservation,
virtually any reference to the color *red* seems to have hyper-
stimulated Hopkins's imagination. But it may as well be a matter
of a common family — what Ong calls an agglomeration — of
images drawn from desultory readings, conversations, retreat sermons, and so on, to which Hopkins would have been exposed
during the whole of his Jesuit life. Thus, I am not trying to com-
pose "The Road to Windhover." Nevertheless, I repeat, the oddity
of language, the discordant tone this poem strikes among all the
other poems, cries out for some explanation. Moreover, if it is
strongly Ignatian, as all commentators have suggested, why not
Spanish imagery and language, rather than French? The use of

the latter is particularly ironic since, as Hopkins certainly knew, Ignatius's wound — with his concomitant "conversion" — was inflicted on him by *French* soldiers.

Again, one is startled how the almost-epic beginning of "The Windhover" jars with its titular subject:

> I caught this morning morning's minion, king-
> dom of daylight's dauphin...

This is the kind of imagery that should suggest something like a *chanson de geste*, or a late medieval legend, or a tale of the Hundred Years War; or it might have suggested something like what in fact does occur in "Book the Second" of Robert Southey's *Joan of Arc, an Epic Poem*, where one reads:

> ...Know thyself my soul!
> Confirm'd thy strength, thy pinions fledged for flight
> Bursting this shell and leaving next thy nest
> Soon upward soaring....

It may be noted that these rather pretentious lines are by Coleridge, later appearing as "The Destiny of Nations" (1817), for whom Hopkins had a considerably higher regard than he did for Southey. But what is more interesting is that Coleridge's last line of his contribution to Southey's poem is: "The Sun, that rose on FREEDOM, set in blood!" — not inconceivably an envisagement of the "ecstacy" opening and the "gash" closing "The Windhover."

Joan herself is described as saving a French nobleman who had been "gashed with wounds." Her mission in Southey's poem and in historical fact is to see the "dauphin" crowned; and she adamantly refused to use any other title for the future king. Moreover, she is contemned by the English leader as "this courtly minion." And when she leads her troops:

> Her foaming courser, of the guiding hand
> Impatient, smote the earth, and toss'd his mane,
> And rear'd aloft with many a froward bound,

> As tho' the Maiden's skill, and his own strength
> Proud to display. The light gale with her plumes
> Wantoned.

In Southey's self-consciously Miltonic "epic," the Maiden first overcomes the temptation to abandon her public mission for the hidden life of the cloister; next she foresees her death by fire; and, finally, she has a vision of the torments suffered by those who exercise their "tyrant power." A "Daemon" punishes them:

> Plunging his dagger in the hearts of some,
> Or probing with a poisoned lance their breasts,
> Or placing coals of fire within their wounds.

Hopkins's disdain for Southey is documented, even to the point of disagreeing with his esteemed Newman, but there is no way at present of knowing if Hopkins was familiar with Southey's youthful effort which anticipates the language and imagery of "The Windhover."

But by 1877 Joan of Arc was a European heroine transcending nationalities, from Schiller's drama to Verdi's opera. According to Jules Michelet — whose fifth volume of the *Histoire de France,* devoted to Joan, was reissued in 1853 — her death established *le droit de la conscience,* and his highly acclaimed and very popular retelling of her life was based on the Passion Narratives, a model later adopted also by Charles Péguy. Michelet went so far as to compare himself to one of the Evangelists. Régine Pernoud in the preface to her collection of original documents, *The Retrial of Joan of Arc* (Eng. trans., 1955), observed: "In 1839 that learned scholar Vallet de Viriville assessed the number of works devoted to Joan of Arc at five hundred; fifty years later the figure had increased fivefold." Part of that increase stemmed from the popularity of Joan as patroness of the French military during the Franco-Prussian War, ended in 1871, when her Catholicism was seen as a bulwark against the forces of what Hopkins himself, four years later in "The Wreck," described as the "beast of the waste wood," symbolized by the "Protestantism" of Martin Luther.

However, that Protestantism and nationalism emerged with regard to Joan much earlier than the Franco-Prussian War. I referred in chapter 1 to Walter Ong's lengthy explication (following a hint from Gardner) of "The Windhover" in the light of Shakespeare's *Henry V.* But in the context of Joan and of "The Windhover," what has received virtually no attention in Hopkins studies is the first part of *Henry VI,* attributed at least in part to Shakespeare, where the dauphin is linked directly to the maid. In act 1, scene 4, there is a bawdy reference to Joan and to the dauphin:

> Pucelle or puzzel, dolphin or dogfish,
> Your hearts I'll stamp out with my horse's heels.

I will not repeat what I have said about the unique proliferation of French imagery in "The Windhover," though one cannot but be surprised by such an unexpected outburst as "O my chevalier," coming as it does after nine almost predominantly Anglo-Saxon lines. Nothing has prepared us for this. Of course, we know in retrospect Joan astonished her followers by her riding skills, and referred to herself as *chef de guerre* (the achieve of). There was subsequently a legend that at the siege of Orleans her mount was *doté du pouvoir de voler* — "how he rung upon the rein." Similarly, there is the startling juxtaposition of the rustic act of "ploughing" with the noble deeds of knighthood, a juxtaposition explained by another historical fact widely attested to and mentioned by several "Witnesses on Her Childhood" (as Régine Pernoud calls friends and relatives): Joan "followed the plough," "went ploughing with her father"; "she went out ploughing, and took her turn guarding the cattle"; and so on.

In fact, if we take Hopkins literally, being a "chevalier" was the direct consequence of "ploughing." No wonder of it, since action flows from being — the external deeds are the epiphany of the interior spirit. And it is obvious how congenial to Hopkins's thinking would be the figure of Joan's "contemplative" life in her native village, and her "active" life as chivalrous savior of her country. Interestingly, Cummins in *The Hound and the Hawk* describes a medieval drawing of "a perch with, left and right, a dove and a hawk, and the rubric *Ecce in eadem pertica sedent accipiter et columba;* the perch is the properly balanced life" of action and contemplation. This balance is also relevant to the story of Joan as it may have "influenced" Hopkins not merely in the conjoining of knightly horsewoman and rural ploughgirl, but in that at her death her executioner reported that a dove was seen hovering over her funeral pyre:* the dovelike fleur-de-lis literally rising from the blue-bleak embers. Thus the poem that begins with the *active* image of the splendid hunting bird — the warrior maid — finds its ending in the flight of Hopkins's *contemplative* "wild wooddove, shy wings shut."

So, in conclusion however tentative, we have not only the dauphin joined to the minion, the chevalier joined to the plougher, but also by rhyme the sillion (Hopkins's chiming orthography) joined to the gold-vermilion. Since Joan of Arc's execution shocked the bystanders, the "ah my dear" might also be read as an outburst of sympathetic horror from those witnessing her death. By this reading, "gold-vermilion" could not refer to the French military standard, "the oriflamme," as Robert Boyle suggested, since this banner was in Paris, then controlled by the English, and for that reason, among others, Joan had designed her own battleflag. It is more likely that Hopkins's yellow-red simply derives from the traditional colors of the flaming "Sacred Heart of Jesus," just as the "Immaculate Heart of Mary" was depicted in shades of blue and white.

I referred earlier in this chapter to the curious cross-gendering of language in Hopkins's text and in the French translation. Regarding the latter, we noted that "windhover" is literally "la *crécerelle,*" but the French translator chose "Le *Faucon,*" and Hopkins uses male pronouns to refer to the bird, even though it is

---

*Vita Sackville-West's impressive biography of Joan concludes with further testimony of the executioner who, although adding sulfur, oil, and other fuels to the pyre, could not reduce her heart to ashes.

the female who provides the poem's central image, and who is, in fact, the *accipiter*. I do not want to weave too many strands into this cable of converging probabilities, but this gender confusion parallels what was viewed as one of Joan's most suspect traits: her cross-dressing vesture — paralleled here by the poem's cross-gendering language. The obsession on the part of her trial judges with her male clothing led to her being questioned repeatedly on the matter, and her refusal to change — even to the point of her being denied Communion — was one of the central factors in her final condemnation, and her execution on *May 30*, 1431.

Now, it would have been common knowledge to anyone like Hopkins, attending daily Mass or following the liturgical office, that in the Catholic calendar commemoration of a newly canonized saint — unless preempted by an earlier or higher-ranking feast — would usually be the day of her or his death. For examples of saints who have figured in this discussion: though canonized in 1930, Jean de Brébeuf's feast day is March 16, the date of his death in 1649. St. Margaret Mary Alacoque's feast day is October 17, the date of her death in 1690. St. Ignatius Loyola's feast day is July 31, the date of his death in 1556. Although Joan of Arc's cause for beatification and canonization, as noted earlier, was introduced during Hopkins's lifetime, she was not canonized, because of political tensions between Rome and Paris, until 1920. Nonetheless, her feast day is *May 30,* the date of her execution in 1431.

The definitive autograph of "The Windhover," representing its third recension by Hopkins and transcribed by Bridges ("after August, 1884," according to MacKenzie), has two changes introduced by Hopkins: the first is the substitution of "AND" for Bridges's ampersand, and the insertion by Hopkins, "St Bueno's. *May 30, 1877*." Hopkins did occasionally insert specific dates in poems from winter and fall of 1877, though the practice is so haphazard, one cannot discern a pattern. But of the seven poems in English MacKenzie estimates or verifies as written in the uniquely productive spring of 1877 — "As kingfishers catch fire," "Spring," "The Sea and the Skylark," "In the Valley of the

Elwy," "The Windhover," "Pied Beauty," and "The Caged Skylark" — only "The Windhover" has a specific date, May 30, even
though Hopkins had corrected all of these poems for Bridges's
final transcription. The question arises why this is the only poem
so amended.

There may be a partial answer in the fact that the poem was
originally written eight years after the most illustrious liberal
prelate in France, Félix Dupanloup, esteemed ally of Newman,
had initiated the proceedings ultimately leading to the canonization of Joan of Arc. Even more significant is the additional
fact that Hopkins remembered this particular date seven years
after he had written "The Windhover." Thus the most likely answer is that this date had some special meaning for him. While I
admit this is speculative, all the indications in this entire discussion of dates converge on the figure of Joan of Arc. Concerning
the dating, Norman White speaks for everyone knowledgeable
about Hopkins's sense of "divine synchronism": "The mystical
value of anniversaries was an aspect of Catholicism which Hopkins, even before his conversion, found congenial. There is a
naivety *in his welcoming of anniversaries and numerical coinci-
dences as inscapes of divine origin,* which displayed to mankind
the connectedness of apparently haphazard aspects of experience"
(emphasis added).

Lastly, if my broad hypothesis that the figure of Joan hovers
over the entire poem has validity, then one has a response to the
carping criticism, first launched by Winters, that the poem is in effect schizoid because the "unexplained ecstasy which hangs over
the octet" is *not* explained in the sestet. But it is explained in
terms of Francophonic language tying together the two parts of
the sonnet; it is explained in terms of imagery, "dauphin," "minion," "chevalier," "sillion." Finally, it is explained in terms of
theme: the balance of the bird's flight parallels that of Joan's life;
the "achieve" of the bird is that of Joan as *chef*; the lowly and
the lofty flight of the bird parallels the lowly and the lofty life
of the maiden; and so on with the other junctures I have pointed
out above.

Walter Ong follows John Glavin in comparing "Lycidas" with "The Wreck" to "show that Hopkins had 'Lycidas' consciously *or unconsciously* in mind when he wrote the poem" (emphasis added). I don't find the relationship alleged of the two poems convincing, but I would embrace the language — though repeating my doubts about psychological surmisals — and thus feel free to say that Hopkins had Joan "consciously or unconsciously in mind" when writing "The Windhover."

Thus, I find it difficult to doubt that somehow — though perhaps not precisely as I have delineated it — her image along with that of the North American Jesuit martyrs is stamped on Hopkins's sonnet.

VII: *Dialectical Synthesis*

"Be in at the End"

It was to Bridges that Hopkins wrote (October 22, 1879): "I think then no one can admire beauty of the body more than I do.... Then comes the beauty of the mind, such as genius.... And more beautiful than the beauty of the mind is beauty of character." He then went on to explain this in terms of what "we Aristotelian Catholics say," that is, in terms of conventional hylomorphism ("the soul is the form of the body"), not as noted in the previous chapter, in terms of Scotist *haecceitas*. Shortly after, in a sermon on the humanity of Jesus, he declared: "Now in the third place, far higher than beauty of the body, higher than genius and wisdom the beauty of the mind, comes the beauty of his character."

Four year later, explaining the nature of beauty to Coventry Patmore (September 24, 1883), again, rather than invoking Scotus, Hopkins introduces what he describes as "an old but a very apposite image not easily improved":

> It is certain that in nature outward beauty is the proof of inward beauty. Fineness, proportion, of feature comes from a moulding force which succeeds in asserting itself over the resistance of cumbersome or restraining matter.... The moulding force, the life, is the form in the philosophic sense, and in man this is the soul. But because its available activity is limited the matter it has to struggle with may be too much for it and the wax is either too cold and doughy (so to speak) and will not take or is too hot and boiling blots out the stamp of the seal—I speak under an old..., etc.

The image is indeed old and apposite, being a favorite of Aristotle in *De Anima*.

But what, then, has happened to Scotus? As I suggested earlier, he survives in the poems as an inspiration, and in Hopkins's life as an air, an ethos; he is the icon of the singular, the unique, the individual. In some of Hopkins's sketchy theological speculations, as we have seen, Scotus's writings do play an active, even a controlling, role. But in the poems, his function is largely symbolic. In fact, the poems can be read, with no loss whatsoever, in the light of the same Aristotelian/Thomist tradition that Hopkins invoked in his letters to Bridges and Patmore — or even in the light of the Hegelian dialectic, which Hopkins had condemned to Bridges and others.

With or without Scotus the structure of the poems is triadic: soul and body, though distinct, are co-principles of one substance just as the wax and the seal of the stamp though distinct constitute one substance. Soul is correlative to body and exists only in the determination and realization of body. Thus one can reread "The Lantern out of Doors":

> Men go by me, whom either beauty bright
> In mould or mind or what not else makes rare...

The "what not else" need not be *haecceitas* — in fact the introduction of the latter would violate the axiom of another Franciscan philosopher that entities should not be multiplied without necessity.

Because the *je ne sais quoi* here is the substantial union of "mould" and "mind," they are the co-principles of the "beauty bright" that constitutes "personness." And so important is this complementarity that "mind" separated from "mould" is an incomplete entity. "Mould" then is not a mere negation or privation; it has its own "eros," its own positive tendency toward being determined by "mind." Even in what is Hopkins's most elaborate and intense meditation on the uniqueness of the self, his retreat notes on the Foundation (August 20, 1880), where he makes the memorable statement: "Nothing else in nature comes near this unspeakable stress of pitch, distinctiveness, and selving, this selfbeing of my own" — even in this detailed reflection, Scotus is present merely as inspiration and "aura." And indeed the entire meditation, concluding to a subtle argument for the existence of a Creator, can only make sense if read in light of Aquinas on the creature's participation in the "light of the divine Countenance" signed on the human mind (*signatum est lumen*) as the individual *intellectus agens* which Hopkins mistakenly identified with the universal agent intellect of those whom he refers to as "Averrhoists" (*sic*). Clearly we are here expanding the horizons of Aristotle, as Aristotle expanded those of Plato. From a radical dualism in which the physical world is "but a spume" that mimes the ideal world, to a moderate dualism in which matter is a co-principle, however subordinate, with form, we are moving in the direction of complementarity. For critical analysis of the poems the following traditional polarizations may be treated as analogous, not homologous, with one another: potency/actuality, essence/existence, accident/substance, matter/form, body/soul, *ratio/intellectus,* particle/wave, and, yes, also Hopkins's diatonic/chromatic.

Night/Light

These co-principles of a higher entity are evident in several poems that I want now to examine. I have already referred to the relationship between "The Windhover" and "The Starlight Night," and have rejected as academic overreaching the notion that the repetition of "look" is connected to auctioneering. This is to fail to enter into the spirit of this *puer aeternus* who is simply overwhelmed by the light of the stars; not by past evocative memories, as with Wordsworth, but by present instantaneous images. The poem is not set in the past tense, is not called "The Starlit Night." Moreover, the images for this *anima candida* are from a child's experience. We have the fairy-tale-like: fire-folk, who are *sitting* (not suspended) in the air; the stars are elves-eyes, and are living gold, are a May-mess; and finally, they are every child's delight:

"flake-doves sent floating forth at a farmyard scare." How could one not be reminded of John Whiteside's daughter, harrying the "lazy geese, like a snow cloud / Dripping their snow on the green grass"? — (not only buy and bid, but Ransom as well).

In the octave alone, there are seven lines on the beauty and wonder of the sight, with no adult, sermonic allusions to the "heavens telling forth the glory of God." Then, almost as an afterthought, one line of "grown-up" self-consciousness, self-reflection, and acquisitiveness ("all a purchase"), followed by another such line at the *volta* ("buy then"); and five more lines of ecstatic admiration ("look" thrice repeated), then ending with the *communio* of, "Christ and his mother and all his hallows."

> Look at the stars! look, look up at the skies!
>   O look at all the fire-folk sitting in the air!
>   The bright boroughs, the circle-citadels there!
> Down in dim woods the diamond delves! the elves'-
>   eyes!
> The grey lawns cold where gold, where quickgold lies!
>   Wind-beat whitebeam! airy abeles set on a flare!
>   Flake-doves sent floating forth at a farmyard
>   scare! —
> Ah well! it is all a purchase, all is a prize.
>
> Buy then! bid then! — What? — Prayer, patience, alms,
>   vows.
> Look, look: a May-mess, like on orchard boughs!
>   Look! March-bloom, like on mealed-with-yellow
>   sallows!
> These are indeed the barn; withindoors house
> The shocks. This piece-bright paling shuts the spouse
>   Christ home, Christ and his mother and all his
>   hallows.

The sestet contains two progressively more remarkable subtle touches. First, the answer to Hopkins's question about what to bid is both original *and* traditional. Concerning the latter, there is the catechism formula: acts related to God and acts related to one's neighbor. But the originality is in the interfusing of both of these "objects." The structure is chiastic because God is in our neighbor and our neighbor — particularly emphasized in the last tercet — is in God:

prayer (to God)	patience (to neighbor)
alms (to neighbor)	vows (to God)

Second, there is the curious seasonal displacement, with May preceding March, intensified by the fact that the underside of willow leaves certainly becomes gold-flecked well before trees blossom. Nor can this displacement be attributed to the demands of the rhyme scheme because, as noted earlier, we know such artifice never controls Hopkins's choice of words, and because he is blissfully inconsistent in the patterning of his sestets. Of course, one might make the case that the speaker is so excited by the beauty of the night sky that he simply overlooks the normal sequence of the months. But this could hardly be true to the practice of so meticulous a craftsman, and so ceaseless a reviser, as Hopkins. The explanation can be only that just as the climax is outside the realm of conventional time (heaven and the heavens "[shut] the spouse / Christ home"), so too is the childlike vision transtemporal. Moreover, the tradition has it that in "paradise" sequential time ceases. We are no longer in the world of organized and regimented experience (children "walking two and two"; "metres meet"), but in the world of true innocence (Blake in his own way being also an *anima candida*), that is, in the world of the mystic's *nunc stans.**

---

*The poetic parallel is Keats's blending of the seasons in the fifth stanza of "Ode to a Nightingale," where he "guesses" the transtemporal bliss that would follow the acceptance of death when all seasons are one: mid-May, summer eves, flowers covered up in the leaves of fall; similarly with the fusion of the senses: taste (sweet), sight (white hawthorn), hear (murmurous haunt). The religious parallel would be Newman's attempt to make eternal punishment "less terrible" to the mind and imagination by showing that eternity is not time extended, but an ever-present nowness with no temporal succession, and hence no anticipation and no recollection. He develops this theme in *A Grammar of Assent* (chapter 10, nos. 2 and 3); cf. also *Sermons on Subjects of the Day* (London, 1834), 76; and *Discourses to Mixed Congregations* (London, 1849), 36ff.

The whole of "The Starlight Night" is modeled on the Lord's Prayer, where after five descriptive laudations (or "Thou" petitions) the speaker introduces the self-reflective "we" petitions — where the parallel structure imitates the Psalms — relating to bread, debts, and deliverance. The bridge between "Thou" and "we" is the phrase "in heaven and on earth," in *that* order in both the Greek and Latin, as Hopkins would have read or recited the prayer; not, as in most vernaculars, "on earth as it is in heaven."

The prayer then turns away from "earthly" self-concerns and back to the external and eternal, concluding with the "Thou" *altitudo,* from the *Didache:* "for Thine is the kingdom, and the power, and the glory . . . " — a doxology which in the Byzantine rite parallels the poem even more closely by adding the words: "Father, Son and Holy Ghost, now and forever, and world without end." Thus the structure of the poem "modeled" on the prayer is from the infinite (Thou) to the finite (we), and then again back out to the infinite. It is a structure depicted in the *carmen figuratum of* "Easter Wings," and described — as we have seen over and over — in the classic journey motif: *ingressus, progressus, regressus.* Moreover, here the *regressus* echoes St. Paul: "You are no longer strangers and foreigners, but fellow citizens with the saints and members of the household ['withindoors house'] of God" (Ephesians 2:19). This is the epistle read on St. Matthias Day, February 24, the date of Hopkins's composition of the poem.

But it is the hylomorphic complementarity engendering the transcending hypostasis that is of primary interest now, as in:

Down in dim woods/the diamond delves/the elves'-eyes

Here the material moulding of dim woods co-responds with diamond delves, and engenders the living "beauty bright" of elves' eyes. Similarly the next line, running in tandem:

The grey-lawns cold/where gold/where quickgold lies

Thus we have these triads:

dim woods	grey lawns
diamond	gold
elves'-eyes	quickgold

In each case, the density of matter (dim, grey), informed by the shimmering form (diamond, gold), engenders the substantial individuated being in all its unique selfness. Elves are preternaturally alive, and "quick" is a synonym for "life," as in "the quick and the dead." And it may also be noted that quickgold plays back to quicksilver, the "preternatural" hermetic medium.

Similarly with the final tercet:

> These are indeed the barn; withindoors house
> The shocks. This piece-bright paling shuts the spouse
> Christ home...

>> barn
>> shocks
>> Christ

But this is not only the concluding tercet; it is the climactic one as well. Here the enveloping barn, the mould or container, is electrified (shocks = shook foil) by the grandeur of God manifest now in the *super*natural living presence of Christ.

I have already stressed the basic triadic structure in "The Lantern out of Doors": "...mould or mind or what not else makes rare." And I have pointed out that the "what not else" represents uncertainty on the poet's part about what to call this synthesized entity: *haecceitas, hypostasis,* substantial unit...? "Now no matter..., the name," it is the ubiquity of the structure that is important. Thus it appears in "Spring and Fall":

mouth/mind	expressed
heart	heard
ghost	guessed

Or, again, in "The Handsome Heart":

> handsome face
> heart mannerly
> hallowing grace

And, finally, in "Henry Purcell":

> sweet notes
> mood/meaning
> forgèd feature

•

THE LANTERN OUT OF DOORS

Sometimes a lantern moves along the night,
  That interests our eyes. And who goes there?
  I think; where from and bound, I wonder, where,
With, all down darkness wide, his wading light?

Men go by me, whom either beauty bright
  In mould or mind or what not else makes rare:
  They rain against our much-thick and marsh air
Rich beams, till death or distance buys them quite.

Death or distance soon consumes them: wind
  What most I may eye after, be in at the end
I cannot, and out of sight is out of mind.

Christ minds: Christ's interest, what to avow or amend
  There, eyes them, heart wants, care haunts, foot
      follows kind,
  Their ransom, their rescue, and first, fast, last friend.

I parse and paraphrase as follows.

First, we are in the realm of transcendent freedom, of the unpredictability of spirit: "*Sometimes* a lantern moves along the
night, / That interests our *eyes.* [Initially the adventitious sense experience, the purely visual; then the conceptual recollection.] And
who goes there? / I *think* ... [And finally, the unknown]; where
from and bound, I *wonder,* where, / With, all down darkness

[cf. 'Comus,' 251–52] wide, his wading light? [So, again, we have the 'material' visible, then the 'formal' thoughtful, and finally the mysterious unnamed composite about which we are uncertain and wondering]."

Second, the "men" carrying their lanterns "rain against our much-thick and marsh air [and, again, the material component is cast in pejorative terms, as in the references in 'The Starlight Night': 'dim woods,' 'grey lawns' — but here defined as 'thick' and 'malarial'] / Rich beams, till death or distance buys them quite. / Death or distance soon consumes [meaning, *not* 'devours,' but 'consummates']."

Third, the *thick* marsh air is conjoined to its complement, "rich beams," which again engender the unnamed and unknown. However, we do know that "God is light," which "interests" the *eye*; God being the "bright essence," the inter-*esse* that penetrates our material density by the "bright effluence" of its very be-am-ness. And, as in "The Starlight Night," we have both a conclusion and a climax in the final tercet — which I shall analyze shortly.

But in the penultimate tercet we have the most wondrously concise depiction in the entire literature of the stumbling, tortuous convolutions of the viator's *regressus* — far eclipsing Donne's "Hymne to God my God, in my sicknesse," Vaughan's "Retreate," or Bishop King's "Exequy": "...wind, / What most I may eye after, be in at the end / I cannot..." And since this is a difficult journey back "home," the line is filled with inversions, with stumbling hurdles demanding a pause on the part of the reader ("I may eye"), with reversals ("be in at the end"), and with recognizable dejecting blockage ("I cannot").

Thus we return to the initial conclusion of the triad: "and out of sight is out of mind." But as in the first stanza we went from the material visible to the spiritual conceptual: "eyes"/"think," here we have sure knowledge, not the final "wonderment" of the first stanza. Moreover, this knowledge is confirmed by taking the form of a universally recognized "old *saw*": out of sight is out of mind. So the stanza ends on a note of near-despairing pessimism. But we *are* in the realm of total freedom, of the totally unpredictable; in short, the realm of grace. And therefore, surprisingly, the next stanza begins with no conjunction or connective with the terminal and seemingly terminating: out of sight is out of mind.

"Christ minds," we are told as we leap from natural wisdom (*saw* = sage) to supernatural insight, and to the realization that human existence is an *itinerarium mentis in Deum*. This is the climax prepared for by the two previous triads:

> sight   thick air
> thought   rich beams
> wonder   death *or* distance

So the coda to this miniature interweaving symphonic fugue is:

> . . . Christ's interest, what to avow or amend
> There, eyes them, heart wants, care haunts, foot follows
>   kind,
> Their ransom, their rescue, and first, fast, last friend.

But however rich the be-am-ness of lost temporal friends, it is as poverty compared to the wealth stored in heaven by the supernatural inter-*esse* of Christ who has conquered death. And though Death "buys them *quite*," the infinite *esse* of Christ ransoms them back. Thus Christ is the one Friend with whom we earthly *viatores* can journey from beginning ("first") through the "middle passage" where we are joined ("fast") to him, and up to the end ("last") of the way. And though Death "buys them," Christ "eyes them" — and keeps them ever in sight. Moreover, he not only sees their "mould" but also tends to their interior needs ("care haunts"), because he is akin ("kind") to them.

Now, Hopkins had joined himself to Newman and Keble as *poets* of the same school. The three may also be joined together as *religious* believers by this poem. In the *Apologia* after describing his first meeting with Keble, Newman wrote: "Mr. Keble used to quote the words of the Psalm: 'I will guide thee with mine *eye*.' This is the very difference, he used to say, between slaves and friends or children. Friends do not ask for literal commands; but from their knowledge of the speaker, they understand his half-words." Newman went on to observe that in one of Keble's poems there is a reference to the "Eye of God's word."

Whether those texts influenced Hopkins may be debatable, but it seems likely that "The Lantern..." owes much to Luke 24, where Jesus explains ("what to avow or amend") the scripture to two disciples whom he describes as "slow of heart." But afterwards, the two disciples' "heart wants" are so satisfied they persuade Jesus to stay with them at Emmaus. *The New American Bible* translates the pertinent passage as follows: "By now they were near the village to which they were going, and *he acted as if he were going farther.* But they pressed him: 'Stay with us. It is nearly evening — the day is practically over.' So he went in to stay with them." Being "kind" he responds to their plea, and stays with them "at the end." Moreover, his "rich beams" prevent the darkness from threatening them, since he has already redeemed ("their ransom, their rescue") them by his death in Jerusalem. Finally, his kinship and friendship with them at the end of daylight are evident in his breaking of the bread (companions) so that as he "eyes them," "their *eyes* were opened." Later the disciples describe how his "heart wants" left their hearts "burning inside" them at hearing his words.

Spring/Springs

One of the earliest commentaries (1970), that of Paul Mariani, notes of "Spring" that it "does not appear to have the complex underthought" of two other poems, which I have already examined, "God's Grandeur" and "The Starlight Night." Yet by my reading it is the paradigmatic Hopkinsian poem precisely because sustaining its deceptively simple "beautiful, vital recreation of the joys of spring" (Mariani) is a harmonious structural pattern and a range of imagery eclipsing any sonnet previously considered here, not excluding "The Windhover."

But since *one* of the central structural patterns in "Spring" is the parenthetic insertion — which we have encountered earlier in the discussion of "Pied Beauty" — I want to preface these remarks with a brief treatment of such ejaculations in "In the Valley of the Elwy." I do this to emphasize their importance as keys to understanding both poems. First, "In the Valley...":

> I remember a house where all were good
>> To me, *God knows,* deserving no such thing:
>> Comforting smell breathed at very entering,
> Fetched fresh, *as I suppose,* off some sweet wood.

(*Parenthetically,* one may note the enjambement in the first line where "good" overflows — illustrating once more the axiom *bonum est diffusivum sui.*)

This first quatrain's parentheses express, again, the kenotic descent from the infinite to the finite; again, a descent from *in caelo* to *in terra.* But also a descent from absolute certitude ("God knows") to contingent tentativeness ("I suppose"). This central focus is maintained in the next quatrain:

> That cordial air made those kind people a hood
>> All over, as a bevy of eggs the mothering wing
>> Will, or mild nights the new morsels of Spring:
> Why, it seemed *of course;* seemed *of right* it should.

The realm of the "of course" is the natural, entropic, flowing realm of time. The realm of the "of right" is the supernatural realm of eternal and divine decree. The chiastic structure (absolute-contingent/contingent-absolute) encoded in the complete octave betokens therefore a "confluence" between these symbolic extremes: God knows–I suppose / of course–of right.

The sestet is devoted to the nature of this confluence and to its fuller implications:

> Lovely the woods, waters, meadows, combes, vales,
> All the air things wear that build this world of Wales;
>> Only the inmate does not correspond:

> God, lover of souls, swaying considerate scales,
> Complete thy creature dear O where it fails,
>> Being mighty a master, being a father and fond.

In the first tercet the unsullied physical beauty of the Welsh coun-
tryside is equated with the divine totality, and fallen humanity is
equated with the fractious and fragmented — these latter terms
are cognate and correlative of the contingent finite. Lines 9 and
10 are, respectively, corpuscular and cymatic (or hylo/morphic),
but in this poem matter and spirit explicitly do not co-respond.
The "creature" fails because only the supernatural can fuse the
divided image, can truly heal the schism between appearance and
reality, body and soul, matter and form. This means that in the
present, post-Edenic condition to be an authentic human being,
to be a true *imago Dei*, requires "a point of contact" for divine
intervention. This is what Karl Rahner calls the "supernatural
existential," the claim that the creature has on the Creator to
be "justified," to be made holy and whole — or in Hopkins's
language, to be "completed."

Moreover, only a principle of perfect mediation can bridge the
gap between creature and Creator, infinite and finite, a principle
which Hopkins would have defined as "incarnation." By incarnation the natural is harmonized with the supernatural; it is "in
balance" with it in the starry "scales." Or, in the precise terms
of the concluding tercet, the Old Testament God of the natural order, the mighty master who draws the creature by all the
cords of Adam, is in balance with the New Testament Father,
after whom all paternity in heaven and earth is named, and who
is loving and fond. The very pattern of the coda expresses, again,
the axiom of Scholastic theology: not chronologically but onto-
logically, "grace presupposes nature," as the father presupposes
the master, as New Testament presupposes Old Testament.

Returning now to "Spring," I will begin with the parenthetic
insertions, and then move on to the more complicated pattern.
Concerning the former, what is unusual is that they appear to be
arbitrary, completely unintegrated with the rest of the poem, and,
as is not unusual with what is on the surface inexplicable, they
have generally been misunderstood or written-off as ambiguous
flaws. But apart from their deeper function as structures of the
primordial sigh (Romans 8, again) concealed at the heart of real-

ity, it is this very arbitrariness that now underlines their purpose. In the structural sense their unpredictability serves to bring out most sharply the sheer gratuity of this eruption of the infinite through the finite:

> Nothing is so beautiful as spring —
>   When weeds, in wheels, shoot long and lovely and
>   lush;
>   Thrush's eggs look little low heavens, and thrush
> Through the echoing timber does so rinse and wring
> The ear, it strikes like lightnings to hear him sing;
>   The glassy peartree leaves and blooms, they brush
>   The descending blue; that blue is all in a rush
> With richness; the racing lambs too have fair their fling.
>
> What is all this juice and all this joy?
>   A strain of the earth's sweet being in the beginning
> In Eden garden. — Have, get before it cloy,
>
>   Before it cloud, *Christ, lord,* and sour with sinning,
> Innocent mind and Mayday in girl and boy,
>   Most, O *maid's child*, thy choice and worthy the
>   winning.

The parenthetic insertions are what Herbert, Vaughan, and their tradition called "spiritual ejaculations," spontaneous prayers or invocations that were to punctuate all the activities of Christian life and thus spiritualize the temporal — just as the strain of Eden Garden punctuates the spring scene. "Strain" is cognate of "structure" and here has the dual sense of a "trace" and of a musical melody. In this latter sense, Hopkins is anticipating a successor poet: this musical "air" (*aria* = *spiritus*) is a strain of earth's "being," is indeed the structure of that Being. *So,* one has *the* final emendation: not, the evangelist's "in the beginning was the Word," nor the Faustian "in the beginning was the Deed," nor the musicologist's (Schenker's) "in the beginning was the contents," but the poet's (Rilke's) "in the beginning was the Song" — or more melodically: *"Gesang ist Dasein."*

But from a more conventional critical perspective, however arbitrary appear to be those parenthetic expressions I underlined above, they may still be integrated into the overall organization of "Spring" — that organization being another variation on the kenotic pattern in several poems considered earlier. The octave moves from an *absolute* statement about spring — "*nothing* is *so* beautiful" — to the description of the playful, utterly contingent newborn lambs; while the sestet moves from the indeterminate past to the particular present — from earth's being in the beginning to Mayday in girl and boy. The first parenthetic outburst calls upon the *Kyrios Christos* (on which W. Bousset wrote the classic study), the pantocrator and absolute ruler of the universe, and thus relates directly to the absoluteness and undefinability at the beginning of octave and sestet. The second outburst, "O maid's child," calls upon the newborn Jesus who is also the *agnus Dei* and, as such, the mediating link (racing lambs) that binds together the closing line of each of the two parts of the whole poem. I shall return to these two invocations shortly.

As with so many of Hopkins's sonnets — and with the classic sonnet in general — we begin in the octave with the visible, factual phenomenon, and then move after the *volta* to the self-reflective noumenal mystery: "What is all this juice and all this joy?" Concerning this octave, it should be noted that it satisfies Hopkins's definition of "mortal" beauty ("mortal" meaning more than merely bodily). "The O-seal-that-*so* feature" evokes as well Aristotle's co-principles of seal and wax. But both "O" and "*so*" suggest perfection and finality, suggest the Anselmian "than which nothing greater can be conceived." How seal it? *So.* "Thou art *so* truth," says Donne as he deifies his beloved. And Crashaw in the "Hymn of the Nativity," when the fitting resting place for the "maid's child" has been found, declares: "no way but *so.*" Nothing more can be said. For in the theological tradition God is the self-answering question. But Hopkins's phrase "O so" conveys more than divine finality and absolutehood; it is an ecstatic utterance which harks back to the ancient symbol of perfection, two spheres linked by the snakelike arabesque: OSO, akin to the *T'ai-chi tu.* But this OSO is beautiful before it is "clouded" and "soured," before it is "seared" and "smeared." Post-Edenic humanity transforms that enthusiastic harmonious OSO into the tortured and fractured image Dante saw in the countenance of everyman: OMO who dwells in the "bent world."

So, again, it is nature that best figures forth the divine perfection of circularity ("weeds in wheels") and that best reflects *in terra,* "Abba" who is *in caelis* ("thrush's eggs look little low heavens"). That last image evokes the Holy Ghost "brooding," as the everyday dawn "springs." And just as the "brooding" plays back to the "ooze of oil," so here the thrush's song, like that in "The Sea and the Skylark," complementarily plays back to "the shining from shook foil" ("it strikes like lightnings"). Similarly, the creative superabundance of absolute Being, the ultimate Good whose nature is *diffusivum sui,* is expressed by the overflowing enjambement describing [the] thrush and its song.

There is no need to explain the omission of the bracketed article in the preceding sentence by introducing the notion of a regional British dialect here. I have already pointed out this omission as an expression of the *anima naturaliter candida,* of the childlike vision of the poet. And in this Hopkins is paralleled only by the Blake of the "Innocence" songs and by Keats — even as here the "echoing timber" parallels "the ecchoing green" and "the melodious plot," all as sign of the remarriage of animate and inanimate creation.

This remarriage is emphasized by the play on "echoing timbre," the latter cognate of tympanum, timbrel, tambourine; and more precisely, cognate of the verb "tabour" in the fragment designated "Ashboughs" where the boughs of the tree "touch heaven, tabour on it" — even as the boughs of the peartree in "Spring" "brush the descending blue," that is, both "rub up" against the sky *and* "paint" it more richly.

But the ancestral passage is, of course, from the "Intimations Ode," which Hopkins professed to admire:

> Then sing, ye Birds, sing, sing a joyous song!
> And let the young Lambs bound
> As to the tabor's sound!

So the echoing "timbre" prepares us for the conclusion of the octave: "the racing lambs too have fair their fling." Indeed, we have the echoes themselves in the successive chiming of "rush," "rich," "race." We also have the whole octave expressing the circularity the poem celebrates. It begins with a brief flat, factual statement (no Wordsworthian exclamations here) of a natural phenomenon: "Nothing is so beautiful as Spring"; and it ends in precisely the same fashion: "the racing lambs too have fair their fling."

But there are two more themes to be emphasized in this richest of octaves. If it is of Eden Garden that all poets write, and if the imagination may be compared to Adam's dream, then as we have seen all divisions, all schisms and schizophrenias, all sectioning-off and sexual separations are virtually dissolved, including as well such postlapsarian polarizations as creature/ creator, inanimate/animate, earth/ heaven, body/soul, accident/ substance, essence/existence, having/being, and so on.

All divisions and separations dissolve when creation returns to the Edenic state, when foot feels being unshod, when the world-wielding hills themselves fling the innocent creature into the arms of the celestial bridegroom. In a journal entry (April 16, 1871) Hopkins describes the newborn lambs: "They toss and toss; it is as if it were the earth that flung them, not themselves." But, of course, it is both: the heart half-hurls earth from under itself, and the earth reciprocates in this consummation of the union of creature and Creator.

Furthermore, even as "the self selves," so also "Spring springs," and "What I *do is* me." Again *doing,* the objective, external "mould," is the co-principle of *being,* of the subjective, interior "mind" — which two conjoined are the mysterious "what not else" that constitutes "my" inscape: What *I* do is *me.* My subjective I-ness and my objective me-ness are paradoxically joined by my objective "doing" and my subjective "being." So, now, one amends to "What I *do is* me." "Doing" and "being" are one, exterior and interior are one, verb and subject are one; and thus when the poet says, "the glassy peartree leaves and blooms," he is again affirming this primordial unity: that the leaves (substantive) leaf (active verb), and the blooms (substantive) bloom (active verb). So, just as the "self selves," the leaves leaf, and the blooms bloom. What they *do* is what they *are*.

The second theme in the octave, relating back to the omission of the specifying article "the" in reference to [the] thrush, illustrates, again, the childlike vision of the poem. Thrush, we are told, "does *so* rinse and wring the ear." But precisely how it does "so" is left indeterminate. "Rinse" indicates washing in water, and given the other images of liquidity ("lush" and subsequently, "juice") conjoined to those of "lightnings," suggests the *photismos,* the illuminating, baptismal cleansing referred to earlier.

But I am struck by the "rinsing" of the ear, a child's experience, and the "wringing" of the ear — a verb which certainly plays off "ringing" ears. But a ringing and a wringing in and of the ears are dissonant experiences, whereas this is clearly ecstatic. It is the ecstasy of a child discovering its own world (remember: [*the*] thrush does), and discovering the whorls and swirls of its own auricular canal. If the poem echoes the "Intimations Ode," it also echoes a poem examined earlier, "The Kind Betrothal," where are also foreshadowed the themes of song, "tabor," and sheep:

> Elected Silence, sing to me
> And beat upon my *whorlèd* ear,
> Pipe me to pastures still and be
> The music that I care to hear.

(For parallel, consider another *anima naturaliter candida,* not a Jesuit priest but a medical doctor, William Carlos Williams, writing in "Smell" [the smell smells] of his own nose: "Oh strong ridged and deeply hollowed / nose of mine!... boney nose....") But "rinse and wring" do pertain to washing in water, and since "faith comes from hearing," we are now more open to the divine "lightnings" which, in the next stanza, are identical with "this juice." And this identicalness returns the reader to the original complementarity of "spark" and "soup."

Lastly, in "Spring" there is also the complementarity of the two parenthetic insertions which opened this discussion. I do not want to suggest that Hopkins was composing either a *summa theologica* or a *summa sociologica,* but such is the ubiquitousness of these structural formats that they must be recognized as undergirding many of our models (Ong's "unconsciously in mind") for comprehending the religious as well as the social order. For Bousset, to whom I have already referred, the *Kyrios Christos* is the theocratic deity (Hopkins's "Christ, lord") with affinities to Pauline doctrine who displaced the eschatological "Son of Man" (Hopkins's "maid's child") with affinities to Johannine doctrine: the institutional God thus displaced the God of the people. The broad lines of this thesis seem to me accurately drawn, though it has been contested by the Catholic L. Cerfaux and the Protestant O. Cullmann. But what Hopkins may be said to be doing in this little poem through its structure is fusing those two religious traditions. By further extension, and now in the language of Max Weber and Ernst Troeltsch, the structure of Hopkins's poem may thus also be said to represent a synthesis of *Gesellschaft* and *Gemeinschaft* and of church and sect.

Thus the "complex underthought," which Mariani found somewhat lacking in the poem, is not only abundantly present, but the poem represents that complementarity of traditional religious, esthetic, social, and cultural themes which is the titular subject of this book, and which is unparalleled in any other sonnets of that *annus mirabilis,* 1877. Finally, because the poem transcends merely personal experience in its origins and in its application — unlike "The Windhover" — and expands outward to a universal horizon, it may be Hopkins's most Catholic and catholic sonnet.

Free Falls

Before ending this sequence with Hopkins's autumnal poem, "Hurrahing in Harvest," I want to look briefly at the only poem from this period to which I have made no prior reference, "The Caged Skylark." The brevity results from the fact that this is Hopkins's most conventional sonnet — a judgment strengthened by the copious classical "metaphors of the limitations imposed by body on soul" in MacKenzie's 1992 edition: Hebrew Bible, much Plato, echoed by Cicero, Macrobius, Shakespeare, John Webster, Francis Quarles, St. Ignatius, et al., followed by various modern commentators, some pursuing but not attaining novel interpretations of this traditional topos.

Written roughly two months after "The Windhover," the poem transforms the falcon into a "skylark" with no gale to dare, no big wind to rebuff:

> As a dare-gale skylark scanted in a dull cage,
>   Man's mounting spirit in his bone-house, mean house
>   dwells —
>   That bird beyond the remembering his free fells;
> This in drudgery, day-labouring-out life's age.
>
> Though aloft on turf or perch or poor low stage
>   Both sing sometimes the sweetest, sweetest spells,
>   Yet both droop deadly sometimes in their cells
> Or wring their barriers in bursts of fear or rage.
>
> Not that the sweet-fowl, song-fowl, needs no rest —
> Why, hear him, hear him babble and drop down to his
>   nest,
>   But his own nest, wild nest, no prison.
>
> Man's spirit will be flesh-bound, when found at best,
> But uncumbered: meadow-down is not distressed
>   For a rainbow footing it nor he for his bones risen.

But unlike all commentaries I have read, the octave should *not* be interpreted as anything other than the kind of factual phenomenological observation that opened, for example, "Spring." Certainly this is not a prelude to the terrible sonnets, or even a poem of frustration — save inasmuch as it is an "empiric" objective assessment of the nature of human existence. And if it is Platonic, it is a highly Christianized and — I would emphasize — Wordsworthian Platonism: bone-house is a nonpejorative kenning, and "mean house" is not to be equated, say, with the youthful Milton's "darksome house of mortal clay." Rather it is the "meanwhile," the intermediate condition between *ingressus* and *regressus.*

What we certainly do not have here is the bitterness of "The Shepherd's Brow" of twelve years later:

> But man — we, scaffold of score brittle bones;
> . . . .
> He! Hand to mouth he lives, and voids with shame...

Moreover, there is a curious absence in "The Caged Skylark" of the anticipated parallelism in lines 3 and 4: "That" bird has no memory of freedom; and one would certainly expect, "This" man is also "beyond the remembering." But this is a re-ligious poet, a poet by free vocation committed to re-membering, and thus the "day-labouring-out life's age" anticipates the "glorious day" Alphonsus Rodriguez shared with more famous martyred Jesuits. Moreover, the Miltonic allusion ("day-labouring") is more than merely echoic; both sonnets begin with an air of "murmuring" against necessity, and both end with their authors' embracing their destiny: in Milton's case the "mild yoke"; in Hopkins's, the "bound flesh."

The octave glosses the *"natural* supernaturalism" of the "Intimations Ode," the sestet, the "natural *supernaturalism"* of Hopkins's religious vision. The skylark is *beyond* remembering his free fells and falls, but man experiences his "mounting" aspirations, even though in the natural order "a dull dough sours" the "selfyeast of spirit" ("I wake and feel"). And even though man is destined to "drudgery," it is this "dragging" (cognate of "drudgery") that makes the plough down sillion shine. With "newly-learned art" both "frame their song" on their poor low "humorous stage" down to "palsied age." But it is their *natural* fate that these brief phases of joy, these spiels of sweetness, are precisely "spells," merely caducous delusions among the "deadly droopings" of their "earthly freight."

The "turn" of the sonnet corresponds to section IX of the "Intimations Ode." But where Wordsworth falls back on self-generated and self-willed synthetic exclamations of past memory ("O joy! that in our embers / Is something that doth live, / That nature yet remembers / What was so fugitive!"), Hopkins looks to the future, to the eschatological eternal "rest" with the "God, who is our home." And both bird and man must return to the "heaven-haven" "that lies about us in our infancy." As noted, *infans* means nonspeaking, and *a fortiori* nonsinging, and therefore both bird and man *"babble"* as they realize with St. Paul that "we have not here a lasting city," but look to our "own nest, wild nest, no prison."

Man will no longer dwell in the "mean house" of this intermediate spell, but when he returns (*regressus*) to his highest and "best" state, his intermediate dwelling place will also be transfigured ("I saw a new heaven and a new earth" [Revelation 21:l]) as flesh is spirit and spirit is flesh. And as with the use of the aphorism, "out of sight is out of mind," so here too the poet clinches his argument by an empiric truism: the rainbow *beautifies,* not burdens, the field that it touches. The image is particularly apposite both because most paintings of the Transfiguration of Jesus show him hovering over Mount Tabor (on which Hopkins has a lengthy sermon note), and because one of the traits of this beautified "risen body" in Scholastic theology was a rainbow-like *claritas:* sheen is *schön.*

"Hurrahing in Harvest" is also a poem of the harmonizing of dualities, but here not merely a marriage of heaven and earth in the *admirabile commercium* of octave and sestet, but rather a ravishing *conquest* of earth by heaven. Whence, again, the puzzling intrusion of "celestial" Latinity (here italicized) into the "terrestrial" world of the "Anglo-Saxon":

> Summer ends now; now, *barbarous* in beauty, the
>   stooks rise
> Around; up above, what wind-walks! what lovely
>   behaviour
> Of silk-sack clouds! has wilder, wilful-wavier
> Meal-drift moulded ever and melted across skies?
>
> I walk, I lift up, I lift up heart, eyes,
> Down all that glory in the heavens to glean our Saviour;
> And, eyes, heart, what looks, what lips yet gave you a
> *Rapturous* love's greeting of realer, of rounder replies?
>
> And the *azurous* hung hills are his world-wielding
>   shoulder
> *Majestic* — as a *stallion* stalwart, very-*violet*-sweet! —
> These things, these things were here and but the
>   beholder
> Wanting; which two when they once meet,
> The heart rears wings bold and bolder
> And hurls for him, O half hurls earth for him off under
>   his feet.

Summer is over, even the harvest is over; and as with Keats, the eschaton approaches. There is a sense of fulfillment here missing from all preceding poems. Not only is there no tone of child-like innocence, but these are not the songs of spring that flow *suaviter*. Autumn has its music too, a music of reaping and rapture which is explicitly barbarous and which flows *fortiter*. So, although we have the same "up-down" trajectory encountered in "The Starlight Night," the Savior here is seen in the guise of the *tremendum* as opposed to the *fascinosum* of the earlier poem ("the spouse Christ"), or of "The Lantern out of Doors," where Christ is the "first, fast, last friend."

In "Hurrahing in Harvest" the Savior comes as "this tremendous lover," to employ the apt title of a celebrated work of spiritual theology by the Trappist, Eugene Boylan. And whereas in "The Starlight Night," creaturely agency is emphasized ("bid then" essentially with prayer, and then with patience, alms, vows), in "Hurrahing," the divine agency dominates, so that the creature can merely "glean" divinity's presence. Moreover, the creature knows this is the season of fulfillment since the two lengthy questions that constitute the octave go unanswered, indeed, seem to be dismissed as irrelevant speculation in light of the imminent coming of the stalwart lover. The creature knows that nothing in the past ("what lips *yet gave*") could induce this rapturous love which is consummated in this eschatological autumn.

This sense of the pleromatic, I have already pointed out, is evident in the swelling ("rounder") and the Keatsian "o'er brimming" of the rhopalic line: "I walk, I lift up, I lift up heart." There is something lit-*urgi*cal ("barbarous," "wilder") about this autumnal *admirabile commercium,* which suggests the transverberating mystical-death throes of St. Teresa or the ecstatic raptures of Crashaw's Magdalen. We are at the core of final union, and here the "greeting" of Christ, as in the medieval "psychology" of love, enters through the eyes, bypasses the mind (the poem's speculative questions are mere rhetorical strategies), and pierces the heart. This explains the paradox that though "greetings" are heard, and that though faith comes *ex auditu,* unlike the "Spring" poem, the *ears* are not mentioned. We have *heart* and *eyes* because we are now transcending faith; we are now beyond the spring of *ingressus,* and into the final phase of visual union, the autumn of *visio beatifica.* This final union, beyond faith, is where in Cardinal Newman's motto, *"cor ad cor loquitur"* (which should be translated "heart to heart by Logos"), comes into play, and we attain the transforming *coro*nation of beatific *vis*ion ("heart, eyes"). The imagery is traditional, and evokes Donne:

> Reason your viceroy in mee, mee should defend,
> But is captiv'd, and proves weake or untrue....
> . . . .
> Take mee to you, imprison mee, for I
> Except you enthrall mee, never shall be free,
> Nor ever chaste, except you ravish me.

We are thus prepared for the ultimate marriage of heaven and earth ("the azurous hung hills") and the ultimate marriage to the Savior, originally glimpsed in the barbarous beauty and rapturous greeting of nature. The early references to "eyes" and the subsequent reference to "hills" suggest Psalm 121: "I will lift up my eyes to the hills — from whence comes my help." But now in the antechamber of union we can recognize the Savior directly in all his "bridal-mystical," supragendered, paradoxic, and paroxysmal reality ("stallion stalwart, very violet sweet"). The entire poem glosses Psalm 19 by way of Wordsworth's *Prelude*. Both Hopkins and Wordsworth were alone, returning home, after what Hopkins in a letter to Bridges (July 16, 1878) described as "extreme enthusiasm," and what Wordsworth in *The Prelude* described as "magnificent...in memorable pomp":

> The solid mountains shone, bright as the clouds,
> Grain tinctured, drenched in empyrean light....
> (IV, 328–29)

And as Hopkins, unbidding, received into his heart the greeting of realer and rounder replies, so too Wordsworth could say, "My heart was full; I made no vows, but vows / Were then made for me." But with Hopkins this is no panentheist experience. It is an encounter with the Sun of Justice, the Savior, who "comes forth like the groom" from the bridal chamber, and is like an Atlantean giant ("world-wielding shoulder") "joyfully running his course" (Psalm 19). And it may also be noted that Wordsworth's "grain" relates not only to Hopkins's "meal-drift" but also, in the sense of "tinted red," to Hopkins's "violet sweet."

But what is for Wordsworth a poetic commission, is for Hopkins a mystical bond with an incarnate deity. Language here, of course, balks at its own constituent hurdles. The paradoxes of incarnation are multiple: "masculine" stallion stalwart melds with "feminine" violet sweet; "violet" evokes the fragile flower and the delicate Herbartian sweetness. But "violet" also evokes its chiming mate "violent," while also suggesting the fusion of spectrumly physical hot red and spiritual cool blue.

But when the creature encounters this violet reality, when the creature hears this incarnate and incoronate *sursum corda,* it wrings its barriers in bursts of fear or rage, as does Keats in "The Ode to a Nightingale." I thus read the "O" of Hopkins's last line as a cry of anguish and frustration — like the "oh, air," of "The Windhover," or the "O where it fails" at the end of "In the Valley of the Elwy." No matter how boldly the heart rears wings, it is still "flesh-bound," it is still in the earthly antechamber of union.

To go beyond this, Hopkins would have had to introduce the death-resurrection theme of Herbert's "Easter Wings." Only by "imping" its wings to those of the Savior can the creature not just *half*-hurl, but successfully *hurl* earth *off* under his feet. Now more than ever does it seem rich to die in the final melting union of the feast of St. Agnes, of the "racing lambs." But, when is that "now"? It is, as Keats says in "To Autumn," when the "stubble-plains" (Hopkins's "barbarous stooks") are touched with rosy hue (Hopkins's "violet sweet"), and "barred clouds bloom the soft-dying day" (Hopkins's "silk-sack clouds" melting across skies).

Since this is the final poem to be analyzed, I want to elaborate, first, on its unifying principles; and, second, on its incorporation of all the major poetical/sexual/theological figures treated in this book, that is, on its unique status in the Hopkins canon as *epitome troparum ac schematum.*

As I have observed, the octave centers on the heavenly, and the sestet centers on the terrestrial, with the complete poem devoted to the marriage of the two, the marriage of heaven and earth. Similarly, as in "God's Grandeur," we have a gap between the two sections of the sonnet, between the supernatural and the natural (though reversed in "God's Grandeur"), which understandably again leads the reader to expect a contrast or adversarial relation between these two distinct orders of existence. Yet for Hopkins the two orders, as we have seen, are in a state of harmony, so that the adversative, "but," is transformed into the coordinative "and." There is, then, really no conflict between the Savior's "reply" at the close of the octave, and the sudden reference to the hills as "his world-wielding shoulder" in the first line of the sestet. Both are expressions of the cosmically unifying incarnational "Word": first, is the word heard from within, the eternal Logos whose countenance is signed *upon the human intelligence;* second, is the word as "blueprint" made visible *in creation.*

So, too, the octave centers on the present ("now; now"), while the sestet centers on the eschatological future ("when they once meet"). Using that same developmental structure, the first quatrain emphasizes the dispassionate consideration of the objective world in terms that are acquiescent and preludial (in Hopkins's Anglo-Saxon, translate: "foreplaying"): "ends," "behaviour," "mould," "melt." And the "wild" and "wilful" of this first quatrain prepare for the second quatrain's ardor and urgency as subject responds to object, creature to Creator, while together they move toward eschatological "rapturous love." The sestet carries on that development as one moves from present to future, and from domination of the subject by the object.

I have already referred to the presence and the significance of such Latinate exotica as "barbarous," "rapturous," "azurous." In a similar vein, I want to look at the import of the two words, one in the octave and one in the sestet, with "be" prefixes. "Be" in this context is a spatial/temporal intensifier. "Behaviour" suggests not only a fusion of the polarities of being and having (*être et avoir*), but also "moral agency" on the part of nature (*age quod agis*); a steadiness and stability on its part in revealing the *vestigia* which the creature gleans in order that the Savior is revealed.

But the "be" in "beholder" indicates not a transient state of holding or clasping, but as temporal intensifier, the "be" indicates a permanent state, an eschatological fulfillment of permanently being-held in the embrace of the Godhead. Thus "Hurrahing in Harvest" is Hopkins's real epithalamion — his real marriage hymn — not for an earthly wedding, but for a wedding of the soul. And since the latter is for Hopkins and his tradition the theme of all poetry, one would expect this poem to embody all the central tropes and figurations of union.

I have previously emphasized the expansionary, rhopalic character of the beginning of the second quatrain: "I walk, I lift up, I lift up heart" — indicating the gradual acceleration of mood as the poet approaches the oncoming eschaton. But this first line is also corpuscular in pattern, and plays off its complementary twin: "Down all that glory in the heavens to glean our Saviour." And this complementarity is reversed (temporal priority is of no significance here):

> And the azurous hung hills are his world-wielding
> shoulder
> Majestic — as a *st*allion *st*alwar*t,* ver*y*-viole*t*-swee*t!*

So, too, with the intermingling and fusion of polarities in the chiastic pattern:

> heart   eyes
> eyes   heart

We also have two clearly different overflowing lines, though both reflect the basic notion of enjambement as the trope of transcendence, that is, of breaking through the barriers that encage us, and of attaining to union with the "other." (In *Celestial Pantomime* I cite a score of texts on human love — literally on "kissing" — whereas here we have to do with the "rapturous love" of near-mystical union.) In the first of these instances, we also have the *anima candida* character, now matured, that be-speaks all of Hopkins's poetry of the *via unitiva:*

> And, eyes, heart, what looks, what lips yet gave you a
> *R*-apturous love's greeting of realer, of rounder replies?

That we have to do with the overflowing of subject into object is patent. What is incredibly and uniquely Hopkinsian is the chiming of "behaviour/Saviour" with the enjambed (and here italicized), "gave you a *R.*"

The enjambement in the sestet though less naive and less visual is equally effective:

> These things, these things were here and but the
> beholder
> Wanting...

The beholder's longing is so intense that like Chagall as lover, his elongated neck extends around the corner of the door frame to glimpse the beloved, just as here the line extends itself around the verse frame so the "beholder" can glimpse the object of his "wanting."

But in terms of the transparency of innocence, there is also the seemingly uncontrollable and enthusiastic repetition of "these things, these things," of the "now; now," in the first line, and the concluding "bold and bolder." All would be as flaws to the sophisticated poet or critic, but for the *anima naturaliter candida*, they are as natural as the *claritas*, the transparency and the openness, of a St. Francis or a Father Zossima — or a Father Hopkins.

Index of Names

Index of Titles or First Lines